Africa Now

Africa Now is an exciting new series, publi[ ]
in association with the internationally resp[ ]
Institute. Featuring high-quality, cutting-edge research from
leading academics, the series addresses the big issues confronting
Africa today. Accessible but in-depth, and wide-ranging in its
scope, Africa Now engages with the critical political, economic,
sociological and development debates affecting the continent,
shedding new light on pressing concerns.

Nordic Africa Institute

The Nordic Africa Institute (Nordiska Afrikainstitutet) is a centre
for research, documentation and information on modern Africa.
Based in Uppsala, Sweden, the Institute is dedicated to providing
timely, critical and alternative research and analysis of Africa and
to cooperating with African researchers. As a hub and a meeting
place for a growing field of research and analysis, the Institute
strives to put knowledge of African issues within reach for scholars,
policy-makers, politicians, the media, students and the general
public. The Institute is financed jointly by the Nordic countries
(Denmark, Finland, Iceland, Norway and Sweden).

www.nai.uu.se

Forthcoming titles

Prosper B. Matondi, Kjell Havnevik and Atakilte Beyene (eds),
  Biofuels, Land Grabbing and Food Security in Africa
Mats Utas (ed.), *African Conflicts and Informal Power: Big Men and
  Networks*

Titles already published

Fantu Cheru and Cyril Obi (eds), *The Rise of China and India in
  Africa: Challenges, Opportunities and Critical Interventions*
Ilda Lindell (ed.), *Africa's Informal Workers: Collective Agency,
  Alliances and Transnational Organizing in Urban Africa*
Iman Hashim and Dorte Thorsen, *Child Migration in Africa*
Cyril Obi and Siri Aas Rustad (eds), *Oil and Insurgency in the Niger
  Delta: Managing the Complex Politics of Petro-violence*

About the editors

Cyril Obi is a senior researcher, and leader, Research Cluster on Conflict, Displacement and Transformation, at the Nordic Africa Institute, Uppsala, Sweden. He has been on leave since 2005 from the Nigerian Institute of International Affairs (NIIA), Lagos, where he is an associate research professor. In 2004, Dr Obi became the second Claude Ake Visiting Professor at the University of Uppsala. He is the recipient of the following international recognition/awards: Council for the Development of Social Science Research in Africa (CODESRIA) Governance Institute Fellow in 1993; fellow of the Salzburg Seminar 1994; SSRC-MacArthur Foundation visiting fellow in 1996; visiting fellow to the Africa Studies Centre (ASC), Leiden; and visiting fellow and senior research associate, St Antony's College, Oxford, from October 1999 to March 2000. In 2001, he was a fellow of the 21st Century Trust conference on 'Rethinking security for the 21st century', also held at Oxford. He is a contributing editor to the *Review of African Political Economy*, and is on the editorial board of the *African Journal of International Affairs*, the *African Security Review* and the *Review of Leadership in Africa*. Dr Obi has been a guest editor of journals such as *African and Asian Studies* and the *African Journal of International Affairs*. His most recent book, co-edited with Fantu Cheru, is *The Rise of China and India in Africa* (Zed Books, 2010).

Siri Aas Rustad is a researcher at the Centre for the Study of Civil War at the Peace Research Institute Oslo. Her research is mainly concerned with post-conflict natural resource management, with a particular focus on Nigeria. Other research interests include the role of natural resources in conflict and the geography of conflict.

Oil and insurgency in the Niger Delta

Managing the complex politics of petro-violence

edited by Cyril Obi and Siri Aas Rustad

Nordiska Afrikainstitutet
The Nordic Africa Institute

Zed Books
LONDON | NEW YORK

Oil and insurgency in the Niger Delta: Managing the complex politics of petro-violence was first published in association with the Nordic Africa Institute, PO Box 1703, SE-751 47 Uppsala, Sweden in 2010 by Zed Books Ltd, 7 Cynthia Street, London N1 9JF, UK and Room 400, 175 Fifth Avenue, New York, NY 10010, USA

www.zedbooks.co.uk
www.nai.uu.se

Set in OurType Arnhem, Monotype Gill Sans Heavy by Ewan Smith, London
Index: ed.emery@thefreeuniversity.net
Cover designed by Rogue Four Design
Printed and bound in Great Britain by the MPG Books Group, King's Lynn and Bodmin

Distributed in the USA exclusively by Palgrave Macmillan, a division of St Martin's Press, LLC, 175 Fifth Avenue, New York, NY 10010, USA

A catalogue record for this book is available from the British Library
Library of Congress Cataloging in Publication Data available

ISBN 978 1 84813 808 7 hb
ISBN 978 1 84813 807 0 pb
ISBN 978 1 84813 809 4 eb

Contents

Tables, figures and maps

Acronyms

CASS	Centre for Advanced Social Science
CD	Community Development
CEO	chief executive officer
COMA	Coalition for Militant Action in the Niger Delta
CSR	Corporate Social Responsibility
DDR	disarmament, demobilization and reintegration
ECOWAS	Economic Community of West African States
EIA	environmental impact assessment
EITI	Extractive Industry Transparency Initiative
EU	European Union
FAL	fusil automatique leger (light automatic rifle)
FNC	fabrique nationale carabine (assault rifle)
FNDIC	Federated Niger Delta Ijaw Communities
GDP	gross domestic product
GMoU	Global Memorandum of Understanding
ICG	International Crisis Group
ILO	International Labour Organization
INC	Ijaw National Congress
INYM	Ijaw National Youth Movement
IOC	international oil company
IYC	Ijaw Youth Council
JRC	Joint Revolutionary Council
JTF	Joint Task Force
JVA	joint venture agreement
LUA	Land Use Act
MEND	Movement for the Emancipation of the Niger Delta
MNC	multinational corporation
MOSIEND	Movement for the Survival of the Ijaw Ethnic Nationality in the Niger Delta
MOSOP	Movement for the Survival of Ogoni People
MoU	memorandum of understanding
N	naira
NAOC	Nigerian Agip Oil Company
NDDB	Niger Delta Development Board
NDDC	Niger Delta Development Commission
NDPVF	Niger Delta People's Volunteer Force

NDVS	Niger Delta Vigilante Service
NEITI	Nigeria Extractive Industry Transparency Initiative
NGO	non-governmental organization
NN	Nigerian Navy
NNPC	Nigerian National Petroleum Corporation
NPRC	National Political Reform Conference
OBR	Ogoni Bill of Rights
OMPADEC	Oil Mineral Producing Areas Development Commission
OPEC	Organization of the Petroleum Exporting Countries
PDP	People's Democratic Party
SALW	small arms and light weapons
SCD	Sustainable Community Development
SPDC	Shell Petroleum Development Company
TCND	Technical Committee on the Niger Delta
TNC	transnational corporation
UN	United Nations
UNECE	UN Economic Commission for Europe

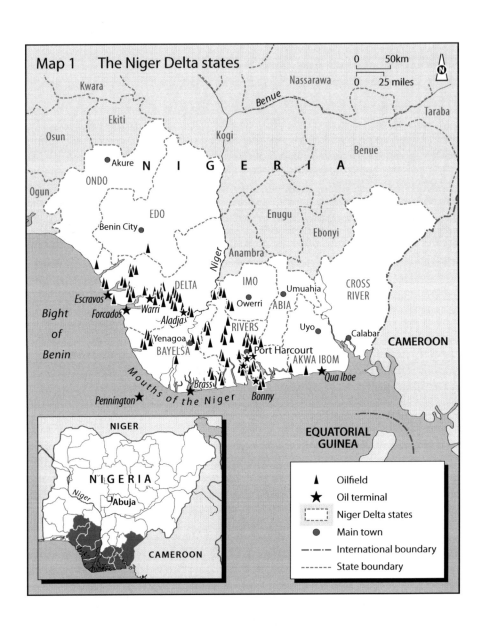

Map 1   The Niger Delta states

0   50km
0   25 miles

Kwara   Nassarawa   Taraba

Ekiti   Benue

Osun   Kogi   Benue

Ogun   Akure   N I G E R I A

ONDO

EDO   Enugu

Benin City   Ebonyi

Anambra

Niger

IMO   CROSS
Owerri   RIVER

DELTA   ABIA

Escravos   Warri   Umuahia

Bight   Forcados   Aladja   Uyo   Calabar   CAMEROON

of   Yenagoa   RIVERS

Benin   BAYELSA   Port Harcourt

AKWA IBOM

Mouths   Qua Iboe

Brass   Bonny

Pennington   of the Niger

NIGER

NIGERIA

Niger   Abuja

CAMEROON

EQUATORIAL
GUINEA

▲ Oilfield
★ Oil terminal
▢ Niger Delta states
● Main town
—·— International boundary
- - - State boundary

Introduction: Petro-violence in the Niger Delta – the complex politics of an insurgency

Cyril Obi and Siri Aas Rustad

The explosion of two car bombs near the regional governor's office in the oil city of Warri in Nigeria's western delta on 15 March 2010, shortly after an on-line warning issued by the Movement for the Emancipation of the Niger Delta (MEND), served as a rude reminder of the militia's existence. It showed that, despite the acceptance of an amnesty programme announced in June 2009 by President Umaru Yar'Adua by leading members of ethnic minority militias, and the conclusion of a disarmament process, other factions which felt that the amnesty and post-amnesty process did not address the root causes of the Niger Delta conflict were willing to continue using violence to press home their demands. Apart from disrupting a high-level post-amnesty conference, the bombings once more demonstrated the deep-seated nature of the conflict, and how solutions that do not go far enough serve only to ensure that the struggle for power over, and access to the benefits of, oil remains at the core of insurgent violence in the Niger Delta.

Given Nigeria's position as Africa's leading oil producer and exporter, with a partly explored huge gas potential, the 'oil war' in the Niger Delta (Nigeria's main source of oil and gas) is of critical importance to Nigeria's economic growth and political stability. The connection between oil-related conflict and the March bombings underscores the need to further explore the causes, dynamics and politics underpinning violent conflict in Nigeria's main oil-producing region, which until very recently had assumed insurgent proportions, threatening oil production and billions of dollars' worth of Western investments, export revenues, as well as the stability of Nigeria and its immediate sub-region. Such an understanding of the 'violence that so often attends the extraction of oil (and necessarily the ecological devastation which is its handmaiden) – petro-violence' (Watts 1999: 1) is central to the search for sustainable conflict resolution in the Niger Delta, with its attendant local, national and global ramifications.

Since 2006, petro-violence has for strategic, economic and political reasons brought the Niger Delta to the forefront of international energy and security concerns. It is therefore important to unpack and understand the complex drivers of the conflict. These show how the crisis is linked to Nigeria's history, internal contradictions and politics, as well as to the nature of the integration of the Niger Delta into the international political economy of oil in ways that have simultaneously enriched international oil companies and their partners – national and local elites – and contributed to the disempowerment and impoverishment of local peoples, through direct dispossession, repression and the pollution of the air, lands and waters of the region (see Ukiwo, Ukeje, Bøås, Emeseh, and Oluwaniyi, this volume).

Equally relevant are the contradictions within Nigeria's ethnicized politics and its centralist form of federalism, particularly in the ways in which ethnic minority agitation for local autonomy and resource control (Ako, Ukiwo, this volume) have metamorphosed (before and after oil became a strong national factor) from non-violent protest to militant resistance. Oil politics in Nigeria has been defined by the high stakes involved in controlling power at any cost (including the subversion of 2003 and 2007 elections in the Niger Delta), by the tensions in the country's fiscal federalism between hegemonic federal elites that dominate the control of oil rents derived from oil production in the Niger Delta (by oil multinationals) and the ethnic minorities of the Niger Delta who are marginalized in the distribution of those rents. Of significance is the collective desire of Niger Delta people to win back the control of their resources – the most politically significant being oil and land – and their local affairs. However, such high-stake oil politics is underpinned by competing class and factional interests that also allow for expedient and fluid alliances within which erstwhile enemies become partners or vice versa, while the people remain largely alienated or victimized, manipulated by the various contending forces.

Perhaps most relevant are the ways in which the high stakes involved have fed into a vicious cycle of exploitation, protest, repression, resistance, militarization and the descent into a volatile mix of insurgent violence and criminality. It is important not to ignore the complex webs of petro-violence, which call for nuanced analysis based on the recognition of the confluence of, or interaction between, many factors – domestic and international – rather than the imposition of a single narrative or 'cause' as being responsible for the violence in the oil-rich but impoverished region. The Niger Delta case shows why it is necessary to understand the historic, socio-economic and political context of conflict, and its fluid dynamics, including the ways in which global forces are implicated in, and benefit from, oil extracted under conditions of structural violence and inequity.

The turn to violent resistance took place in the context of prolonged military rule, marginalization and repression of community protests. It has involved government armed forces and then community vigilantes/armed groups and local militias. While government forces engage in pacifying protesting or feuding communities, or fighting local militias resisting exploitation and marginalization by the Nigerian state and its partners, the oil multinationals (MNCs) (Ukeje, this volume), armed groups have been involved in intra- or inter-communal violence, turf wars or criminal activities, including kidnapping, oil theft (illegal oil bunkering) and brigandage (Ikelegbe, Bøås, and Duquet, this volume). Militias riding on the back of widespread frustration that non-violent protests were not having the desired effect on petro-business resorted to violence: attacking oil installations and kidnapping expatriate oil workers, first as a strategy for drawing attention to their cause. But the activities of some militias later began to acquire other characteristics and goals different from the initial ones of protest, resistance and the demand for resource control. It is important to recognize the problematic nature of the notion of the 'militant' and 'militancy' in the volatile context of the Niger Delta. This is because the lines between militancy and criminality have become blurred or fluid (Bøås, Ikelegbe, this volume).

Militancy is also linked to the generational power shift from local chiefs and elites to younger people that took place in the late 1990s (Obi 2006; Ukiwo, Ako, this volume) and the widespread view among the emergent forces of protest that the only language that the state and oil MNCs would listen to was the use of force (Obi 2009a, 2010; Watts 2007; Ikelegbe 2006a, also this volume). However, the abandonment of peaceful protest and dialogue, in favour of violent protest and militancy, involved calculations of expediency embracing various actors: the armed groups, cults and militias, the Nigerian state and the military, local political elites, youth, ethnic identity movements/associations, oil multinationals (MNCs), security advisers and the international community, further complicating the conflict and its resolution (see Ukiwo, Ikelegbe, Duquet, this volume).

In this the 'local' and the 'global' forces in the Niger Delta are enmeshed and implicated in the violent conflict either as supporters of the state-backed transnational extractors of oil or as allies of local resistance movements and rights advocacy groups. This recognition is critical both to the understanding of the nature of violent oil-related conflict and its wide ramifications, and to various levels of engagement for an alternative project of conflict resolution. These considerations form the basis of, and define the scope of, the empirically based, analytical and policy-oriented chapters of this book.

The Niger Delta and oil

The Niger Delta is a vast coastal plain in the southernmost part of Nigeria, where one of West Africa's longest rivers empties into the Atlantic Ocean between the Bights of Benin and Biafra, in the Gulf of Guinea. Estimated to cover about 75,000 square kilometres, it is the largest wetland in Africa and one of the largest in the world, supporting a wide range of biodiversity (Obi 2010: 222) and an estimated population of 31 million people. The swampy terrain and fragile ecology pose several challenges, including land scarcity and supporting a high-level population density (TCND 2008: 6). They also define the livelihoods of the local people – as farmers, fishers, traders, food processors and local manufacturers of items linked to the principal subsistence economies. The

Niger Delta, given its centrality to Nigeria's political economy, has also been defined in geopolitical terms. In this regard, it is made up of nine states (out of Nigeria's thirty-six): Abia, Akwa-Ibom, Cross River, Rivers, Bayelsa, Delta, Imo, Ondo and Edo. In terms of oil production and petro-violence, three states are of key importance: Bayelsa, Delta and Rivers.

The prominent place the Niger Delta occupies in national and global consciousness is linked to its strategic importance as the source of over 75 per cent of Nigeria's petroleum production and exports. The Niger Delta presently hosts Nigeria's oil industry, including oil multinationals, state and local oil companies, oil service companies, 'thousands of kilometers of oil pipelines, ten export terminals, four refineries and a massive liquefied natural gas (LNG) sector' (Watts 2007: 639). This makes the region both a site of global oil production and international relations (Soremekun, this volume) bringing the 'local' into close proximity with the 'global'.

At the national level two issues are important. Oil accounts for over 80 per cent of official revenues and 90 per cent of export earnings, making it the fiscal basis of both state and federal power and economic development. Also relevant is the fact that over 95 per cent of the oil is produced by local subsidiaries of vertically integrated oil multinationals: Shell, Chevron Texaco, ExxonMobil, Total and Agip (Eni), which are bound to the 'Nigerian state through contracts, underpinning the transnational nature of oil extraction and the sharing of profits' (Obi 2010: 224). This means that Nigeria is dependent on oil earnings, and its economy is vulnerable to fluctuations in global oil prices. Dependence on oil rents paid by MNCs that also control the technical processes of oil production makes the Nigerian state more of an oil gatekeeper and oil revenue collector, operating in partnership with, and beholden to, oil MNCs.

Since most of the oil is from an ethnic minority region, its political and economic significance makes it a key factor in national politics and ethnic minority–ethnic majority relations, particularly with regard to the struggle over access, control and distribution of oil revenues in a multi-ethnic federation. It also means that the rural communities of this region host some of the most sophisticated multinationals on earth, and also suffer the direct devastating environmental impact of oil production and oil accidents, making it 'one of the world's most severely petroleum impacted ecosystems and one of the 5 most petroleum-polluted environments in the world' (Niger Delta Natural Damage Assessment and Restoration Project 2006). This also implies that the environmental impact of oil production in the context of state oil dependence, lax regulation and implementation of environmental laws[1] and state expropriation of land 'for oil development' threatens destruction of local livelihoods and subsistence economies in the region. Beyond that the Niger Delta, with one of the world's highest rates of gas flaring, contributes to global warming and climate change, which in turn contributes to the destruction of the fragile delta ecosystem.

The interaction between the global, national and local around oil production makes explicit the connections that define the high stakes involved and the ways in which globalized oil production simultaneously generates wealth for a 'few' and impoverishment for 'many'. Global oil giants sit cheek by jowl with poor rural oil communities in the Niger Delta. The fundamental questions of how such relations have been structured and (mis)managed over time to become a factor in the violent conflict are addressed in this book, alongside the various options for resolving such conflicts.

Background to the conflict in the Niger Delta

The background to the conflict in the Niger Delta is embedded in a long history of struggles for self-determination and local autonomy by the people of the region, and the political and socio-economic impact of transatlantic trade on the region.[2] The quest by the British for imperial glory and control of the trade in palm oil (largely dominated by local merchant-princes and kings) were important factors in the conquest of the region (after fierce resistance had been overcome), as a stepping stone to the eventual colonization of Nigeria in 1914. The creation of Nigeria and its division into three regions by the British meant that the trading states of the Niger Delta and the local entrepreneurial class were subdued. Also, the people of the Niger Delta became relegated to an ethnic minority status in relation to the numerically superior ethnic groups that dominated political life in the old Western (Yoruba), Eastern (Igbo) and Northern (Hausa-Fulani) regions of Nigeria.

In 1954, Nigeria was transformed into a federation with three strong regions and a rather weak central government. The institutionalization of revenue-sharing, political representation and power distribution along these regional lines reinforced ethnic majority hegemony, and rivalry, which also meant that ethnic minorities often lost out, or were marginalized, in the power equation at the regional and national levels. As independence became imminent, ethnic minorities in southern and northern Nigeria agitated for self-determination by demanding the creation of autonomous ethnic minority regions/states within a free Nigeria. However, such demands were unmet.

The feelings of marginalization gained ground even after independence in 1960, particularly after political elites became locked in a bitter struggle for power and resources at the regional and federal levels. In spite of the pressures for states creation, only one ethnic minorities' state, the Midwest region, was created, in what was considered a plot by the Northern Peoples' Congress (NPC)–National Convention of Nigerian Citizens' (NCNC) ruling coalition to split the Action Group (AG)-dominated Western region into two, and effectively reduce the political base of the Yoruba majority ethnic group.

Although oil was discovered in commercial quantities by Shell-BP in 1956 in Oloibiri (now in Bayelsa state),[3] oil exports did not commence until two years later. Initially oil contributed very little to national revenues, which were dominated by earnings from cash crop and mineral exports (based on production in all regions). Thus, it was not until the mid-1960s that the rising profile of oil exports (in the face of declining cash crop earnings) began to attract some political attention. The early oil industry was dominated by Shell-BP, which was later joined (in the Niger Delta) by other Western oil MNCs after Nigeria's independence in 1960, while indigenous participation in, and regulation of, the oil industry remained minimal until the 1970s.

In 1966 there was an abortive attempt at secession aimed at forcibly asserting ethnic minority regional autonomy by a group of ethnic Ijaw youth, the Niger Delta Volunteer Force (NDVF), led by Isaac Adaka Boro, who wanted to create a Niger Delta republic that would ensure, among other things, Ijaw self-determination, ownership and control of the oil in its territory (Obi 2010: 225). This revolt was partly driven by Boro's concern that the Eastern region (of which the Niger Delta was a part), dominated by the Igbo elite, and the federal government (after the January 1966 coup), under the control of an Igbo army general (Aguiyi Ironsi), would purloin the oil resources in the Niger Delta. Boro and his lieutenants were captured, tried and found guilty of treason, but got a reprieve after the second coup in July 1966 resulted in Yakubu Gowon, a northern ethnic minority army officer, becoming the head of state. The new government subsequently freed Boro and his men and created twelve new states in 1967, of which three, the Midwest, Rivers and Southeast, were in the Niger Delta (ibid.: 226). This move was resisted by the military governor of the Eastern region, Colonel Odumegwu Ojukwu, who led the Biafran secession, ostensibly to fight for Igbo self-determination (against perceived northern domination), but also to assert control over the Niger Delta oilfields (located in the Eastern region). Boro joined the federal war against Biafra, in defence of Ijaw territory and to repel Biafran claims to Niger Delta oil, and died shortly before the war ended in 1970, after which he assumed the status of a martyr in the cause for ethnic minority self-determination in the Niger Delta.

Several developments during and after the Nigerian civil war had implications for the agitation for minority rights in the Niger Delta. The first was that the oil from the region became the main source of national revenues and export earnings. Second, the federal military government had taken over control of oil through Decree No. 51/Petroleum Act of 1969. Specifically, the Petroleum Act provided that 'the entire ownership and control of all petroleum in, under or upon any lands [...] shall be vested in the state'. In Section 2, the Act granted the federal oil minister 'the sole right to grant oil mining leases to oil companies'. This Act expropriated oil from the Niger Delta, much to the chagrin of the ethnic minorities of the region, who hoped that the (ethnic minority) states would own the oil within their territories. It also meant that a structural change had occurred in Nigeria's federalism under the military: the shift in power from the regions/states to the federal government, underscored by the centralization of power over oil.

These feelings of exclusion, dispossession and disappointment were further reinforced by the progressive downward revision of the derivation principle of revenue allocation,[4] which effectively reduced the 'share' of federal allocations to oil-producing ethnic minority states from 50 per cent in 1966 to 3 per cent in the mid-1990s. In 1999, partly in response to the protests from the region, and to lend legitimacy to the new democratic government, the allocation was raised to 13 per cent. In spite of this, the agitation for self-determination has continued, driven by the demand by Niger Delta ethnic minorities to control the oil from their states by embarking on the campaign for 'resource control'. At its heart is the strong feeling among the ethnic/oil minorities of the Niger Delta that the non-oil-producing ethnic majority groups that dominate the federal government also control the oil wealth, while they who produce the oil suffer (unjustly) from neglect, exploitation and pollution.

The Land Use Act (LUA) of 1979 (now updated in the Laws of the Federation of Nigeria [LFN] 1990 and LFN CAP L5, 2004) has effectively placed all land in the country under the control of the state government. Although some customary claims to community land are still recognized by the Act, the state government can acquire such land 'in the public interest'. In the Niger Delta, with its high population density, it has meant a loss of power over 'scarce' (oil-rich) land for local people, and loss of compensation for the full value of appropriated land, save for compensation for trees/crops or property on the surface of such land. It also meant that oil MNCs could directly get oil and land leases from the government without recourse to local communities. The alienation of the people from their land and the oil produced from it feeds local grievances. While the federal government is seen as neglecting and slowly 'killing the goose that laid the golden eggs', the oil MNCs are seen as its partner and the visible and actual perpetrators of neglect and exploitation of the region's resources, and the pollution of its lands and waters (Obi 2010).

It was against this background that the Movement for the Survival of Ogoni People (MOSOP), representing one of the smallest ethnic groups in the Niger Delta, the Ogoni, presented the Ogoni Bill of Rights (OBR) to the federal government in 1990. The OBR demanded, among other things, local autonomy, Ogoni right to control of Ogoni resources (oil), and compensation for the exploitation of oil and oil pollution, which were believed to be threatening the existence and survival of the Ogoni people. When there was no response to the OBR from government, MOSOP internationalized its demands, targeting Shell, the oldest and largest oil operator in the country. Its international campaign was coordinated by Ken Saro-Wiwa, a writer and Ogoni ethnic minority rights activist, who successfully framed Ogoni grievances in the discourse of indigenous peoples/ethnic minorities and environmental rights. By linking up with global rights advocacy networks, MOSOP waged effective local non-violent protest and a global campaign that placed the Nigerian government and Shell under immense pressure for their roles in the abuse of human rights, exploitation and pollution of Ogoniland, eventually forcing the latter to stop their operations there.

What followed was a systematic repression of Ogoni protest, including military raids on Ogoni villages and the arrest of suspected MOSOP cadres and sympathizers. After a trial widely held as flawed, Saro-Wiwa and eight MOSOP members were found guilty by a special tribunal of inciting a mob to murder four allegedly pro-government chiefs/elites and, in spite of worldwide pleas for clemency, were hanged in a Port Harcourt prison on 10 November 1995. The execution of the 'Ogoni nine' was followed by a wave of state terror against Ogoniland in what the commander of the Rivers State Internal Security Task Force, Major Paul Okutimo, called 'wasting operations' directed at crushing the MOSOP protest.

The lessons from the MOSOP struggle and Boro's earlier heroic exploits informed the emergence of a new ethnic minority resistance movement in the Niger Delta led by the Ijaw. Ijaw ethnic minority youth from six states in the Niger Delta met in Kaiama, the place of birth of the Ijaw martyr Isaac Boro. At the end of the meeting they formed themselves into the Ijaw Youth Council (IYC) and issued the Kaiama Declaration (KD) on 11 December 1998. Through the KD, the IYC asserted that 'all land and natural resources (including mineral resources) within the Ijaw territory belong to the Ijaw communities and are the basis of our survival'. Of particular note was the resolution that the Ijaw 'cease to recognize all undemocratic laws that rob our people/communities of the right to ownership and control of our lives and resources, which were enacted without our participation and consent. These include the Land Use Decree and Petroleum Act' (United Ijaw States 2010). On the basis of the KD, the IYC issued an ultimatum to all oil companies to leave the Niger Delta by 30 December 1998. The response of the federal military government was to declare a state of emergency in the Niger Delta and flood the region with troops. Protesting Ijaw youth were shot at by anti-riot policemen, while checkpoints were set up to stop the movement of suspected IYC sympathizers and the potential for the protests to spread. The protest was crushed without addressing the grievances of the IYC.

Nigeria's return to democratic rule in 1999 raised expectations within the Niger Delta both that a new basis would be set for the demilitarization of the region and that the elected leaders would better address the grievances of the people. At the same time, some elements of the youth, long exposed to military repression, had become socialized into a belief that non-violent protests were not of much use, as the state–oil alliance had always ignored peaceful demands and resorted to repression when confronted with demands for redress. For this group and their co-travellers violence was a legitimate weapon of protest when peaceful protest fell on deaf ears. Their resolve was reinforced by the retention of federal control of oil by Section 44(3) of the 1999 constitution, and state control of land through the LUA, in spite of protests against such laws. The last straw was the deadlock between northern and southern delegates at the 2005 National Political Reform Conference, over the demand of delegates from the Niger Delta for an increase in the oil derivation allocation from 13 to 25 per cent. The result of the deadlock was that the Niger Delta delegation left the conference in protest.

The return to democracy also had wider ramifications for the human rights and pro-democracy movement, even as politicians of the Niger Delta tapped into the groundswell of popular anger among the large number of unemployed or alienated youth in the region. Some of these youths became ready tools of politicians, feeding into a spiral of local violence in the 1999 and 2003 elections, which connected with communal conflicts, politics of local resistance and the struggle for resource control, and evolved into a full insurgency by 2006. The insurgency was initially rooted in the militarization and coming together of youth groups and their protests at several levels, but quickly took on other agendas and dimensions. The complex conflict involved broad militant alliances like MEND (with ambivalent links to some local politicians), which combined lethal attacks and sabotage of oil installations with the effective use of global media to publicize its campaign of 'fighting for the control of oil revenues by indigenes of the Niger Delta'.

The inability of the government military Joint Task Force (JTF) to rein in MEND, and the success of the latter in forcing a shutdown of a third of Nigeria's oil production (resulting in huge losses to oil companies and the state), and growing domestic and international concerns, formed the background for the granting of a presidential amnesty to Niger Delta militants in 2009 (see Ukiwo, this volume). This was accepted by the main militia leaders, while a faction of MEND remained opposed to the amnesty (amid reports that some militia leaders were co-opted by top government officials of Niger Delta origin). The amnesty has been followed by a marked reduction in the level of conflict in the region, but it is not clear that the conditions for a permanent peace are yet prevalent (see Obi and Rustad, this volume).

Scope of the book

Oil and violent conflict in the Niger Delta The relationship between oil and violence cannot be understood outside of ongoing debates between those that subscribe in varying degrees to some form of linkage between oil endowment and violent conflict, and others who call for more nuanced, balanced and radical perspectives. Nowhere is this more evident, directly and indirectly, than in recent literature on African petro-states (Shaxson 2007; Ghazvinian 2007; Oliveira 2007; Watts 2007), particularly in relation to the ways in which oil fuels corruption or neo-patrimonialism among African ruling states/elites and the complicity between oil MNCs and African 'petro-elites', resulting in dysfunctional or failing states, which can neither govern effectively nor guarantee political stability and security (Watts 2007: 648–51).

While some scholars point to greed and personal enrichment as motivation for conflict (Collier and Hoeffler 2004), there is a growing quantitative literature pointing at resource-related grievances as explanation for the statistical correlation between, particularly, oil and conflict. Østby et al. (2009) find that regions with high levels of horizontal inequalities, i.e. inequalities between groups, combined with resource endowment have a higher risk of conflict outbreak. Furthermore, natural resources can be both a curse and a blessing. Mehlum et al. (2006) argue that the economic performance of resource-rich countries is highly dependent on the quality of institutions. The case of the Niger Delta brings some of these issues to the fore. Beyond this it captures the history, the role of various actors, and the dynamics and implications of violent conflict in oil-rich enclaves of the world.

The dominant global perspective of petro-violence in the Niger Delta has been the securitization of the region as a source of strategic oil supplies to oil-dependent global powers. The acts and rhetoric of MEND, which has led the insurgency, including attacks on Shell's offshore Bonga oil platform, has attracted the attention of Western powers, particularly the United States, whose energy security is at stake on account of its dependence on imports of Nigeria's favoured high-quality light crude. Nigeria is currently the fifth-largest oil supplier to the United States. Two US oil MNCs (ExxonMobil and Chevron Texaco) operate in the Niger Delta, which together with other states in the Gulf of Guinea provide between 12 and 18 per cent of US oil imports (estimated to increase to 25 per cent by 2020, overtaking oil imports from Saudi Arabia). In a context where the USA is keen on diversifying its dependence on Middle East oil, the Niger Delta as part of the West African oil frontier is of key strategic importance to US energy security and national interests (Klare and Volman 2006; Obi 2007, 2009b), to be secured, if need be, by military means. Apart from criminalizing the militias, the West and the USA have stepped up support for the security apparatus of the Nigerian state (see Ukeje, this volume), while putting pressure on the government to rein in the militias.

The fourteen chapters of this book are broadly divided into three parts: causes of conflict, state (in)capacities; conflict actors' dynamics; and oil MNCs' response(s). They explore various aspects of the complex causes and dimensions of petro-violence and insecurity in the Niger Delta, reflecting the various perspectives and debates on the oil–conflict nexus, and the prospects for sustainable peace.

Part One: Causes of conflict, state (in)capacities Various chapters explore the causes of the conflict, reaching a broad consensus that most of the factors are embedded in the grievances of the people about the alienation from the oil wealth produced in their region. Several also point to the complications created by the nature or limitations of the state's response to the crisis (Ukiwo, Ahonsi, Ako, Ukeje, Soremekun, this volume). While noting the contribution of the 'resource war' perspective to violent conflict, Ukoha Ukiwo argues with regard to the Niger Delta that attention should be focused on alienation and despair, or 'accumulation by dispossession', as being at the heart of the violent conflict. In his view, the technologies and politics of dispossession fuel alienation and grievance, and underpin the transition from ethnic minority civil protest to militant agitation.

Several chapters are critical of the nature of the state's response(s) to the conflict, and are of the view that the Niger Delta crisis can best be addressed by entrenching the principles of community participation, ownership and control in the context of democratic governance, representative leadership, accountability and sustainable development. Babatunde Ahonsi's chapter identifies the lack of adequate state response and capacity as being at the root of Nigeria's inability to autonomously fashion and implement a permanent solution to the Niger Delta conflict. Suggestions for overcoming these inadequate state institutional and policy responses include strategic human development and institutional strengthening of public service at all levels, and a dedicated democratic political leadership across the tiers of governance.

Another perspective is provided by the chapter by Rhuks Ako, based on a radical interrogation of the resource-control discourse. Ako argues against a one-sided reading of the discourse, noting that, even if it were granted, the states of the Niger Delta lack the capacity to implement resource control, a situation that is worsened by corruption[5] and internal contradictions and divisions within the Niger Delta elite. Still on the issue of state incapacity, the chapter by Engobo Emeseh identifies the state's inability to provide access to justice, and the lack of capacity of judicial institutions to provide redress for grievances and compensation for damage to property and the environment by oil operations, as important factors explaining the resort to the alternative (violent) methods of seeking redress by the aggrieved. Writing on the Ijaw National Congress (INC), an ethnic minority elite association, Ibaba Samuel Ibaba analyses how its efforts have been undermined both by the state and by the oil companies, which have largely ignored the INC's offers to mediate in some conflicts in the region. The point is also made that the corruption within the Niger Delta states, and the contradictions within the elite, have limited the impact that non-violent organizations like the INC could have had on conflict resolution in the region.

In the sixth chapter, the state's security response to the conflict is analysed. Charles Ukeje focuses on the history of the militarization of the region, showing how oil became a factor in the region's conflict through the securitization of its extraction by the Nigerian state and its partners – the oil MNCs. It is noted that the state's military response has not resolved the conflict, but rather has dialectically fed into the militarization of the response(s) from sections of Niger Delta society. On this basis, Ukeje suggests the demilitarization of the region and the adoption of non-violent, democratic methods in resolving the crisis.

Kayode Soremekun's chapter analyses how the Nigerian state has responded to the growing influence of local and transnational non-state actors in the Niger Delta conflict. It provides a historical background to oil – which was a critical weapon in Nigeria's activist pan-African foreign policy in the 1970s – noting that from the 1990s its role was somewhat transformed into an instrument for the transnationalization of the Niger Delta, manifested in the increased struggles between global extractive actors (backed by the state) and non-state forces of local resistance (backed by global activist networks). By also demonstrating how the Niger Delta crisis has reduced the potency of oil as a tool of Nigeria's diplomacy, the chapter analyses the state–oil partnership, and explains why the Nigerian state has become more amenable to the energy security interests of the world's powers, further complicating the nature and ramifications of the conflict in the oil-rich region.

Part Two: Conflict actors' dynamics The chapters in this section of the book identify and analyse the role of various conflict actors in the Niger Delta crisis: the militias, armed groups/cults, the military JTF (made up of units drawn up from the army, air force, navy, police and security services) and the oil companies. They underscore the complex nature of the conflict actors, particularly the ambiguities that underpin their motives and actions. The chapter by Morten Bøås situates the roots of ethnic minority militias in unaddressed grievances, and provides a framework for understanding their tactical and strategic agency in the Niger Delta insurgency. He unpacks the ambiguous relationship of attachment and opposition to such militias, and their resistance towards various manifestations of the Nigerian state. Arguing that the profit motive does not explain why such groups deviate from their original political agendas, the chapter shows how situations of marginalization and exclusion in neo-patrimonial societies such as those of the Niger Delta can be used to explain why the MEND rebellion against a corrupt Nigerian state had over time begun to manifest perverse forms.

The chapter that follows analyses Niger Delta militias in terms of their use of popular and criminal violence in advancing their struggles. Augustine Ikelegbe categorizes ethnic minority militias as insurgent, deviant insurgent and criminal, and provides interesting insights into the complex nature, motives and ambiguities of, and methods used by, these groups, particularly the factors that inform the blurring of boundaries between rebellion and criminality. Violence is treated as a mode of 'empowerment' for alienated youth. In another perspective on conflict actors, Nils Duquet provides an analysis of the linkage between demand-driven proliferation of small arms and light weapons (SALW) and violence in the region. Several chapters also analyse how payments from oil MNCs to some militias for 'stay-at-home, surveillance or security contracts', and payments to the military for 'special allowances/welfare' and security/protection, have gone into arms purchases or acted as incentives to engage in violent activities (Bøås, Ikelegbe, Duquet). They also note how 'rogue' military personnel and state elites cooperate with militias in illegal oil bunkering,[6] providing funds for arms proliferation.

Focusing on a gendered dimension to the conflict actors, Oluwatoyin Oluwaniyi relates women's protests in the Niger Delta to the double-layered exploitation of women, first by men, and second as a result of their exclusion from the benefits of the oil economy, including their victimization by state repression of protests. The ways women organize to resist the various forms of oppression and marginalization which they face is also analysed.

Part Three: Oil MNCs' response(s) Most chapters in this book point to the implication of oil MNCs in the Niger Delta conflict. The official response(s) of oil MNCs to charges of contributing to the violent conflict in the region has been one of outright denial, placing most of the responsibility on the government and criminal elements in the region. Contributors to this section demonstrate how the extractive activities of the companies adversely affect the locality and people, and provide interesting insights into the oil MNCs' response to the demands and grievances of the oil-producing communities.

Uwafiokun Idemudia's chapter explores how oil companies can build a more business-friendly environment in the Niger Delta, as opposed to the existing hostile context, by tapping into Corporate Social Responsibility (CSR). It provides a history and analysis of oil company CSR policies in the Niger Delta, and examines the prospects for new corporate business practices that can prevent or address the conflict. In her chapter, Anna Zalik focuses on a less-explored dimension of how the securitization of Niger Delta oil – in the form of the criminalization of 'stolen' oil and community protest – constitutes a new strategy in the oil MNCs' response to perceived threats to their profit motives in the region. She argues that this strategy has underpinned industrial interventions by global oil companies in the form of discursive reframing of profiteering (campaigning for the fingerprinting of stolen crude oil) through the use of the legaloil.com website, and Global Memoranda of Understanding (GMoU), which outlaw protest, jointly signed with oil-producing communities in the Niger Delta. Based on fieldwork in communities around the Soku gas plant in the Niger Delta, the chapter analyses the context and content of the GMoU signed by Shell with local communities to establish the way in which the new conditionalities for corporate-supported community development projects reflect corporate hegemony over the concept of 'legality' in the region as a means of criminalizing protest and the campaign for resource control.

In the concluding chapter, Cyril Obi and Siri Rustad provide an analysis of the most recent attempt by the Nigerian government to address the insurgency in the region, through the amnesty and post-amnesty programmes, noting that the window of opportunity is still open for radical reforms that can address the roots of the conflict and brighten the prospects for sustainable peace, but that this opening should not be taken for granted.

PART ONE

Causes of conflict, state (in)capacities

1 | The Nigerian state, oil and the Niger Delta crisis

Ukoha Ukiwo

Introduction

The government of Umaru Musa Yar'Adua recorded a remarkable feat when it finally got Niger Delta militants to accept the presidential proclamation of amnesty at the eleventh hour. The proclamation gave unconditional pardon to all those standing trial for militant activities and those involved in such activities once they gave up their arms and embraced peaceful resolution of the crisis. Acceptance of the amnesty generated much excitement and relief in political and oil industry circles as there was palpable concern that yet another major government initiative to resolve the long-running crisis would flounder after so much investment of political capital.

The government's initial plan to organize a high-profile summit on the Niger Delta had failed as a result of the rejection of the appointment of Professor Ibrahim Gambari as its convener.[1] The government subsequently established the Technical Committee on the Niger Delta (TCND) to collate previous policy recommendations for addressing the crisis in the region (see International Crisis Group 2009: 7; TCND 2008).[2] Although the TCND submitted a report to government in November 2008, nothing much was heard from government afterwards.[3] Rather, in April 2009 the government authorized a military offensive against the Movement for the Emancipation of the Niger Delta (MEND).[4]

Pressure from the world's oil-dependent powers and oil multinationals, as well as the limited success of the military approach, influenced the government to release Henry Okah (a MEND leader standing trial) and announce an amnesty for militants. President Yar'Adua, who described the acceptance of amnesty as 'an Independence anniversary gift',[5] promised his government 'shall do everything to ensure that the conditions that make people take arms against the nation and subject themselves to inhuman conditions in the creeks are ameliorated'.[6]

This commitment signalled a shift from the prevalent perspective that criminalized the Niger Delta militants. The criminalization of Delta militants stemmed largely from their alleged involvement in underground or illegal economic activities, such as hostage-taking, protection rackets, political thuggery, theft of crude oil or illegal 'oil bunkering' and weapons proliferation (Human Rights Watch 2002, 2003, 2004; International Crisis Group 2006a: 6, 2006b: 8–10; Asuni 2009; Davies 2009).

Militancy in the Niger Delta has been troubling for the international community as a result of the region's rising strategic importance. Nigeria accounts for about 10 per cent of US oil imports (the equivalent of about 40 per cent of Nigeria's oil exports), and the Niger Delta has loomed large in the security interests of the USA, as it has for the EU and other major oil-importing nations such as China and India, especially with security challenges in the Middle East since September 11 (see Lubeck et al. 2007: 3; Watts 2007). According to Obi (2008a: 428): 'The globalisation of the Niger Delta's oil has gone side-by-side with its "securitisation", in which global hegemonic forces see the oil as a vital "globally-needed" resource, whose continued "uninterrupted" flow along with the safety of (transnational) oil investments and oil workers must be protected at all costs, including military means.'

As the global interest in uninterrupted oil production coincides with the interests of the Nigerian rentier state and its dominant social forces that depend on oil revenues – accounting for over 90 per cent of government revenue – oil production has also become a national security concern. The Nigerian government has not only welcomed international military support for safeguarding oil production (Asuni 2009) but has also deployed serving and retired military officers to troubleshoot in the region.[7] Massive troop deployments to the region have made the ratio of security personnel to oil workers expand beyond affordable and sustainable limits. It is hardly surprising that a sizeable proportion of the federal government's budgetary allocation to the Niger Delta in 2008 was allocated to security, even though the military and police had among the largest chunk of the budget (International Crisis Group 2007: 6).

The desperation of both dominant global and national social forces for oil production to continue at all costs has also indirectly boosted the militancy. It showed militants just how vulnerable the state and global oil markets were to attacks on oil investments in the creeks. It is no wonder that MEND always ensured that reports of its attacks were sent to newswires and reverberated in the global oil markets. The staying power of the militants was due not to the strength of their numbers and arsenal or popular support for insurgency, but rather to their calculation that dominant national and global social forces had more to lose from prolongation of the insurgency.

This chapter sheds light on the root causes of conflict, the responses of the Nigerian state, and what needs to be addressed if the post-amnesty programme is to lead to sustainable peace and development.[8] It includes a critique of the dominant narratives of the crisis. The ways in which the technology of oil production and the politics of oil revenue distribution lie at the heart of the conflict in the region are also explored. This lays the basis for the analysis of the transition from civil protest to violent mobilization. In the concluding section, some suggestions are proffered for resolving the crisis.

Revisiting the 'resource war' perspective to violent conflict

Post-Cold War studies of armed conflict have been dominated by the 'resource war' perspective, which privileges economic motives of armed groups. Two broad versions of this perspective have been applied in the analysis of the violent conflicts between militant groups and the state and oil companies in the Niger Delta.[9] The first version argues that 'greed' is the primary motivation of Niger Delta militants. It posits that though militant groups claim community grievance, their primary motivation lies in opportunities to plunder resources to actualize visions of a better life for themselves (see Reno 2000; Collier et al. 2006; Oyefusi 2007). The second version argues that though the primary motivation may be group grievance, the opportunities for plunder create an incentive for perpetuating the conflict. Thus, far from triggering conflict, greed exacerbates and makes it intractable (Ikelegbe 2006a). Analysts increasingly refer to the transformation or evolution of grievance into greed (Watts 2007: 637).

Against this background, commentators started differentiating groups that are motivated purely by grievance from those motivated by greed. While the former were recognized as genuine *militants* fighting the just cause of the Niger Delta, the latter were dismissed as *criminals* that deployed the rhetoric of self-determination for filthy lucre. This approach is common to scholars and government officials alike, as well as some militants who threatened to apprehend criminals masquerading as militants.[10]

Although the resource war perspective contributes to our understanding of the multiple and complex motivations of insurgent groups, it overlooks the historical and structural causes of violent conflicts. It also serves hegemonic interests as the economic interests of state actors hardly become the focus of its lens (Le Billon and El Khatib 2004; Keen 2007; Kabia 2008). Moreover, the focus on the criminal intentions of insurgents often leads to the adoption of a securitized solution and neglect of the imperatives of redressing more fundamental issues of injustice and horizontal inequalities. The position taken in this chapter is that violent conflicts in the Niger Delta can be traced to alienation and despair over what Watts (2007) has described as 'accumulation by dispossession'. The section that follows discusses the modalities of accumulation by dispossession in the Niger Delta.

The technologies and politics of dispossession

Technology and power are central to the exploration and production of oil. While technology provides the technical know-how, power provides the legal framework of exploration and exploitation. Oil begins to flow only when the interests of technology and power coincide. The terms of agreement that govern exploration and production define who partakes in the production and distribution of oil revenues. This section shows how the technologies and politics of oil production marginalize oil-producing communities and generate violent conflicts.

Technology of oil exploration and exploitation Seventy years after the *potopoto*[11] people of the Niger Delta first witnessed the ritual of oil exploration the experience has remained alienating to them. The hallmark of the entire process of exploration, concession and exploitation is the non-involvement of the *potopoto* people. The oil industry is an enclave economy par excellence as the oil companies enter the community with their capital and labour en suite. Most of the oil facilities are prefabricated and can easily be dismantled and relocated. The *potopoto* people are made to understand that they lack the skills to be employed in the highly technical industry. The only contribution of the people to the process is that they are titular owners of the land and water on which the activity is taking place. However, this contribution is tenuous because their title to land is customary and not legal. This is because, with the enactment of the Land Use Act of 1979, all land belongs to the state. The process is also alienating in the sense that the *potopoto* people have nothing to do with the inputs and outputs of the company. The company has no connection with the local market.

Even the process of the oil company's entry is alienating as it is the government that unilaterally grants it the licence to operate. It is assumed that the villagers have tacitly consented to the concession because they did not object when the government called for objections – a ritual that precedes oil licensing. The fact is, however, that the newspapers in which the oil concession notices are published do not get to the village, and the villagers who are likely to have radio sets do not pay attention to such announcements. Thus, even the means of consultation and communication is alienating.

When in the 1980s the people intensified their complaints about pipes that criss-crossed their communities and intermittently leaked into their farmlands and rivers, as well as the unquenchable gas flares that generated much heat but no light for their communities, another ritual of consultation was introduced. Community activists argue that this new ritual, called environmental impact assessment (EIA), offered only an opportunity for the people to talk but not to decide whether or not the company should be admitted to their communities (see Okonta and Douglas 2001; PEFS 2004; Omeje 2006a).

The *potopoto* people contrast their experiences of alienation and exploitation in their relations with government and oil companies with their previous relations with the global market. The slave trade and palm oil trade required community participation as they entailed massive mobilization of local labour and capital. Surpluses and rents which accrued to the local elite contributed to class formation and the consolidation of dynastic rule in some of the prominent communities. This explains why Niger Delta elites were relatively privileged in the early colonial period, though some Niger Delta inhabitants resented their loss of influence and wealth with the imposition of formal colonial rule (Ekeh 1996).

The fortunes of Niger Delta elites worsened with the regionalization of politics and the transformation of Nigeria's disparate ethnic groups into 'majority' and 'minority' ethnic groups in the mid-1940s. Regionalization transformed Niger Delta ethnic groups into ethnic minorities in the Eastern and Western regions. Surpluses appropriated by regional governments through the marketing boards furthered class formation and capital accumulation among elites of the emergent major ethnic groups in the regions.

The political economy of oil revenue allocation This is because the prevailing revenue allocation formula allowed the regions from which cash crops were derived to retain 50 per cent of the revenue. However, the derivation principle, which was one of the major building blocks of Nigeria's federalism, was de-emphasized with the advent of oil as a major source of revenue in the late 1960s. Successive reviews of the revenue allocation formula witnessed the reduction of the derivation component (see the Introduction to this volume; Uche and Uche 2004). This generated resentment which snowballed into militancy in the region. It is instructive that the MEND emerged shortly after the 2005 National Political Reform Conference (NPRC) failed to accept the recommendation of Niger Delta delegates on the pegging of the percentage of revenue allocated on the basis of derivation at 25 per cent (see Ukiwo 2007).

The Nigerian state and dominant social forces embarked on the ingenious construction of oil as a *national* asset in order to devalue the derivation principle. The regional identities of cocoa, groundnut, palm oil and rubber, which entitled the regions to collect surplus values from their respective cash crops, were discouraged when oil became the major source of revenue. The nationalization of oil was evidenced by the naming of marketing companies, the granting of subsidies to oil products to guarantee a flat pump price across the nation, and the construction of the oil revenues as the *national cake* (Apter 2005: 24–5; Ukiwo 2008a: 74). The naming of certain types of oil and some oilfields after local oil-bearing communities was only symbolic and had no economic value.

The nationalization project has been alienating to oil-producing communities in all its ramifications. First, while oil wealth was deployed to foster unity among Nigerians through the construction of roads and bridges, no effort was made to construct similar roads and bridges to foster unity among Niger Delta peoples.

Second, the appropriation of oil wealth and its transfer to non-oil-producing states to give them a sense of *national belonging* and guarantee them a *minimum national standard* of living have come at the cost of alienating the 'goose that lays the golden egg'.

Third, while concerted efforts were made to transport petroleum products to non-oil-producing sections of the country and therefore guarantee national

21

access at a subsidized rate, no corresponding effort was made to guarantee access to people from whose backyard oil is extracted.

Finally, the nationalization project is alienating to the peoples of the Niger Delta because it is specific to oil. Oil, found *only* in the Niger Delta, is the *only* resource in the country that is represented as a *national* resource. As Okilo aptly puts it:

> This is worse than apartheid [...] Some parts of the country have freedom to exploit minerals found in their country, while in others a whole gamut of laws prevents them from doing same. Solid minerals, wherever you find it, some Nigerians are free to exploit it and people in those areas do. But when you get liquid minerals (*potopoto*), Nigerian laws catch you. But when you are lucky to have solid minerals, no law affects you.[12]

It is evident that central to understanding the current insurgency in the Niger Delta are the competing constructions of oil as a national and a local community resource. The dominant discourse of oil as a national resource to be harnessed to build a virile nation has been associated with the pauperization and disempowerment of oil-producing communities.

Alienation, group mobilization and violent conflicts

Movements for self-determination in the Niger Delta pre-date the advent of the oil complex. Since the late nineteenth century, various resistance movements have mobilized against external domination and/or exploitation in the region. The first set of movements was initiated by merchant-kings against the intrusion of British traders and proto-administrators (see Ikime 1968).

The 1950s witnessed the emergence of another set of resistance movements that were concerned about the marginalization of the Niger Delta in the emergent regional politics of Nigeria. These movements, namely the Mid West State Movement (MWSM), the Calabar Ogoja Rivers State Movement (CORM) and the Conference of Rivers Chiefs and Peoples, were also elitist (Vickers 2000).

The Niger Delta Volunteer Force (NDVF), led by Isaac Jasper Adaka Boro, rebelled against the authority of the Nigerian federal government under General Aguiyi Ironsi by declaring a Niger Delta Republic in February 1966. The resistance was different from political mobilizations in the 1950s because it was a non-elite resistance movement. The rebellion was quashed and Boro later died fighting as a combatant on the federal side in the Nigerian civil war.

Isaac Boro was politically reincarnated three decades later as the icon of Ijaw youths who, like him, were disenchanted with oil exploitation and unimpressed by the efforts of the mainstream leadership to get a better deal for their people (see Nwajiaku 2005). The Ijaw youths were also inspired by Ken Saro-Wiwa, the writer and environmental activist who spearheaded anti-state and anti-oil company mobilizations among the Ogoni people.

Saro-Wiwa avoided Boro's militant tactics, adopting a pacifist strategy instead. He took great pains to consult extensively among various segments of the Ogoni community – a tragic oversight on Boro's part. He put his skills as a writer to use by preparing a very effective international campaign and grassroots mobilization based on the ideology of Ethnic Autonomy, Resource and Environmental Control (ERECTISM).[13] Saro-Wiwa rightly reckoned that the Movement for the Survival of Ogoni People (MOSOP) would be more effective if it took Nigeria and Shell – the main oil company in Ogoniland – to the global court of public opinion. He therefore embarked on the construction of the Ogoni as an endangered indigenous people. The discourse of endangerment struck the right chord with resurgent international minority and environmental rights organizations, which massively mobilized global support for MOSOP (see Okonta 2008a).

Ijaw youths under the aegis of the Ijaw Youth Council (IYC) adopted all of MOSOP's strategies but also tried to do what Saro-Wiwa did not proactively attempt, namely to cultivate a pan-Niger Delta platform. They were aided by two significant factors. First, it was easier for the Ijaw as the most populous group in the region to lead the initiative. Second, the emergence of the IYC in 1998 and its presentation of the Kaiama Declaration roughly coincided with the most recent transition to civil rule in Nigeria. The transition to democracy was significant because it removed a major barrier between political elites and youths and other subaltern groups in the region. Throughout the period of military rule, especially when non-indigenous governors and administrators were in charge of states in the region, elite accumulation and reproduction required alliances with dominant interests in the Nigerian state system.

However, the reconfiguration of power occasioned by the election of indigenous governors bridged the gulf between the elites and the youths. Recognizing the popularity of the cause promoted by the youth groups, a cause that had been enshrined in a couple of bills of rights of ethnic minority communities in the region (see ERA 1999; Raji et al. 2000), and *ipso facto* the political dividend they could harness by becoming patrons of the campaign for a greater transfer of resources to the oil-producing region, the Nigerian elites jumped on to the bandwagon of the resource control struggle (Ukiwo 2007).

The defining moment of unprecedented unity among Niger Delta social forces was the decision of Niger Delta delegates to walk out of the NPRC in 2005 after northern delegates rejected the proposed 25 per cent increase in derivation revenues. The aftermath of the botched conference enhanced the profile of Delta elites as trusted representatives after the turbulent 1990s, which witnessed the decapitation and banishment of some chiefs. At the national level, many Delta chieftains and politicians regained relevance as eminent persons whose good offices were sought for the mediation of conflicts between youths, the state and oil companies.

The context for this was the proliferation and militarization of youth movements amid increased opportunities for local political patronage, security contracts with oil companies and the heavy-handed response of the Nigerian state to civil protest in the Delta (see Ukeje 2001a). The invasion and destruction of the sleepy Odi community in central Niger Delta by Nigerian soldiers in search of the killers of twelve of their colleagues was a turning point. That this armed onslaught against Odi occurred under a democratic government convinced most hardliners that only armed resistance could counter the extractive and exploitative designs of the government and oil companies and force them to pay attention to local demands.

This perception partly contributed to the proliferation of small arms and light weapons as groups procured weapons to overpower poorly armed security agents and defend their communities. Proliferation of weapons was also driven by the penchant of power-hungry elites to arm youths during elections, chieftaincy disputes and communal conflicts, as well as oil bunkering (Ibeanu and Mohammed 2001; Hazen and Horner 2007; Asuni 2009).

The critical factors explaining the transition from civil protest to militant agitation can be discerned at different levels. At the regional level the rapprochement between elite and non-elite groups, the popularization of the resource control agenda and the proliferation of youth organizations were crucial. At the national level, the continued dependence of the Nigerian state on oil and the determination of dominant social forces to control oil wealth by all means were crucial. At the international level, the increasing reliance of the global oil markets on Nigerian oil amid deteriorating security conditions in the Middle East, developments in information technology and communications and proliferation of small arms and light weapons were crucial. The capacity of MEND to attack strategic oil infrastructure and kidnap oil workers otherwise protected by state security exposed the weaknesses and capacity problems of the military and police forces.[14] In a region saturated with weapons the success of MEND in partially crippling oil production and exports and pushing up world oil market prices inspired other armed groups to jump into the fray.[15]

It should be noted that the Niger Delta is not the poorest region in the country. The region is doing relatively well on some human development indicators (see UNDP 2006). It is, however, the region with the highest rates of youth unemployment and income inequality. Violent conflicts in the region are thus driven by perceptions of alienation and exclusion. As a World Bank study puts it:

> The widespread perception of relative deprivation in the core Niger Delta states
> is driven by the considerable mismatch between the level of wealth extracted
> from the region and the benefits accruing to the region and its people. Levels of
> self-assessed poverty are much higher in the Delta than those revealed by household income and expenditure data. In the South South zone, over three quarters

of the population (77 percent) consider themselves to be living in poverty, compared to the official figure of one third (35 percent). (World Bank 2008: 8–9)

Factors that account for the high perception of relative deprivation include the inflationary effects of high incomes in the oil industry, declining opportunities for gainful employment in the oil industry for youths from oil-producing communities, and high levels of corruption in public service and oil companies. It is important to underscore the fact that souring relations between oil-producing communities and oil companies coincided with the implementation of the wage liberalization regime of structural adjustment programmes in the early 1990s. This policy, which transformed the fortunes of oil workers at a time when wages in the public sector were stagnating, triggered competition for jobs in the oil industry. The competition seemed more intense as the liberalization regime had led to the closure of industries and the introduction of embargoes on recruitment into the civil service.

Job seekers from the region could not compete effectively for jobs in the industry and began to identify some institutional factors that placed them in a disadvantageous position. These include the location of the headquarters and/or personnel departments of most companies in Lagos and the mandatory one-year national youth service. They alleged that oil company staffers, who were mostly from non-Niger Delta areas, favoured non-Niger Delta applicants in the recruitment exercises. There were also allegations that statutory positions for junior staff that should have been reserved for 'indigenes' had been allocated to 'non-indigenes'. As unemployed youths from oil-producing communities began to besiege oil companies in search of jobs, the companies began attempting to buy peace by paying the youths monthly allowances. The handouts ironically created an impression of the industry as a place to scrounge free money. The failure of such handouts to sustain peace led the oil companies to hire some youths as security consultants to protect facilities. The favoured youth contractors deployed some portion of the payments they had received to purchase weapons. Free money and light weapons had a destabilizing effect on many communities as different youth groups formed their own companies or gangs to compete for security contracts from oil companies (see WAC Global Services 2003; International Crisis Group 2006a, 2006b).

The situation was further complicated by the advent of democratization in the late 1990s as politicians secured the services of the security outfits and gangs to manipulate the electoral process (Human Rights Watch 2003). The colossal scale of corruption in the Niger Delta between 1999 and 2003, in which public office-holders privatized oil revenues and bamboozled the people with ill-gotten wealth, increased the stakes for political power. This formed the context for the violence in the 2003 elections across the region. Politicians either secured the services of existing cults and gangs or facilitated the formation of new ones to attain their electoral objectives.

Conclusion: the imperative of resource ownership and control

The consequences of the violent conflicts discussed above are ubiquitous and depressing. They include decaying community governance structures, violent and violated environments that can no longer sustain livelihoods, declining social capital and pervasive distrust of public institutions and officer-holders, and the internalization of the culture of militarism. The danger of not addressing these consequences is that each has the capacity to trigger another cycle of violence. This explains why governments and civil society organizations at the regional, national and international levels have demonstrated commitments towards addressing them. However, these investments in resolving the Niger Delta crisis have yielded few dividends because little attention has been paid to addressing the fundamental causes of violent conflicts in the region discussed in this chapter.

A cursory examination of the policies introduced to tackle the Niger Delta crisis reveals the privileging of security and governance perspectives. The security perspective is based on the assumption that the violent conflicts are due to the activities of criminals and vested interests. It therefore adopts a law-and-order approach. It suggests stiffer penalties for criminal activities,[16] more investments in security to enable the security agencies to contain criminality, and social policies such as recruitment of unemployed youths into the police force to prevent them from being recruited into criminal networks and activities.[17]

The governance perspective assumes that the violent conflicts in the region are the result of the absence of development, democracy and good governance. There is thus a concentration of effort in bringing about development and good governance through a range of activities in the Niger Delta that include establishment of a development board, construction of roads, provision of amenities, forceful impeachment of corrupt governors, promoting transparency in public budgeting and supporting monitoring of oil revenues.

Some of these initiatives are laudable and need to be strengthened. They have, however, failed to realize their noble objectives because they are being pursued in lieu of addressing the fundamental issue of alienation which arises from the political question of resource control. In fact, proponents of the security and governance perspectives dismiss the quest for resource control on the grounds that the 13 per cent derivation revenues awarded by the 1999 constitution made a difference only to the bank accounts of politicians and not to the lives of Niger Delta peoples. Presented in this top-down and patronizing fashion, these perspectives offend the sensibilities of the Niger Delta people.[18] Both approaches privilege the criminalization discourse. Essentially, while the security perspective incriminates subaltern classes, the governance perspective blames the woes of the region on corrupt practices by its elites.

Evidence from best practices in the region suggests that the solution to violent conflicts is addressing alienation by entrenching community participation, ownership and control. A case in point is the community trust funds operational in Akassa, Bayelsa state (Ibeanu 2008). By institutionalizing community ownership, the model has provided the community with an objective interest in protecting oil company facilities. Thus, a rare phenomenon was reported in Akassa, where community leaders rounded up and handed over youths who attacked the oil company facility to law enforcement agencies. The trend across the region is for aggrieved community members to turn a blind eye to 'oil bunkering' activities taking place in their neighbourhood. The Akassa model is currently in high demand across the Niger Delta because the dominant practice that drives conflict is one in which, according to Ledum Mitee, the president of MOSOP, the oil-producing communities 'have nothing to lose if oil stops flowing'.[19]

There is a groundswell of opinion in favour of resource control across the region. For instance, 5,000 Ogoni leaders, youths, professionals and women met on 19 July 2008 to approve the framework of benchmarks to be met by prospective operators.[20] The Petroleum Industry Bill (PIB), which is currently being considered by the National Assembly and provides for direct transfer of 10 per cent of oil revenues to oil-producing communities, represents an opportunity to mainstream community participation (Transnational Crisis Project 2010).

The second proposal to address alienation in the Delta is directed at the political economy of oil revenue allocation. There is a need to redesign the modality of the Federation Account with a view to enabling oil-producing states to collect oil revenues and remit an agreed percentage to the account. This reform is highly needed in Nigeria's fiscal federalism as it would reduce dependency on oil and provide an incentive for non-oil-producing states to harness resources that are currently neglected.

Finally, to address alienation there is a need to institutionalize free and fair elections and make elected officials accountable and responsible to the people. Fraudulent elections produce fraudulent leaders. Militancy has thrived in the region because guns rather than votes count during elections. The gains of the amnesty programme will be lost if the politicians rearm the youths in future elections.

2 | Capacity and governance deficits in the response to the Niger Delta crisis

Babatunde A. Ahonsi

Introduction

The Niger Delta crisis has in the last decade attracted significant research attention and progressively expanding policy engagement. Much has been written by way of analysis of the remote and immediate causes of the crisis and its recent escalation. Equally, many attempts have been made over the last three decades by all levels of government, oil MNCs, international development agencies and other stakeholders to implement interventions designed to end the crisis and put the region on a path of sustainable development.

Yet the crisis remains intractable, partly because of the larger national crisis of governance related to the accelerating decline in institutional and human capacity. The gap represented by capacity deficits as an aspect of the crisis of response to the conflict does not feature prominently in scholarly and popular studies of the escalating violence in the Niger Delta. It is also not fully taken into account in planned or recommended response interventions.

Salient dimensions of the Niger Delta conflict

There is a broad enough consensus about the characterization of the Niger Delta conflict as an extreme manifestation of Nigeria's larger and long-standing twin crises of underdevelopment and nation-building (FGN 2009; Obi 2006; Kew and Phillips 2007; UNDP 2006). We identify five interrelated dimensions of the conflict that feature prominently in much of the relevant literature. These are the struggle for resource control and ownership by the oil-bearing communities and its increasingly militant and violent nature, severe environmental degradation, the abject lack of political participation and democratic accountability, infrastructural underdevelopment, and deep and widespread poverty, especially youth unemployment. Each is deserving of some brief elaboration.

The resource control/ownership question and its increasingly violent character The Niger Delta has endured a long history of exploitation in the sense that for four decades it has accounted for much of Nigeria's foreign exchange earnings (over 90 per cent), national GDP (over 40 per cent) and total government revenue (over 80 per cent), but has enjoyed only a small portion of these

(UNDP 2006; Kew and Phillips 2007; Albin-Lackey 2007). For example, it has since the early 1970s produced several hundred billion dollars' worth of oil and gas with its net oil revenues alone (to Nigeria) exceeding $45 billion in 2005, and yet most of its peoples and communities remain poor and unemployed while a few oil companies and individuals (predominantly from outside the region) have amassed and continue to amass stupendous wealth.

Over 85 per cent of the region's working population have no connection with the oil and gas industry, with low-wage/low-productivity informal enterprises as its primary source of livelihood (UNDP 2006). This situation has fostered a widespread sense of extreme relative deprivation. It is a significant factor in the growing resentment and increasingly militant demand for greater access and control over the oil resources of the region by its peoples and leaders.

The continuing lack of response to this demand, and the widespread perception that it may never be peacefully met by government, seem to be fuelling the increasingly violent insurgency within the Niger Delta. But further compounding the conflict is the astronomical increase, especially since 2003, in the incidence of violent clashes between relatively organized youths in local communities and the personnel of oil and gas companies and the military/law enforcement agencies that protect them. One notable consequence of this situation has been a sharp rise in the kidnapping for ransom of oil company executives (especially the expatriates), top political and administrative office-holders, business tycoons and their relatives.

Some of these militant groups, having recently developed a life of their own, and no longer depending on their original patrons among the political elite (FGN 2009; Kew and Phillips 2007; CSN 2006), have very quickly hijacked what was once a peaceful and is still a very popular struggle for resource control to create a booming underground economy (see Bøås, Ikelegbe, Duquet, this volume). It is an economy built around an intricate web of oil-stealing, arms proliferation and hostage-taking rings. Such groups would therefore not be expected to have much interest in a speedy, peaceful and comprehensive negotiated resolution of the conflict, especially given their increasing integration into the highly lucrative regional and transnational trade in illegally sourced crude oil (Cole 2008). Nigeria's national security and economic stability are now in extreme jeopardy as a result of this increasingly international criminal component of the conflict and the recent calamitous increase in the disruption of oil production due to militant activities.

Environmental degradation There is no doubt that the Niger Delta is one of the most environmentally degraded regions in the world. Prior to the discovery of petroleum in commercial quantities in 1956 and commencement of its exportation in 1958, the Niger Delta region had the most extensive lowland tropical and fresh forests, aquatic ecosystems and biodiversity in West Africa. It supported a large percentage of Nigeria's fisheries industry, huge and diverse medicinal and forest resources, wood for energy and shelter, as well as a stable fertile soil for farming and a hospitable habitat for increasingly endangered wildlife such as the Delta elephant and the river hippopotamus. These resource endowments served to provide relatively sustainable means of livelihood for millions of people across the region

But drawing on several sources, a recent study captures as follows the extent and impact of the degradation of the Niger Delta environment associated with crude oil exploration:

> [...] 1.5 million tons of oil has spilled into the Niger Delta over the past 50 years, making the region one of the five most polluted locations on earth. Oil slicks cover the region; blowouts and leaks affect creeks, streams and related traditional sources of livelihood, destroying mangrove forests, eroding soil plots, and killing aqua life. Hundreds of well-sites have flares, which come from the burning of associated gas. [...] Resulting sulfuric acid mists damage plants and forests. Flares pollute rainwater, cause acid rain and contribute to climate change. [...] Amid this pollution many Niger Delta residents suffer from oil poisoning. [...] Oil poisoning causes respiratory ailments. In addition, residents suffer from a plethora of waterborne diseases such as malaria, dysentery, tuberculosis, typhoid and cholera. Life expectancy is low [...] (Kew and Phillips 2007: 159–60)

One consequence of this hazardous environmental situation is the exacerbation of intra- and inter-regional youth migration to the cities. This worsens the urban unemployment situation and contributes to the intensification of numerous social pathologies. Prominent among these are cultism, gangster activities, a growing sex industry, high rates of unwanted pregnancy and sexually transmitted infections, spontaneous violence, and family instability, which have all become prominent features of life in urban centres across the region (UNDP 2006; NDDC 2006; Albin-Lackey 2007; Kew and Phillips 2007).

Furthermore, there seems to be a lack of will and capacity on the part of the federal and state governments to compel the oil-exploring companies to clean up the region, pay adequate compensation to degraded and polluted communities, and improve the safety standards of oil industry operations. This apparent official indifference is frequently cited by leading resource control advocates as strong grounds for the oil-bearing communities to have greater participation in and ownership of the oil and gas industry (CSN 2006; Manifesto of the Niger Delta 2006). Indeed, without enhanced community engagement, it is difficult to see how, within Nigeria's presently warped federal structure, the unholy alliance between the oil MNCs and the federal and state governments can be broken to enable better environmental monitoring, remediation and restoration.

Lack of political participation and democratic accountability It is the case that both during the long period of military rule (especially between 1983 and 1999) and since the return to civil rule in May 1999, the peoples of the Niger Delta have experienced no real sense of political participation or responsiveness of the national, state and local council leaders to their needs and concerns (Ibaba, Ako, Idemudia, this volume). It seems, on the one hand, that with every election in Nigeria as a whole and in the Niger Delta in particular the people's votes count for less and less as elections are more and more blatantly rigged (Kew and Phillips 2007). On the other hand, national campaigns by civil society groups and social movements in the region demanding greater political and fiscal autonomy have intensified since the early 1990s. Similarly, at the state level, such demands on the governments in the region to become more responsive to the needs and aspirations of the people and their local communities through improved governance and more devolution of power to the local council and community levels have significantly expanded (Ibeanu 2006). But these demands for change are increasingly frustrated by Nigeria's unyielding, godfather-centred *unitary* federalism (Albin-Lackey 2007; Manifesto of the Niger Delta 2006; Kew and Phillips 2007).

It has been argued that the rapid proliferation of militant groups in the Niger Delta is partly a result of the powerlessness and frustrations that the ordinary people of the region, especially the youths, feel in the face of a persistent lack of democratic choice and the prevalence of unaccountable, anti-people governance across the three tiers of Nigeria's federal system (Obi 2004a, 2006; Kew and Phillips 2007).

Infrastructural underdevelopment Despite the stupendous amount of resources extracted from this region, it remains grossly underdeveloped. According to the Niger Delta Regional Development Master Plan, despite the largely riverine terrain of the region, the state of water transport infrastructure is so poor that the cost of water transport for goods and people is typically higher than for road transport, and transport time is often longer by water than by road. Even so, 40 per cent of the total length of paved roads in the region remains in poor condition, with most of the wetland areas being without roads and therefore inaccessible. The region lacks rail transportation, possesses very poor housing stock, and over 36 per cent of the households therein lack access to electricity supply and over 60 per cent to potable water respectively. Only about 10 per cent of the region is served by the national postal system and the number of telephone users per 100 people is one of the lowest in the world (NDDC 2006: 81–6).

Given the vast amount of oil wealth generated from the Niger Delta, its state of infrastructure development can only be described as abysmally poor. From the agitation of nearly all the well-known resource control movements and from several needs assessments that have been conducted within the region, it is clear that massive but effective investment in infrastructure by government and oil MNCs aimed at alleviating the suffering of the people has to be a major component of any comprehensive response to the Niger Delta conflict (FGN 2009; Ojakorotu 2008; CSN 2006; NDDC 2006; Manifesto of the Niger Delta 2006; OVPN 2007).

Poverty and unemployment The relatively high levels of poverty in the Niger Delta in the midst of stupendous oil wealth have led to a large and growing proportion of the youth population seeing violence as a solution to their problems (Albin-Lackey 2007; Obi 2006). Many unemployed young persons are easily attracted to the militias rampaging across the region by the immediate prospects of highly rewarding employment in the violent underground economy described previously.

Comprising over a fifth of Nigeria's total population of about 145 million, the inhabitants of the Niger Delta are spread across nine states, residing mostly in largely rural communities in dispersed village settlements. The region's unemployment levels are higher than the national average (put at 5 per cent in 2000), reaching 16–19 per cent in three of the constituent states and manifesting as one in every seven young people in the region being unemployed (FGN 2009: 105). And while its adult literacy rate (78 per cent) is significantly higher than the national average of 54 per cent, more than a third of the region's under-five children are either severely or moderately malnourished, a strong indication of high levels of household poverty (UNDP 2006: 13–15). In much of the region, life-chance-enhancing social amenities are concentrated in the state capitals, and while its overall poverty situation is not the worst in Nigeria, it is exceptionally high when compared to other oil-producing regions of the world, as the following extract from a recent report by the UNDP (ibid.: 15) makes clear:

> The region's human development index (HDI) score, a measure of well-being encompassing the longevity of life, knowledge and a decent standard of living, remains at a low value of 0.564 (with 1 being the highest score). While these ratings put the Niger Delta at a slightly higher level than Nigeria's overall HDI of 0.453, the area rates far below countries or regions with similar oil and gas resources.

Elements of a comprehensive response

Both in scholarly and public policy circles, a widely held view is that for any response to the Niger Delta conflict to stand any chance of success it has to be holistic, multi-sectoral, long-ranging, and based on broad-based political consensus among the key stakeholders within the conflict. Indeed, a similar inference has emerged from the most recent broad-based response to the crisis led by the federal government (FGN 2009). In September 2008, President Yar'Adua constituted the Ledum Mitee-led Niger Delta Technical Committee and charged it with preparing a compendium of key recommendations from the reports of all previous committees set up to proffer solutions to the Niger Delta crisis, from the 1958 Willinks Commission report to the 2001 Ogomudia Committee report, and other major reports and studies on the subject.

It may be surmised from the main recommendations of the Mitee Committee, the implications of the conclusions from several studies, and the codified demands by several social movements across the oil-bearing communities of the Niger Delta (ibid.; OVPN 2007) that a comprehensive response to the conflict must begin with some highly visible, quick-impact, targeted improvements in the infrastructural and security situation of the region in the context of a longer-term development and peace-building strategy.

The goal in the immediate term would be to create public confidence, reduce the deep-seated distrust of the state and oil multinationals within the oil-bearing communities, and generate the goodwill required to take on the more difficult and long-term aspects of the response. Among such measures would be the full implementation of all outstanding promises, court rulings and memoranda of understanding (MoU) between oil companies and relevant host communities (OVPN 2007; Manifesto of the Niger Delta 2006). Others are speedy and negotiated consultations with militants and credible community leaders to establish a durable ceasefire, the activation of high-powered institutional machinery to manage an expanded Niger Delta response initiative, and the simultaneous rehabilitation of strategic roads, bridges and water transport infrastructure across the region (FGN 2009; Manifesto of the Niger Delta 2006).

In the medium term, provided an improved security situation can be sustained, the broad consensus seems to be that some sort of 'Marshall Plan' for the region, focusing on extensive infrastructural development projects and economic growth, based upon the Niger Delta Regional Development Master Plan prepared in 2006 by the Niger Delta Development Commission, would have to be efficiently and effectively implemented. In its current formulation, the plan requires fifteen years to be fully executed at a cost of $50 billion (in 2004 prices) based on a public–private partnership strategy (NDDC 2006). The plan essentially entails the pursuit of improved agricultural productivity, the development of micro and small-scale enterprises, the establishment of improved infrastructure and medium- to large-scale industries, accelerated human resource development interventions, and improved environmental protection and restoration as the basis for poverty eradication, wealth creation and sustainable development.

Finally, a flexible but sequential, multi-step approach is widely envisaged for a consensus-building process that would bring together all the parties to the conflict for a thorough negotiation of a binding set of agreements around a detailed plan for resolving all the major outstanding issues in the conflict.

Prominent among these are resource ownership and control; intergovernmental relations; local government area and state creation; citizenship, residence and movement; environmental monitoring and protection; electoral reform; and the termination of militant activities (including amnesty for and reintegration of militia leaders).

The issue that immediately arises, therefore, is why, despite the apparently fairly broad consensus about what needs to be done, it has been difficult to make modest progress in implementation. The commonly given response to this question is that Nigeria's dysfunctional unitary or centralized federalism, widespread official corruption associated with the patronage-driven redistribution of petroleum and gas revenues, and the deeply ingrained exploitative character of the business and community development activities of the oil multinationals have been and remain the main barriers to the implementation of a holistic response (ARD Inc. 2006; Okonta and Douglas 2001; Albin-Lackey 2007; Kew and Phillips 2007). But is this interpretation adequate, given that a comprehensive response to the Niger Delta conflict is a major and very complex undertaking?

Capacity and governance aspects of the response crisis

It is legitimate to question whether the Nigerian state could lead and implement an effective response to the Niger Delta conflict. This is because such a response clearly requires a robust and strong capacity to plan, implement and monitor a complex series of interventions over a sustained period, which the Nigerian state has increasingly shown itself to be lacking. Recently developed research-based indices of state weakness, constructed according to relative performance of the core functions of statehood, all classify Nigeria as a critically weak or fragile state – that is, a country that lacks the essential capacity and/ or willingness to fulfil four sets of critical governmental responsibilities (Rice and Patrick 2008; Versi 2007). These are: fostering an enabling environment for sustainable and equitable economic growth; establishing and sustaining legitimate, transparent and accountable political institutions; protection of citizens from violent conflicts and securing the country's territorial integrity; and meeting the basic human needs of the population.

One could easily dismiss such indices for being high on description and low on analytical and predictive utility. But Nigeria is in a situation in which its military, even with help from the oil companies, can no longer protect oil installations that are located 120 kilometres off the coast of the country, with perhaps over 25 per cent of its daily oil exports being illegal (Cole 2008; also see Ukeje, this volume). Moreover, the presidency was unable for over fourteen months (June 2007–July 2008) to establish a national consultative and dialogue process for a conflict that threatens Nigeria's corporate existence. Even the series of initiatives by the Yar'Adua administration to frontally address the crisis through the creation of a Niger Delta ministry, and granting of presidential amnesty to all militants that agree to disarm, have so far yielded less than satisfactory outcomes (Ogbodo 2009).

Moreover, the evidence is clear that increased military presence and official consultative actions aimed at reducing unrest in the region have been accompanied since the return to civil rule in 1999 by geometric increases in shutdown of oil production via destruction or violent occupation of oil installations, kidnapping of oil workers, gang wars, communal conflicts, armed robbery, election violence and hijacking of oil tankers or ships (Ibeanu 2006; Nodland and Hjellestad 2007; FGN 2009). Oil and gas pipeline vandalization by youth militias in the region, for example, witnessed an eightfold increase between 1999 and 2007 in near-concurrence with the federal government's intensification of its response to the crisis (FGN 2009: 114). This pattern in the impact of a dominant response to the crisis demands that we give more serious consideration to the issue of whether Nigeria truly possesses the human and institutional capacity to end and resolve the violent conflict in the Niger Delta.

It is important to stress that even on issues as simple and basic as childhood immunization coverage, access to potable water and maintenance of public safety, Nigeria ranks as poorly as countries in severe conflict or post-conflict situations such as Zimbabwe, Sierra Leone, Myanmar and Nepal (Chankova et al. 2007; Horwood 2008).

It seems, therefore, that part of the challenge that we have to interrogate is the huge capacity/governance deficits that may be severely hindering the country from being able to autonomously fashion and implement a permanent solution to the long-standing Niger Delta conflict. A state that is failing to deliver basic social, economic and political goods to its citizens should not be expected to competently manage a response to a complex, long-running crisis. It may, of course, be argued that such a failure is much more a consequence of a lack of political will and commitment to good governance than of a lack of human and institutional capacity.

It is therefore important at this juncture to clarify the sense in which the concepts of *capacity* and *governance* are used here and why they may be usefully interlinked for an assessment of the different phases of the official response to the Niger Delta conflict. Governance is here conceived broadly in terms of the process by which the relationship between the rulers and the ruled, the state and the individual, is managed to produce the delivery of services that meet the needs of the latter without threatening the stability and orderly change of the larger society. Central to this conception is the role of the state as the main vehicle for the exercise of political power in the management of a country's affairs such that the majority of citizens can enhance their chances of enjoying a good-quality life (Guhan 2000).

Governance, therefore, has both political and technocratic dimensions – that is, issues of transparency, accountability and participation are as important as those of economic efficiency and management effectiveness in the conduct of governmental activities if the goal is promotion of the good life of the citizen. The capacity of the state to deliver programmes and services through which this goal is achieved is thus an intrinsic part of governance (Ake 1996).

Capacity is the aggregate of human skills and competencies, organizational structures and institutional procedures and systems through which identified collective needs or problems are effectively responded to. It is necessary, as Ake (ibid.: 3) argues, to think in terms of *aggregations of capacities, especially in the context of national development, which requires networks of interconnected capacities*. Inherent to this conception of capacity is the notion of empowerment vis-à-vis the ability of people and organizations to take control of activities and processes that affect their lives or desired outcomes.

Thus, when a country has a paucity both of trained and skilled human resources and of strong institutions required to tackle its particular problems, it will struggle to resolve its development and nation-building challenges (ibid.; Juma 2006). For example, we know that Nigeria has a severe shortage of engineers and technologists, with the situation in the Niger Delta being worse than that of the more developed south-west region (UNDP 2005; FME 2006). Yet, as made clear by Juma (2006), a country's ability to initiate and sustain economic growth and sustainable development depends in part on its capabilities in engineering and technology, which in turn determine the ability to provide clean water, good healthcare and adequate infrastructure.

The implication is that without addressing the critical capacity deficits facing Nigeria as a whole, and the Niger Delta (with its more challenging terrain of creeks and swamps) in particular, resolving the Niger Delta conflict through the comprehensive response described earlier would be made doubly difficult. Such an eventuality may not necessarily be made less likely by increased technical and financial support from the oil MNCs and international development agencies, since the resolution of the Niger Delta crisis cannot be achieved without the full involvement of the region and its peoples. None of the previous state-led interventions in the crisis has, for example, enabled the people of the Niger Delta to substantially tap directly into the oil industry benefits such as employment and equity stakes because of their continued lack of skills and financial capital (UNDP 2006). This general point would be made clearer by a brief review of the three broad phases of the official response to the crisis and conflict to date.

1960–89 The main response during this period was informed by the early recognition by the federal government of the special developmental attention that the region deserved. This led to the establishment in 1960 of the Niger Delta Development Board (NDDB) to manage the developmental challenges of the region. But it achieved very little in its seven years of operation and, following the cessation of the 1967–70 civil war, the resources meant for its activities were diverted to fund a massive rehabilitation and construction programme in different parts of the country (NDDC 2006). A second attempt was made during the Shagari administration (1979–83) to refocus attention on the growing developmental challenges of the region with the establishment of a Presidential Task Force to manage the allocation of 1.5 per cent of the federation account for tackling the special needs of the region. Again, by the time its lifespan expired in 1991/92, only a few projects had been completed, with little or no positive developmental impact on the oil-bearing communities.

The failure of governance vis-à-vis the lack of capacity to seriously respond to an emergency was a defining feature of this phase of missed opportunities to nip the emergent Niger Delta crisis in the bud. One assessment of this early phase of the official response was even more pointed in attributing its minimal impact to planning and management capacity deficits, describing the NDDB as having 'no clear idea of its objectives or how [...] it should set about the task of sorting out desirable projects into priority order' (Manifesto of the Niger Delta 2006: 31). Logically, one would expect this early-phase capacity shortfall in the response to carry over into later phases at an increasing rate as the crisis in the region became more complicated without the implementation of a carefully designed, large-scale capacity-building intervention to date.

1990–99 This period witnessed the intensification of discontent and restiveness in the region. In response the Babangida administration (1985–93) set up the Oil Mineral Producing Areas Development Commission (OMPADEC) in 1992. It was allocated 3 per cent of federal oil revenue to tackle the developmental challenges of the oil-bearing communities. Yet capacity-governance gaps vis-à-vis major planning and implementation hiccups feature, though not with enough emphasis, in a recent dispassionate assessment of its performance between 1992 and 1999, when it was wound up:

> OMPADEC completed several projects but bequeathed numerous abandoned or unfinished projects and huge debts. There is no reliable information on the total amount the Commission received from the Federation Account, but what is clear is that OMPADEC suffered from lack of focus, inadequate and irregular funding, official profligacy, corruption, excessive political interference, lack of transparency and accountability, and high overhead expenditure. Most of its projects had little to do with poverty reduction and the vast majority of the people did not benefit from its activities. (NDDC 2006: 102)

The utter failure of OMPADEC marked the beginning of fast-growing disenchantment with the official response to the Niger Delta's crisis of development and environmental deterioration, and distrust of the sincerity and sustainability of this response. Many of the social movements agitating for greater resource control by the oil-bearing communities also began to increasingly view government special initiatives and their institutional mechanisms as barriers between the people and their resources (see, for example, Manifesto of the Niger Delta 2006: 31).

2000–present The return to civilian democratic rule in May 1999 after nearly sixteen unbroken years of military dictatorship provided Nigeria with a new opportunity to fashion a lasting solution to the growing restiveness in the Niger Delta. In response, the NDDC was inaugurated in December 2000 with provisions for generous funding, mainly from 15 per cent of the monthly allocation from the federation account, oil- and gas-processing companies' contribution of 3 per cent of their total budget, and 50 per cent of the Ecological Fund allocations due to the nine states that make up the region (NDDC 2006). Furthermore, in line with the provisions of the 1999 constitution, 13 per cent of total oil revenues have been allocated on a monthly basis since 2000 to oil-producing states, in addition to their share of federal revenues distributed to all the thirty-six states.

So, with the interventions by NDDC in the region and the hugely increased revenues accruing to the region's state governments (especially the violence-ridden Delta, Rivers and Bayelsa) associated with the extended high price of crude oil on the world markets, one would have expected more rapid development in the region. Instead, the last eight years have witnessed an intensification of the conflict due to the colossal failure of both the NDDC and the region's state governments to deliver on rapid infrastructural development and poverty reduction (see Ukiwo, this volume).

An observation frequently made about the structures of decision-making in the NNDC is that they are not participatory enough and that genuine direct engagement with beneficiary communities as agents in the planning and implementation of development interventions has not been a hallmark of major Niger Delta response measures by the federal and state governments, even with the coming of the NDDC (Ibeanu 2006). Yet providing oil-bearing communities with the skills and resources to take on more responsibility for the development and execution of economic, social and environmental protection programmes and services is crucial for creating an enabling context for permanently resolving the crisis in the region (OVPN 2007).

Predictably, most of the attempts at analysing the causes of this débâcle emphasize the role of official corruption, especially at the state level (see the chapter by Ibaba, this volume), and deliberate underfunding and political interference by the federal government in the operations of the NDDC (Kew and Phillips 2007; Obi 2006; Manifesto of the Niger Delta 2006). The question of whether, with the chronic shortage of skilled human resources in the region and the country as a whole and the associated crisis of programme planning and delivery by the public service at the state and federal levels, the increased amount of funding that became available since 2000 for development interventions in the Niger

Delta could be efficiently deployed and managed is rarely asked. Neither is the likelihood that these capacity deficits have aided resource leakage and funds misappropriation often discussed or analysed. But even the most recent presidential efforts (since January 2009) at resolving the crisis through the creation of a Federal Ministry of the Niger Delta and the granting of amnesty to militants, as part of the process of implementing the recommendations contained in the report of the Technical Committee on the Niger Delta, are already attracting a barrage of criticisms for being superficial, sloppy, haphazard and disjointed in implementation (Abati 2009; Orere et al. 2009).

Nonetheless, many analysts do not seem to notice the contradiction in, on the one hand, bemoaning the underfunding of the NDDC by the federal government and oil and gas multinationals and, on the other hand, highlighting the limited impact of its developmental efforts with the $1.62 billion it received between 2000 and 2006 (see, for example, Ebiri 2008). More fundamentally, such analysts seem not to realize the near-impossibility of progress on a key demand of Niger Delta militants and key opinion leaders regarding greater host-community stakeholding and participation in the oil and gas industry (which is almost completely controlled by the oil MNCs) if the region and Nigeria as a whole do not develop the human capacity and technological know-how to directly prospect for, process and export oil and gas products.

Charting a way forward

What, then, is the way forward? The first step relates to strategic human capital development and the strengthening of the structures and capacities of the public service at the federal, state and local government levels. This needs to be given more prominence and fully integrated across every aspect of the planned official and other responses to the Niger Delta conflict.

Second, there is an immediate need to undertake a rigorous and wide-ranging assessment of the human and institutional capacity requirements for the planning, implementation and management of a comprehensive response to the Niger Delta conflict. A plan for human capital development and institutional strengthening informed by its findings then needs to be developed, budgeted for and integrated into the overall response.

Third, based on the long history of failure of vertical approaches to fielding special development interventions in the region, perhaps it is time to give serious consideration to the scrapping of the NDDC and its state-level equivalents. In their place, a policy of horizontal integration should be instituted that requires all key social service delivery and infrastructural development agencies at the federal level, such as the National Poverty Eradication Programme, the National Directorate of Employment, the Universal Basic Education Commission, the National Primary Health Care Development Agency, the Federal Housing Authority, the Education Trust Fund and the National Agricultural and Cooperative

Bank, and their state-level equivalents to significantly expand their services and interventions in oil-bearing communities in the region. But it would also be necessary in the interests of sustainability and participatory governance to give the local people and governments more responsibility for coordinating and facilitating investments and interventions by the higher tiers of government and the oil MNCs at the community level.

But if this approach would be divisive or too radical in the short term, since it has never been tried before as part of the Niger Delta response, it can be preceded by a back-to-back integration of the implementation processes, with the NDDC or newly created Federal Ministry of the Niger Delta as the fulcrum. The integration would then be structured to ensure that the interventions that are closest to the people, in basic physical and social amenities, are largely designed and executed by organizations and firms that are owned by or based in the local communities.

Fourth, steps need to be taken by the government with support from the oil MNCs and international development agencies, as part of the initial stages of rolling out a comprehensive response, to prepare the oil-bearing communities themselves for more direct engagement with the official response. This would entail the identification and mobilization of community associations such as youth groups and neighbourhood councils, vocational associations and trade groups, women's cooperatives and local faith-based organizations to be formally linked with agencies that are to implement the planned development interventions.

Not only will this approach provide for greater accountability and programme relevance and responsiveness, it would increase the communities' capacities to absorb the increased funding for services and infrastructure that will come with the envisaged expanded response to the conflict. This should not be very hard to accomplish given that many of these groups are already involved in the provisioning of public goods, including road rehabilitation, security, healthcare and education, and generally tend to have an appreciable degree of internal democracy (ARD Inc. 2006). It is in any case a more sustainable approach to capacity-building since it necessarily acknowledges and harnesses local knowledge and expertise.

In the medium to long term, a major implication of the thesis advanced so far is that the planning and implementation of the envisaged comprehensive response to the conflict has to be used to provide Niger Delta residents and public agencies therein (and other Nigerians) with the opportunity to learn and acquire further skills and competencies, and develop structures or mechanisms for self-development, professional excellence and economic empowerment. This may require, for example, that the state and federal governments partner with the oil and gas companies to institute integrated skills training and preferential enterprise mentoring/subcontracting schemes that enable small firms owned and managed by Niger Deltans to implement parts of large infrastructural and service projects.

It may also require that for the sustained dialogue and consensus-building process among all affected stakeholders to conclusively address the key issues that are driving the conflict (poverty, infrastructural development, youth un-employment, security, political/electoral reform, environmental remediation and protection, oil company–community relations), and for it to be perceived as credible and legitimate, stakeholder groups would have to be supported with capacity-building efforts. Affected communities could, for example, be trained to gather data on environmental impacts, mapping community needs and structures, and to improve their negotiating skills and ability to represent their constituencies.

Conclusion

Nigeria's ability to resolve the violent conflict in the Niger Delta will require considerable investment in human capacity and institutional strengthening given the level, density and variety of skills and competencies as well as organ-izational structures and strengths demanded by the frequently advocated com-prehensive response around which a broad consensus seems to have developed. It is a response that demands a central role for the federal, state and local governments as part of a well-coordinated and focused multi-stakeholder net-work of actors, including regional and international development institutions, local and international NGOs with expertise in conflict mediation, peace-building and consensus-building, community associations and donor agencies.

Such committed and sustained engagement with efforts to resolve the Niger Delta conflict is likely to become a great opportunity for the Nigerian state to address some of its critical human resource gaps and organizational manage-ment deficits in ways that better set the country up for its quest to achieve much higher rates of economic growth and social development. This is simply because resolving the Niger Delta conflict will ultimately entail transformative regional and national development interventions and political re-engineering. These, by their very nature, require and generate progressively robust webs of interconnected capacities at the human and institutional levels, provided there is dedicated democratic political leadership across the three tiers of governance.

3 | The struggle for resource control and violence in the Niger Delta

Rhuks Ako

Introduction

The quest for resource control by the people of the Niger Delta lies at the heart of the violence in the region. Resource control is essentially based on claims of ownership, access and equity, and refers to the desire that the region be left to manage its natural resources, particularly its oil, and pay taxes and/or royalties to the federal government. The notion of 'resource control' is grounded in the historical struggles of the people of the Niger Delta for self-determination and local autonomy, particularly in reversing decades of perceived federal marginalization in the distribution of power, and from the benefits accruing from the exploitation of the natural resources in the region. The resource control discourse evolved from the Boro-led Niger Delta Volunteer Force's (NDVF) failed secession from Nigeria in 1966. The group alleged that the existing framework for exploiting oil would not promote the development of the oil-bearing communities. Following this logic, the Movement for the Survival of Ogoni People (MOSOP), through the Ogoni Bill of Rights (OBR), demanded, among other things, 'Ogoni control of Ogoni oil'. These demands also found expression in the rather short-lived campaign of the pan-Delta Chikoko Movement (CM) and that of a number of other ethnic minority associations in the Niger Delta. However, the notion was explicitly and clearly framed in the 1998 Kaiama Declaration of the Ijaw Youth Council.

This chapter explores the various ramifications of the resource control discourse in the context of ongoing violence in the Niger Delta and Nigeria's 'unfinished federal project'. In this regard, the idea of resource control can be broadly conceptualized in three ways. These are 'absolute' resource control, 'principal' resource control and increased derivation. Absolute resource control refers to the aim that all oil resources in the Niger Delta be owned and controlled by the people of the region. The expression of this form of resource control is manifest in the Kaiama Declaration, which asserts in Paragraph (5) that '[E]very region should control its resources 100 per cent from which it will allocate funds for running the central government.' The IYC's proposition is simply that each federating unit in Nigeria should have 'absolute' control of the resources within its geographic territory and make contributions to the central government to fund federal responsibilities.

The definitions proffered by Sagay and Douglas imply 'principal' control. Sagay (2001) defines resource control as the region having 'a direct and decisive role in the exploration for, the exploitation and disposal of, including sales of the harvested resources'. Douglas (2001), in similar vein, posits that resource control 'denotes a compelling desire to regain ownership, control, use and management of resources for the primary benefit of the first owner (the communities and people) on whose land the resources originate'. While Sagay emphasizes 'direct and decisive role' to suggest increased participation of the Niger Delta in the management of the oil industry, Douglas refers to the region 'regaining control' of the oil industry.

For their part, Adesopo and Asaju (2004) define resource control in terms of increased derivation. This refers to the right of the Niger Delta to be allowed to control or manage the revenue accruing from the oil and other natural resources in line with the tenets of true federalism. An interesting observation in this definition is the reference to 'true federalism', a phrase that is often used in the resource control discourse. The OBR, the Kaiama Declaration and politicians from the Niger Delta region have made reference to 'true federalism' consistently. For instance, the governors of the seventeen southern states referred to 'true federalism' in their definition of resource control. According to them, resource control is: 'The practice of true federalism and natural law in which the federating units express their rights to primarily control the natural resources within their borders and make agreed contribution towards the maintenance of common services of the government at the centre.'[1]

Adesopo and Asaju (ibid.) define true federalism as a federal system of government wherein each state would have full control of its resources and contribute an agreed percentage towards the maintenance of the common services of the government at the centre, as the case was in the first republic and as it is being practised in places like Canada, Switzerland, France and even the United States of America, from where Nigeria partly copied its system of governance.

It is imperative to make some clarification regarding the 'true federalism' terminology. There is no doubt that within resource control parlance it refers to the participation of the Niger Delta in either the management of the industry and/or access to adequate pecuniary benefits from the exploitation of the resource. It also signifies shared coequal relations between the tiers of government in the country. However, it is doubtful that this phrase has much traction outside the resource control discourse within Nigeria. Indeed, it is doubtful that any sort of federalism may be correctly described as 'true'. The plausible argument that may be advanced is that, owing to the similarities between Nigeria's federalism and another's (for the sake of argument, the United States of America), the distributive aspect of Nigeria's political arrangement be modelled after the USA's. Hence, the key issue here is the location of the power to control and distribute resources/revenues rather than the 'trueness' or otherwise of a federal model.

The fundamental questions are true federalism for whom, how and why? It is within this context that an exploration of fiscal federalism is necessary.

Federalism is a system of government that emphasizes both vertical power-sharing across different levels of governance and, at the same time, the integration of different territorial and socio-economic units, cultural and ethnic groups in one single polity (McLean and McMillan 2003). The allocation of powers is determined by the (federal) constitution, which is in reality a political and legal response to the underlying social and political realities of different societies.[2] Thus, federalism may have certain practical core values but its application is pragmatic and dependent on each country's peculiar societal circumstances and experiences as dictated by its people. The active involvement of a country's citizens in the constitution-making process underscores the legitimacy of the constitution. This point is most pertinent to this discussion because the lack of public involvement in the making of the Nigerian constitution is a point of argument for the advocates of resource control. The current 1999 constitution was foisted on the country by the military, which had institutionalized a unitary style of federalism (Douglas et al. 2004). The result includes a central government that wields excessive political and economic control over the federating units. Thus, it is not coincidental that the agitation for resource control in Nigeria has economic and political dimensions that cannot be separated. What the advocates of resource control describe when they speak of 'true federalism' is a redress in Nigeria's fiscal federalism wherein the federating units own and manage their resources and revenues, and decide on how much contribution they make to the central government to fund federal responsibilities.

Fiscal federalism is a general normative framework for assignment of functions to the different levels of government and appropriate fiscal instruments for carrying out these functions (Oates 1999). Where natural resource revenues are thrown into the fiscal federalism mix, the level of government that collects resource rents and shares them with the other is determined by two major factors. The first is the level of fiscal decentralization; that is, the extent to which various levels of government have the power to levy taxes generated by non-renewable resources. Second is the issue of revenue-sharing; that is, how resource revenues are allocated, not only among levels of government but between governments at the same level (McKenzie 2006). Consequently, it is erroneous to suggest, as is often suggested in the resource control debate, that central collection and allocation of resource revenues (centralization) is an aberration. In fact, McKenzie argues, 'the conventional economic wisdom in this regard is that taxation of natural resources should be centralized – with the national as opposed to the state – government' (ibid.: 252). If central revenue collection is not an anomaly, revenue allocation has proved to be, and this is what needs to be highlighted. In other words, rather than argue that resource control implies, or is synonymous with, fiscal federalism, the argument should be that irrespective of who collects resource rents under Nigeria's federalism, the issue of revenue allocation must be properly addressed.

Resource control and petro-violence in the Niger Delta

The resource control discourse has become the bedrock of activities for various groups with different intents. These include militant/militia groups that initially conceptualized resource control as the fundamental basis of their struggle. Gangs and other criminal elements have opportunistically latched on to the rhetoric of resource control and operated within the pervasive sense of insecurity in the region to engage in criminal activities for personal gratification. Politicians from the Niger Delta have also taken advantage of, and co-opted the language of, resource control in legitimizing their leadership and facilitating access to political power and increased oil revenues. Politicians routinely proclaim the benefits of resource control and restate their commitment to its achievement, even in the absence of any real intent or evidence on how the core essence of the concept – sustainable development of the region and its inhabitants – is to be attained.

The earliest form of violence-related resource control campaign in post-colonial Nigeria found expression in the Boro-led twelve-day revolution in 1966, which failed to establish a 'Niger Delta Republic'. Subsequent attempts to exert pressure for 'resource control' till the 1990s were mainly political, with the elite engaging the federal government almost exclusively in the discourse through demands made by socio-political, states creation and ethno-cultural movements (Osaghae et al. 2007). MOSOP's entry into the resource control discourse in 1990 changed the face of the struggle. Although the organization employed peaceful means in its struggle to achieve its main objective of 'Ogoni control of Ogoni resources', the response of oil multinationals and federal government ranged from indifference at first to military repression. The region witnessed a period of state-sponsored terrorism as the crackdown on supporters of 'resource control' intensified and resulted in the 'judicial murder' of the 'Ogoni Nine' in November 1995. The high-handed approach adopted by the federal government paradoxically radicalized the Niger Delta youth to become more vocal and proactive in participating in the politics of resource control and local resistance (Ikelegbe 2005a; Osaghae et al. 2007). The Kaiama Declaration and the activities of the IYC quickly caught on, with hitherto passive organizations and communities becoming belligerent (Ukeje 2001a).

On a national level, the post-1999 democratic period deepened the 'militant-ization' of ethno-political groups and ethnic militia. They sought to assert their ethnic minority rights as the struggles against perceived federal exclusion and resources gained prominence (Obi 2006). This period witnessed a shift in the agitation for resource control from elitist organizations to militant youths, which contributed to the exacerbation of violent conflicts in the oil-rich region (ibid.).

However, as noted previously, not all violence in the region is genuinely linked to agitation for resource control. The motivation for recourse to violence determines whether a group is classified as militant or otherwise. According to Osaghae et al. (2007: 16, 21):

> In the Niger-delta, the term 'militants' refers to gunmen who make political demands, including the release of imprisoned leaders, cash reparations for communities, change of electoral candidates and a greater share of oil revenues, among other issues. These political demands distinguish them, albeit tenuously, from criminals who simply kidnap people for money. Militants are also distinct from disaffected communities, whose people may perform kidnappings or attacks in the hopes of getting a clinic, school or cash, but have no overall political aims [...] Cults are [thus] groups of individuals dedicated to providing security and economic opportunities for each other and their respective communities, subscribing to an oath of allegiance and secrecy and relying mostly on violent means to achieve their ends.

These organizations have defined resource control in socio-economic, political and human rights contexts that have appealed to sympathetic observers within and outside the country (Ikelegbe 2006b). Combining the intellectual expression of their agitation for resource control with the consistency of purpose; access to arms and ammunitions; and the dexterity and assiduous planning of their activities have resulted in unprecedented levels of petro-violence experienced in the Niger Delta (see Ikelegbe, Duquet, and Bøås, this volume).

Gangs and cults operating in the context of the insecurity generated by oil-related conflicts also ride on the coat-tails of the agitation for resource control. The main difference between these gangs and militant/militia groups, as noted previously, is the motivation. Gangs and cults are primarily motivated by the financial benefits they gain from indulging in activities such as political thuggery, kidnapping, drug-peddling, stealing, oil bunkering and turf wars to access revenues from other activities that took place or passed through their communities. In reality, it is not easy to draw a line between cultists and militants because the militants also engage in these same activities; albeit with underlying 'identified causes' (Ikelegbe 2006b: 92). Furthermore, the two groups constantly interact in somewhat symbiotic relationships.

The struggle for resource control also has a political dimension that has contributed to the violence in the Niger Delta. With the return to democratic governance in 1999, politicians have become primary drivers for government policies and activities. However, to gain access to political authority, politicians recognize the advantage in aligning with and arming youth organizations that are no longer apolitical and have gained prominence in their communities where they could influence the result of polls (Human Rights Watch 2007b). These already restive youth groups were employed by political parties and politicians mainly to intimidate opponents in elections that were character-ized by the 'commodification of violence' (Joab-Peterside 2007; Human Rights Watch 2008).

After the elections, the Niger Delta political elite politicized the resource control discourse by clamouring for increased derivation and 'true federalism' to alleviate the pervasive state of poverty and underdevelopment in the region. Although the politicians did achieve limited results in the form of increased oil-derivation-based revenue allocations, they subjected the states' resources to personal control and did not better the lot of their states' citizens. These issues, among others, precipitated increased militancy and violence in the region. Between 2006 and 2009, the Movement for the Emancipation of the Niger Delta (MEND) engaged in armed attacks on oil MNC and government targets, determined to 'cripple' oil exports as a strategy of putting pressure on the government, 'following 50 years of beating around the bush' (Baldauf 2009). MEND's reference to 'beating around the bush' may be interpreted to include failed political attempts, among others, at resolving the persistent crises in the oil communities, among them the failed attempt to get the National Political Reform Conference (NPRC) to recommend an increase in derivation percentage and the loss of the Resource Control suit.[3]

There is another interesting dimension to links between Niger Delta politicians, resource control and violence in the Niger Delta. This point is made with particular reference to two former governors of the 'core' Niger Delta, made up of Bayelsa, Delta and Rivers states. Alamieyesiegha (Bayelsa) and Ibori (Delta) were front-line advocates of resource control while in office, but they also allegedly enriched themselves from their state's revenue (mainly from oil derivation funds). Following Alamieyesiegha's arrest on charges of money laundering and consequent jumping of bail in the UK, before returning to Nigeria, where he later stood trial and was convicted, some loyal militant groups increased their attacks on the oil industry as leverage to demand his release (Etekpe 2007a). More recently, youth supporters in Delta state stopped officials from the police and security agencies from arresting Ibori to face charges of corruption. In Ibori's case, it is too early to decipher whether these youths are from militant groups that support the agitation for resource control, political supporters or plain thugs hired by the ex-governor to protect himself. What these instances suggest is that the links between the political class (in this case, the governors), militancy and violence in the Niger Delta straddle personal and group interests.

In conclusion, although the struggle for resource control had peaceful origins and assumed violent dimensions in the late 1990s, it is driven by collective, personal and opportunistic interests. These dimensions should not detract from the reality that the region has been seized by violence arising from the widespread feeling that its people have been severely short-changed within the context of Nigeria's 'unequal' fiscal federalism. It is the feeling that injustice, exclusion and impunity cannot be effectively resisted by non-violent means which has fuelled the actions of various actors engaged in 'petrolized violence'.

Resource control and the future of petro-violence

A common argument is that the attainment of resource control will result in the reduction and possibly the end of violent conflicts in the oil-rich delta. However, it could be argued that it may under certain conditions lead not to peace but rather its opposite – more violence. The problem may not be solved once and for all just on the basis of an increase in oil revenue allocation. To begin with, the proponents of increased derivation argue that the adverse environmental effects that oil exploitation has on the host communities far outweigh the payment the host states receive in derivation (Adesopo and Asaju 2004; Dunmoye 2002). Presently, the Niger Delta states are paid 13 per cent of oil revenues that accrue to the Federation Account as derivation in accordance with Section 162(2) of the 1999 constitution.

If it is assumed that derivation is increased to 50 per cent as is presently being demanded by Niger Delta governors, the main implication of such an increase is that the Niger Delta states (as administrative units) will receive almost four times the amount they currently receive as derivation funds. Their argument is that increased derivation to the states will improve their financial capability to provide the infrastructure necessary to develop their states. They also argue that if state revenues increase, the amount allocated to the local governments will also increase and will instigate development at the grass roots and quell restiveness. However, the possibilities of a converse situation occurring are highlighted below.

First, derivation payments from the federal government are made directly to the states, which then share this and other generated revenues with the local councils, as prescribed by the state legislature. The salient point to note is that since the allocation of revenues from the state is discretionary, the local councils and indeed the citizens may not benefit commensurately from such an increase. Thus, while the states will receive substantially more oil revenues, without any institutional provisions and firm guarantees on the democratic utilization of such funds, the funds may be misappropriated, as had been the case, some argue, with the 13 per cent derivation funds. It may, however, be argued that it is more likely that increased oil funds will go to the state oil-producing areas development commissions (SOPADECs) established by the states in the Niger Delta. These commissions, fashioned after the Niger Delta Development Commission (NDDC), are funded by certain percentages of the derivation funds the states receive and are intended to implement development projects in the oil-bearing communities. However, the evidence shows that, like the NDDC and its progenies, these state commissions are afflicted by the malaises of under-funding, revenue misappropriation and corruption (Emitimi 2009).

Second, increased derivation may increase fraud, corruption and political conflict in some oil-producing states, as past experiences suggest. In accordance with the provisions of the 1999 constitution, derivation to the Niger Delta states was increased to 13 per cent. This increase in derivation-based revenues has not produced any significant increase in the standard of living in the oil-rich region. Rather, the political elite have been engaged in large-scale financial embezzlement and corruption scandals. The profligacy of the governors of the Niger Delta states soon after derivation was increased was scathingly criticized by then president Obasanjo (Peel 2005). The federal government, irked by the alleged rate of financial decadence, subsequently published its allocation of oil revenues to state governments since 2003. Although the federal government was allegedly motivated by the desire to discredit the governors and undermine their agitation for resource control, this does not invalidate their indictment, as the cases against Alamieyesiegha and Ibori particularly indicate (Ibeanu 2004; Ifidon-Ekuerhare 2009). Given these and other cases of mismanagement of increased funds to the Niger Delta, it is doubtful that further increases in derivation without effective democratic participation, accountability and institutional capacities will promote development and reduce conflicts.

It is not far-fetched to suggest that under the current status quo, if derivation is increased to 50 per cent state officials will likely continue to misappropriate funds, and the inhabitants of the oil-rich communities could turn their frustration from the federal government to their state governments. Such a situation will have different repercussions from those pertaining in the current situation, where the federal government in faraway Abuja is held primarily responsible for 'robbing the golden goose', and the mismanagement of oil revenues. Indeed, if the focus shifts to members of the state governments, who live in close proximity and are recognizable to the inhabitants of the oil communities, the repercussions may be serious, as aggrieved persons will be able to personally vent their frustrations on these politicians.

Regarding absolute resource control, there are two probable consequences for the management of the oil industry. The ownership and control of the resource and accruing revenues will go to the Niger Delta states, and they will have to take responsibility for the regulation of the oil industry. Indeed, given the wealth, sophistication and domination of oil technology of the oil MNCs, the Niger Delta states would be in no position to effectively regulate or compete against them. That notwithstanding, with absolute resource control enormous revenues will accrue to the states. Such increases, as noted earlier, do not necessarily translate into improvements to the living standards of the region's inhabitants. Rather, the influx of such astronomical revenues will more likely precipitate struggles among local actors (including politicians, chiefs, the local elite and militants) to gain political, financial and territorial advantage solely to access the accruing oil revenues.

Since 1999, the power struggle between the political class, militants and gangs in the Niger Delta has contributed to violent conflicts in the region. While the politicians armed thugs and colluded with cultists to overwhelm the opposition to gain access to political power and the pecuniary gains from derivation allocations, armed gangs fought for control of the creeks to benefit from oil bunkering (Human Rights Watch 2005a). Such is the allure of allocation revenues in the Niger Delta region that Human Rights Watch (2003: 15) observed with reference to Delta state that 'the control of the government structure of Delta State has become a major prize both for the individuals and the political parties concerned'. With increased revenues accruing directly to the Niger Delta states, the stakes in controlling power at that level have increased, and it is predicted that this will contribute to more petro-violence in the region in the future.

Absolute resource control may also exacerbate land-related conflicts in the region. Land is a scarce resource required by the oil industry for sundry purposes. In the course of oil exploration and production activities, land is subject to pollution and properties susceptible to damage. In Nigeria's oil industry, oil-company payments to landholders for land they require and/or payments for damage done to land (or other property) are the two assured ways in which inhabitants of the region may derive direct pecuniary benefits from the oil industry. In other words, local inhabitants' access to oil money is intrinsically linked to their occupation/control of land. This perception, which already fuels intra- and inter-ethnic conflicts in the region, will in all likelihood fuel violent conflicts in the region with more money from state governments at stake (Obi 2006). Similar tensions are likely to result in the process of selecting locations for development projects by oil companies, because this is dependent on competing local-community customary (and state legal-ownership) claims to the land close to the operations of the company.

Another assumption that needs to be interrogated is that once the Niger Delta states own oil resources they will have exclusive control of the oil industry. The extension of this argument is that such control will lead to stricter operating standards which will reduce occurrences of the negative environmental and social impacts of the industry, and remove some of the reasons for communal restiveness. The question, though, is: what is the likelihood that the Niger Delta states will impose stricter operating standards? While it is not easy to predict what the states will do in this situation, it is safe to assume that there will not be any radical changes in the short to medium term. This proposition is based on the rationale that radical changes, such as an outright ban on gas flaring (rather than the current situation, characterized by oil companies exploiting loopholes in the Associated Gas Reinjection Act of 1979 and paying insignificant fines for violating the law), for example, will result in a drop in production levels and revenues which the country cannot afford. On the other hand, if the status quo of operational standards is maintained, invariably the conflicts based on operational issues will remain. In fact, such conflicts are more likely to increase because the affected communities will interpret the governments' lack of action as 'self-betrayal'.

Also, related to the state governments' control of the oil industry is the question of whether they can develop institutions capable of effectively regulating and supervising the oil multinationals without instigating conflicts. One of the necessities of building effective institutions in the highly sophisticated capital-intensive oil industry is the availability of qualified, professional and experienced manpower. It is difficult to envisage a situation whereby staff recruitment into, and promotion in, institutions will be based on merit, especially given the ethnic preconditions for employment at state levels in Nigeria, where ethnicity is a predominant factor (Lohor 2003). This is rendered even more difficult given the low level of local capacities, a weak industrial base, the lack of backward and forward linkages between the oil industry and the local economy, and the paucity of indigenous capital in the region.

Past experiences in appointing board members to organizations created to develop the Niger Delta region exemplify the deleterious role of ethnic politics in decision-making and the performance of development agencies. With a lot more at stake with the states controlling the oil industry, the potential for conflicts is once again increased. Another factor in terms of violent conflicts breaking out in the context of the Niger Delta states controlling the oil industry is how to manage the challenge this will pose in the face of the federal monopoly on the security and defence forces. The experience of federal military responses to protests or conflicts in Kaiama, Odi, Odioma, Okerenkoko and Umuechem is hardly comforting, and raises the need for the Niger Delta states to deal with the highly politically sensitive issue of organizing regional defence – which will likely put excessive strain on Nigeria's rather fragile federal experiment.

One may be tempted to suggest that the stakes of absolute resource control are too high, and thus the option of principal resource control should be preferable. However, that option is not without its own problems and similar potential for precipitating violent conflicts. Under an arrangement whereby the Niger Delta states will exercise principal resource control, it is expected that both the federal and state governments will jointly own and manage the oil industry. Sagay (2001) suggests that, under this model, a Petroleum Affairs Commission may be established to take over the functions of the minister of petroleum affairs vis-à-vis the management and control of the oil industry.[4] The functions of the commission, as Sagay suggests, will include the issuance of permits and licences and the conclusion of agreements with oil companies, as well as the supervision of all areas of the industry.

Issues relating to the manipulation of ethnicity among the Niger Delta elite may rise to the fore as the selection of board members is likely to be subject to ethno-political considerations rather than merit and commitment to community service. It is pertinent to state that the issue of ethnicity and possible violence in the Niger Delta is not exaggerated. One may argue that the different ethnic groups of the region are 'united' by the common experiences they share as a result of the negative impacts the oil industry has had on them. However, it is posited that the fragile intra- and inter-community relationships in the Niger Delta, braced by their common petro-experiences, will likely fracture once issues of ethnic cleavages and politics within the region come to the fore (Human Rights Watch 2003; Leton 2008). Indeed, extant research reveals that access to oil revenues remains one of the central causes of intra- and inter-communal conflicts in the Niger Delta region (Watts et al. 2004). Arguably, with the Niger Delta states in pole position to control windfall profits from oil production and exports, conflicts in the region will escalate as different groups seek positions of power to benefit themselves, defined either in ethnic or communal terms. As noted in a recent Transnational Crisis Project (2010: 15) publication, 'once locals see oil rents as objects of zero-sum factional warfare, destructive behaviours and perceptions fuel one another in an endless cycle'.

Resource control, peace and sustainable development in the Niger Delta

The previous section has interrogated the assumption that resource control will automatically translate into peace and development by exploring the possibilities of resource control instigating a new crisis and/or exacerbating existing conflicts. This is not to suggest that the idea of resource control is wrong-headed. Indeed, under participatory democratic and equitable conditions, it can produce positive benefits for the majority of the Niger Delta peoples. In essence, the fundamental issues that precipitated the agitation for resource control must be addressed. Thereafter, the most suitable variant of resource control should be adapted alongside appropriate institutions and practices to address the grievances of the people.

The ways in which Nigeria's over-centralized federalism marginalizes the people of the Niger Delta, particularly denying them direct benefits from oil, is the underlying cause of petro-violence in the Niger Delta. The oil industry's regulatory framework was developed mainly during military dictatorships, wherein the objective was to arrogate authority to the centre. Indeed, the control of oil resources and revenues played a significant role in the military's foray into national politics and the desire to concentrate power at the centre (Ako 2008; Oyebode 2004; Soremekun 1995). The military's unitary style of governance, wherein excessive authority is vested in the federal government, permeates the constitution that the military bequeathed to the nation. Consequently, Nigeria has not had the opportunity to develop a constitution that expresses the innate desires of its people. This point is better appreciated by highlighting the example of the 'dictatorial' decision to append the controversial Land Use Act to the 1999 constitution. There is no gainsaying the fact that this law remains one of the main causes of violence in the Niger Delta (Ako 2009).

More worrisome is the fact that the influences of military-ingrained unitary federalism are manifest in Nigeria's contemporary governance structures, where devolution of power is considered an anathema. There is a constant state of conflict in the power relations among structures of governance, with the federal government jealously guarding its overarching authority in relation to the states, and the states acting similarly towards their local councils. While the federal government attempts to fend off state-government-led agitation for resource control, the state governors in particular seem to have hijacked and personalized the struggle. In this scenario, the ordinary person who is the most affected is marginalized and denied active involvement both in the general political process and specifically with regard to the resource control discourse. In the absence of a defined space in which to participate or have their voices heard, it is not surprising that militants initially enjoyed considerable support from the populace. Indeed, if the government's post-amnesty development plans succeed, the populace will consider the violent militant approach to resource control more effective and beneficial than the politicized version.

However, the challenge remains how to resolve the issues that contribute to agitation for resource control, which have become a permanent feature of the instability in the region, leading to hostilities and affecting the economic well-being of the people (Ololajulo 2006). Certainly, Nigeria's federal structure must be transformed to emphasize equal citizenship rights, equity and political accountability, which imply good governance and participatory structures. The important point to note with regard to resource management, particularly in the Niger Delta, is the need to promote the inhabitants' active participation in development/community governance, rather than their being simply their targets.

The 'Akassa model' is an example of the dividends of active public participation in sustainable development process. The model is a development foundation facilitated by Pro Natura International (PNI), funded by Statoil (now StatoilHydro), in alliance with BP (and others) and predicated on communal interactive participation to facilitate development. The community, through different interest groups, participates in identifying, appraising and initiating micro-projects. Decision-making is integral, as representatives of interest groups partake in the process at the village level and village representatives then take part in clan-level planning committees.

A pertinent observation is that the Akassa initiative was started in 1997 – a challenging period in the Niger Delta. The initiative has survived for over fifteen years owing to its emphasis on sustainability reinforced by active public involvement in the development process. The success of this initiative has been replicated in five local government areas in the Oron region of Bayelsa state, where Nexen is working on behalf of Oriental Energy in partnership with PNI (Nigeria). Based on the Akassa model, but suited to its peculiar circumstances, a board of trustees, a transparent governance system and a bank account have been established to achieve sustainable peace and development. Indeed, this model can be scaled up and replicated with modifications to suit peculiar circumstances in the entire Niger Delta. Above all, the Akassa model proves that community participation in the management of oil wealth and benefits is not unachievable. It is important to ensure that governments in the region are based on free and fair elections, hence truly representative of the people's interests. It is also important to choose credible and experienced development partners such as non-governmental organizations (NGOs) and community-based organizations (CBOs) to provide institutional support and capacity-building initiatives in the region.

Regarding the variant of resource control that is best suited to the Niger Delta, it is suggested that increased derivation is the most feasible. This suggestion is made bearing in mind the political and legal realities and difficulties that must be overcome. Also, bearing in mind the difficulties involved in the states' management of the oil industry, some of which have been highlighted earlier, it is preferable that the option of absolute resource control is avoided. With regard to increased derivation, it appears, judging by the political mood in the country, that a political compromise and consensus can be reached on phased increases. The main area of concern is determining what use the increased flow of oil revenues should be put to. While the experience of increased derivation in the Niger Delta has not been encouraging, if elements of democracy, accountability, equity and active public involvement in the management of resource revenues are ingrained in the process, sustainable peace and development can become attainable targets in the Niger Delta.

4 | The Niger Delta crisis and the question of access to justice

Engobo Emeseh

Introduction

This chapter examines the connection between obstacles preventing access to justice by aggrieved oil-producing communities in the Niger Delta and the conflict in the region. Its point of departure is informed by the view that the majority of Niger Delta peoples feel deeply aggrieved because of their political marginalization and alienation from the benefits of oil production and the destruction of the environment and local livelihoods by oil pollution, but also because of their lack of access to justice, redress and compensation. This necessitates exploring the role of the law as an instrument of social order and transformative justice and its place in resolving the crisis in the region. This transcends a purely legalistic or positivist analysis of the relevant laws guiding the operations of the oil industry and the maintenance of law and order in the restive region. By engaging in a socio-legal examination of the Niger Delta crisis, this chapter seeks explanations for the inability of the law – substantive, procedural and institutional – to stem the rising tide of tensions and conflicts in the region. Several questions are relevant in this context: why has the law been unable to sufficiently resolve the crisis, and in what ways do broader socio-economic and political factors constrain the rule of law and access to justice, and with what consequences?

This chapter underscores the need for reviewing the normative content of various laws and legal instruments, starting with the Nigerian federal constitution and laws applying to the Nigerian oil industry, as well as other procedural and institutional gaps and lapses that hinder the effectiveness of the system of justice administration. It is recognized that simply reviewing laws without addressing the prevailing socio-economic and political environment within which they operate cannot effectively resolve the conflict in the Niger Delta.

In the sections that follow, the notion of access to justice is critically explored, followed by a critical overview of the perceived role and function of the law in society, and the processes by which law obtains its legitimacy and authority. This is then applied to an analysis of the Niger Delta situation, highlighting how the processes of law-making, the normative content of the laws, institutional lapses in enforcement, and the use of 'law' by the state engender and reinforce a perception of injustice, and a consequent resort to extralegal means of seeking redress by aggrieved groups. The concluding section includes some recommendations for a holistic and comprehensive approach to addressing the deficits of the law, rather than the ad hoc or piecemeal review of specific legislations.

Access to justice: some conceptual issues

The phrase 'access to justice' is not specifically used or defined in legal instruments. However, access to justice is a well-established legal concept referring to a bundle of rights recognized under various international[1] and national legal instruments, including Section 36 of the Constitution of the Federal Republic of Nigeria 1999. The exact meaning of access to justice is difficult to capture completely in a single definition. It is perhaps more helpful to describe what it means by setting out its key components or attributes.

The principles of equality and fair trial are at the core of the concept of access to justice. The specific components of this right are provided in Articles 7–11 of the United Nations Universal Declaration of Human Rights 1948 (UDHR). These include equal protection of all by law, and equality before the law, effective remedy for wrongs, and freedom from arbitrary arrest, detention or exile. Also included are procedural protections such as the right to a fair and public hearing, independence and impartiality of adjudicators, and the presumption of innocence. The International Covenant on Civil and Political Rights 1966 (ICCPR) and the International Covenant on Economic, Social and Cultural Rights 1966 (ICESCR) reinforce these components of access to justice and apply them to specific areas of focus. In the environmental sphere (environment being a main concern in the Niger Delta) the principle of access to justice was recognized in Principle 10 of the Rio Declaration, and has now been enshrined in the binding UNECE Convention on Access to Information, Public Participation in Decision-making and Access to Justice in Environmental Matters (popularly called the 'Aarhus convention') 1998. Various Nigerian constitutions, including the current one of 1999 (Sections 1(1) and 36), recognize the broad components of this body of rights. However, one key component under Article 8 of the UDHR, the phrase 'effective remedy', is absent from Section 46(1) of the Nigerian constitution, on redress for breaches of the rights protected.

In essence, access to justice means that everyone, irrespective of age, sex, religion, ethnicity, status and other such factors, should have the means of obtaining justice under predetermined rules in an open and fair manner. It is an intrinsic component of the rule of law, which is the bedrock of modern democratic government. This is because the basic tenet of the rule of law, which is equality of all before the law, cannot truly be achieved without access to justice (Penal Reform International and Bluhm Legal Clinic of the Northwestern University School of Law 2007).

It is not uncommon to have a purely procedural approach to evaluating access to justice, thereby focusing on access to the courts, other formal institutions for dispute resolution, and access to proper legal representation before such courts (Le Sueur 2000; Yuille 2004; Pepper 1999). According to Le Sueur (2000: 457), 'Access to justice rights enable people (a) to obtain help and advice about possible litigation; (b) to initiate proceedings; (c) to have a full and proper hearing of their case; and (d) to be granted an effectual remedial order by the court.' Access to law-making powers is itself crucial as political disempowerment of certain groups within society could mean predetermined rules under the law are unfair and the law becomes a tool, which merely legitimizes the interests of the dominant group. Having access to the formal judicial system required legally to uphold such a law is merely having access to the courts and not necessarily access to justice. Real access to justice implies the lack of any impediments to an individual or group seeking redress for perceived wrongs through legitimate means, which includes but transcends the formal judicial system (Schärf and Nina 2001: 40). At the core of this is the existence of a fair set of laws which provide effective remedy. It also entails rights to access legitimately other forums in which to seek redress.

Access to justice is not just the establishment of, and the right of all to access, the formal institutions for dispute resolution, but also the content of the laws themselves, and the enablement of individuals, financially and otherwise, to obtain justice through these institutions (Alston 2000; Lash et al. 1998). As demonstrated in later sections, while everyone has a right of access to the formal judicial system in the Niger Delta, systemic inequalities and the normative contents of certain laws, as well as procedural, financial and other obstacles, have made real access to justice a mirage. The lack of access to justice creates an environment where people, even 'good' ones, may resort to extrajudicial or extralegal means of seeking redress. This reality was encapsulated by the then secretary-general of the UN, Mr Kofi Annan, thus: '[T]he United Nations has learned that the rule of law is not a luxury and that justice is not a side issue [...] without a credible machinery to enforce the law and resolve disputes, people resorted to violence and illegal means [...] the Rule of Law delayed is lasting peace denied, and that justice is a handmaiden of true peace [...]' (Annan 2003). Apart from the current crisis in the Niger Delta, examples abound of other conflicts in resource-rich zones, the cause of which is attributable to lack of access to justice in the face of serious environmental and socio-economic impacts. A recent study by Godnick and co-authors (2008) looks at such resource conflicts in the Andean region of South America, particularly in Colombia, Ecuador and Peru (also see Lyons 2004). Other examples include Papua New Guinea, where there was a full-blown ten-year secessionist insurgency (Islam 1991; Michalski 2006)[2] and Irian Jaya in Indonesia.[3]

Law, legitimacy and access to justice

Generally, law, especially when considered from the point of view of the rule of law in modern democracies, can be perceived to be constructive in social ordering by creating a 'just' society. Indeed, this is arguably one of the main functions of law (Llewellyn 1940). However, the role of law in society is contested. Arguably, as an instrument of control, law can become a vehicle for legitimizing injustice by those who have the power to make or enforce laws, and laws may not always meet the needs of the people (Nonet and Selznick 1978; Alper and Nichols 1981). Thus, Veitch argues that law can be used to legitimize human suffering, and indeed has been complicit in some of the major injustices in the world, such as slavery and colonialism (Veitch 2007: 1). This has resonance with the discourse on the Niger Delta crisis, where provisions within such legal instruments as the Nigerian constitution, the Land Use Act and the Petroleum Act have arguably been the tools legitimizing the disempowering of the people with regard to the control of oil resources in their land.

To some extent, this evaluation of the normative content of law to determine its validity is at the crux of the debate between positivist and naturalist schools of thought (Fuller 1980). However, the intention here is not to dwell on this long-standing debate. Rather, our interest is in the practical implications that perceptions of legitimacy and authority have for compliance. While there are different theories explaining why people comply with or obey laws, one of the crucial factors is belief in or acceptance of the laws' legitimacy because they subscribe to the values or the normative content of the law (Weber 1947: 124–5; Tyler 2006). Indeed, according to the reactance theory, law-takers may deliberately act contrary to laws which are perceived to be unjust or a breach of their human rights (Braithwaite 2002; Brehm 1966). It is therefore the challenge of governments or lawmakers to create in the minds of law-takers an acknowledgement of the legitimacy and authoritativeness of the law through strategies of 'enrolment' (Latour 1986). Governments use a combination of mechanisms to achieve this (Weber 1954; Mertz 1994). Two key examples are coercion and rewards. However, while both of these may be effective in the short term, ultimately there could be long-term problems where this is not combined with strategies which create in the law-taker an acceptance of the inherent legitimacy and authority of the law. Coercive measures alone could fuel a feeling of injustice, while rewards could create an unsustainable rentier culture. As is demonstrated later, the use of mainly coercion and rewards in the Niger Delta has failed to effectively 'enrol' the people to accept the legitimacy and authoritativeness of aspects of the constitution and other relevant laws.

In light of the foregoing, even where there is a legal framework and institutions for seeking redress, if the pre-established principles forming the basis of that framework are perceived to be unjust, there is unlikely to be any real sense of access to justice. Thus, despite legal right of access to the judicial system,

58

'unfair' normative contents of the laws, political and institutional inequalities, systemic biases and practical challenges to litigation create major obstacles to effective access to justice for the Niger Delta people.

Law, the Nigerian state, oil, and the implications for access to justice in the Niger Delta

From a historical perspective, colonial rule displaced the indigenous systems of law and justice that it encountered. This had implications for the Nigerian legal system and issues related to access to justice. In post-colonial Nigeria, indigenous customary law and traditional justice institutions have very limited roles in the legal system and are generally subject to statutes made either during the colonial administration or the various governments post-independence. Such laws have been fashioned after Western systems of jurisprudence and government (Obilade 1979). Moreover, as is usual under military regimes, which have for the most part ruled Nigeria since its independence, laws such as the Petroleum Act 1969 and the Land Use Act of 1979, which effectively alienated the people from the oil wealth from their region, were enacted without the consultations usual in a democratic system.

This raises two key concerns, both of which are part of the central causes of the Niger Delta conflict and pose challenges to its effective resolution. The first has to do with tensions arising from perceptions of the legitimacy of some of these 'new' laws where they do not reflect or are in conflict with established and accepted customary law. Land ownership, which is a main source of conflict in the region, is one area where this is of particular concern, owing to the enactment of the Land Use Act of 1979. It is well established that Western concepts of 'property' and ownership of land significantly differ from those of indigenous peoples and local communities under customary law. Although there is debate as to whether the definition of indigenous people under international law includes local communities such as those in Nigeria (Kingsbury 1998; Scheinin 2005), there are definitely similarities shared between both groups in terms of their relationship with the lands in their territories and the common experience of imposition of 'alien' legal principles or understandings of property rights. Both groups recognize collective ownership of land (Elias 1956; Kiwanuka 1988).[4] Their relationship with the land is also much more intricate, the land and its resources being the main source of subsistence, as well as being closely linked to identity, culture and spiritual issues (Anaya 2004). This much is now recognized under various international instruments, such as Article 13 of the ILO Convention 169.

However, the Land Use Act of 1979, contrary to customary law and even the received English land law, vests all lands 'comprised in the territory of each State in the Federation [...] in the Governor of that State [...]'.[5] The implication of this is that the state can acquire any land whatsoever for the use of oil

59

activities without recourse to the communities. Moreover, communities are entitled to compensation only for 'unexhausted improvements'.[6] Considering that oil production takes place predominantly in rural communities which practise subsistence farming, the improvements on the land are usually not substantial. Rather, the true value of the land is the right to its use for farming and other purposes (including the broader significance of land, which was discussed earlier). The problem is exacerbated by the abysmally low compensation rates for food crops (Omotola 1990; Fekumo 2001). Also, the jurisdiction to consider the adequacy or otherwise of such compensation was given to the relevant Land Allocation Committee and not to the courts, except in cases of damage to third-party rights arising from pollution, where the actual damage caused could be assessed by a court.

The second issue that arises from the colonial legacy is the efficacy of customary law and its institutions even within the limits of their recognition under the current legal system. Since colonial times, there has been continuing erosion of respect for and confidence in traditional customary institutions, especially in matters relating to the state. This is due to the fact that the custodians of these traditional institutions, who now derive their position from and are dependent on the government, have often been used to promote government's agenda, while those who refuse may be removed from office. Although this is not unique to the Niger Delta, it is generally believed that one of the factors leading to the rise in militant activism by the youths of the region is lack of confidence in the elders (the custodians of these customary law institutions) because they are perceived to have been corrupted by the oil companies and indeed the state, and therefore complicit in the marginalization of the region (Osaghae et al. 2007).

This has three significant consequences. First, it partly contributes to lack of respect for or obedience of customary norms which are part of the pluralist legal system of Nigeria. Second, the customary institutions can no longer provide the constraint or the very useful role of alternative dispute-resolution mechanisms, especially where conflict or violence is inter- or intra-communal. Third, the breakdown of traditional institutions creates chaos within communities and lack of clear lines of authority for negotiation between communities, or between communities and the government and/or oil companies.

Nigeria is a federation, with power shared between the centre (federal government) and the constituting regions (state government).[7] The brand of federalism created under the Nigerian constitution significantly concentrates power at the federal level. Some have argued, therefore, especially with regard to resource allocation, that Nigeria does not operate true federalism (Ikein and Briggs-Anigboh 1988). While oil has accounted for a very high proportion of Nigeria's exports and is the main foreign exchange earner (over 95 per cent at its peak) (Khan 1994; Ikein and Briggs-Anigboh 1988; Obi 2007), there are very few tangible benefits to the people of the region. Section 44(3) of the constitution grants ownership of mineral resources to the federal government, and only a small proportion of oil revenue (at one point as low as 3 per cent) derives to the oil-producing states. It is also the federal government which has the power to regulate the oil industry as 'mines and minerals' are an item on the exclusive legislative list reserved for the federal government.[8] However, the ethnic minority people of the Niger Delta have little power or influence at the federal level and consequently on the laws being enacted. This has implications for perceptions of the legitimacy and 'justness' of the relevant laws. Rather, people's perceptions mirror Veitch's (2007) argument as legal instruments and laws (such as the various federal constitutions, the Petroleum Act 1969 and the Land Use Act of 1979) are seen as the tools that 'legitimate human suffering' by alienating and dispossessing the people of the oil produced from their region.

The grievances

The recurring feature of the conflict in the Niger Delta is the presence of the oil industry. On the one hand, there is the industry's impact on the environment and the sociocultural, economic and political lives of the people. On the other hand, there are issues relating to the response of the government and the oil companies to this impact (see chapters by Ukiwo, Ikelegbe, and Bøås, this volume).

For several decades, oil has been the mainstay of the Nigerian economy, accounting for as much as 80 per cent of national revenue (Frynas 2000: 25). However, not much benefit has accrued to the Niger Delta, which produces it, with the region having little or no basic infrastructure and high levels of poverty (UNDP 2006: 17, 56). This is made worse by the attendant environmental degradation of the delicate and rich ecology of the Niger Delta, which traditionally has been the source of livelihood for local communities (Greenpeace 1994; Okonta and Douglas 2001; Asuno 1982; Powell et al. 1985). The industry's activities have been characterized by poor environmental management practices resulting in high numbers and huge volumes of oil spills, devastation of mangrove forests, improper disposal of effluents and other production wastes, and gas flaring. This has resulted in pollution of water resources and farmlands, thereby making fishing and farming, the traditional occupation of the people, unsustainable.

Although in recent times a large percentage of oil spills and pipeline fires has been attributed to sabotage, for several decades, even according to official sources, avoidable problems such as pipeline corrosion were the main cause of spills (Awobajo 1981; Emeseh 2006). While natural gas is potentially a huge money-earner (Okoh 2001), the lackadaisical attitude of the Nigerian government in implementing a policy adopted in the 1960s to develop gas-gathering facilities meant that, for several decades, the country held the dubious record of having the highest volume of gas flares both in absolute and relative terms globally. At one point, Nigeria flared as much as 75 per cent of its gas, with the next-worst culprit, Libya, flaring only 21 per cent (World Bank 1995; Ashton-Jones 1998).

Environmental pollution as well as the presence of the industry have far-reaching health and socio-economic implications. Various studies at the international level show links between oil spills and gas flares, with some very serious ailments such as cancer, asthma and other lung diseases (Epstein and Selber 2002). A study of the health impacts of the *Sea Empress* oil spill of February 1995 in the UK indicated 'possible short-term adverse conditions within the local communities including nausea, headaches and skin irritations; dermatological problems [...] in beach workers not wearing adequate protective clothing' (Edwards and White 1999). Also, analysis of Federal Government of Nigeria surveys of HIV prevalence between 1991 and 2001 shows that the Niger Delta region had the highest prevalence of HIV-infected persons, and the connection was made to the presence of the oil industry in the region (Udonwa et al. 2004; UNDP 2006: 17; TCND 2008: 102).

Other impacts include destruction of roofs from the effects of acid rain (Akpan 2003) and high inflation owing to the presence of highly paid oil industry workers in the region. Research conducted jointly by Nigeria's National Space Research and Development Agency (NASRDA) and the University of Missouri of the United States, which covered the period between 1986 and 2003, shows a huge loss of the mangrove forest (a source of forest products and a natural habitat for fish and other aquatic creatures), attributable in part to oil industry activities (James et al. 2007). This, together with pollution of water and land, has serious implications for the sustainability of fishing and farming, which are the traditional occupations of the local peoples. People in this region are also one of the most likely to be impacted by the effects of climate change, particularly in terms of sea-level rise and loss of fishery resources.

The state has failed to provide effective access to justice by not enacting laws to effectively regulate these impacts and thereby provide an efficient framework for addressing these grievances. The implication of this is that local communities, which cannot see any direct benefits in terms of development from the proceeds of oil revenue individually and collectively, bear the brunt of the activities of the industry. They are the ones who lose their ability to sustain themselves with their traditional sources of livelihood, owing to pollution of their lands and waters. They have to seek alternative sources of water for drinking and other domestic uses when the rivers and streams they previously relied on are polluted by spills, or, as more routinely happens, they have no alternative but to use the polluted water and suffer the consequences. The inhabitants of oil-producing communities also bear the discomfort of the perpetual light, noise and polluted air from gas flares.

In an area with very poor health delivery systems, people suffer from preventable diseases and risk death from pollution-related illnesses (Oluwaniyi, this volume). They also live with the attendant sociocultural implications of the large influx of oil industry workers, into sometimes quite remote communities, subsidizing the oil companies, which do not take into consideration such environmental, social and health costs in making their investment decisions. Worse, the Nigerian state does not plough back the revenue from the industry into developing the region and alleviating the adverse impacts of the industry's operations. Rather, as demonstrated in the section below, the existing laws are aimed at ensuring easy access to the oil wealth for both the government and the oil companies.

The legislative framework

There was no specific focus on the impact of oil on the environment in Nigeria until the 1960s. Early oil legislation was mainly directed at defining the powers of government regarding issues of ownership, participation and control, fiscal regimes and taxes, and regulating the operations of oil companies. Following the 1972 United Nations Conference on Human Environment, and the greater awareness of environmental issues, the first ever conference organized by the government's own national oil company, the Nigerian National Petroleum Corporation (NNPC), in 1979, highlighted the serious environmental impacts of the oil industry and recommended the enactment of relevant legislation to include establishing a regulatory agency fashioned after the United States Environmental Protection Agency. Subsequent conferences in 1981 and 1985 reiterated this point. However, it was only in 1988, sixteen years after the Stockholm Conference, and nine years after the first recommendation from the NNPC conference, that the country enacted such a law.[9] To lend credence to the perception that the inaction over the years was a result of the lack of concern over the environmental impacts of the oil industry, the 1988 framework law came into existence in direct response to an incident unrelated to oil – the dumping of toxic wastes by an Italian company in Koko, Delta state – only months after the incident took place. In addition, the government also enacted at the same time specific legislation on hazardous substances,[10] even though the country had yet to enact a comprehensive law specifically on oil pollution.[11]

Even where laws have been enacted, they are either not sufficiently stringent or have not been followed through. For instance, legislative steps have been taken since 1969 to introduce plans for utilization or reinjection of gas, with a law prohibiting flaring being in place since 1984,[12] but this has yet to be enforced. The fines provided under the law are too insignificant to be sufficient deterrent, and government has continued shifting the gas flare end-date since, with the current deadline being 2012 to accommodate the companies, given what are considered to be the financial implications of enforcement for the country (Next 2010). However, this merely shows a lack of prioritization of environmental concerns, together with short-sightedness on the part of government, since potential revenue from the gas currently being flared is significant.

In contrast, the government has been quick to enact laws for the protection of oil installations. For example, in 1975 the Petroleum Production and Distribution (Anti-Sabotage) Act was enacted, even though at the time sabotage was not a major problem in the country; and in 1984, the Special Tribunal (Miscellaneous Offences) was set up. Both of these provide for stiff penalties (the death penalty and twenty-one years' imprisonment respectively) for tampering with oil installations or otherwise disrupting or disturbing the distribution and marketing of petroleum products. Even more draconian, the Treason and Treasonable Offences Decree of 1993, under which the 'Ogoni nine', including Ken Saro-Wiwa, were tried and executed, provided the government with power to restrain any form of dissent, including disaffection with the impacts of oil pollution. Not only did these actions indicate how seriously the government intended to protect revenue from oil, and by implication the oil companies, but corresponding inaction on behalf of the communities showed its lack of interest in the suffering caused by the impacts of oil operations. Law was used to effectively label acts against oil operations as 'criminal' while the same types of legal measures were not adopted to label the polluters. Rather, what the government did in 1978 was to further erode any rights that the people had with respect to the exploitation of the resources within their communities by enacting the Land Use Act.

Impediments in the judicial system

Although the current regulatory framework is weak, there are provisions creating both civil and criminal liability for environmental pollution from oil industry activities (Emeseh 2006: 583–9). However, the various enforcement agencies have yet to institute any civil or criminal action against any of the oil companies for non-compliance with these laws. This is despite the obvious evidence of pollution, which is readily admitted by the government and its regulatory agencies. For instance, at a public forum in 1999 where oil company representatives were present, the then minister of state for environment, Dr Ime Okopido, attributed much of the restive situation in the Niger Delta to the 'heinous environmental crimes' of multinational oil companies and attributed the 'pathetic environmental' situation in the Niger Delta to the 'breach of good environmental management'. He stated: 'Over the past decades, the Niger Delta terrain has been overrun through deliberate over-exploitation carried out in total disregard of the basic principles of sustainable environmental management [...] From available information, close to 4,000 oil wells have so far been drilled in the Niger Delta and offshore areas since 1937 [...] that constitute potentially polluted sites at which drilling wastes, drill cuttings, oily sludges and various toxic hazardous chemicals have been disposed.' He further observed that 'the patience of the people have [sic] been tried to the limit' (Guardian 1999).

Later, in 2002, another highly placed federal government official, the presidential adviser on petroleum and energy, Rilwanu Lukman, noted that 'operators seemed to have paid little or no attention to the environment', as the impact of spills that had occurred more than thirty years earlier was still evident in parts of the Niger Delta region and new spills that had occurred in recent years were creating further concern. He linked this to weak enforcement of health, safety and environmental guidelines (Guardian 2002). However, the repeated threats to prosecute companies for oil pollution made by the administration of President Obasanjo came to nothing for eight years (1999–2007). The Yar'Adua administration and its newly created agency, the National Oil Spill Detection and Response Agency (NOSDRA), has merely continued to issue similar ineffective threats by accusing the companies of violating existing laws and regulations (This Day Online 2009).

Although the obvious explanation for this situation lies in the lack of capacity and resources, this does not fully explain the total lack of enforcement. Some of the violations are blatant, and even individuals and local communities that are much weaker have successfully sued the companies. Rather, viewed against the backdrop of non-prioritization of legislation for the environment, the answer appears to be lack of political will to strictly enforce laws against an industry which is the main source of national revenue. The broader weak governance and accountability challenges in the country make it difficult to compel the relevant agencies to perform their legal duties. This is exacerbated by the very narrow interpretations given by the judiciary on who has *locus standi* (sufficient interest) to institute actions in court, as demonstrated in *Oronto Douglas* v. *Shell Petroleum Development Company Ltd and others*.[13]

In light of the failure of regulatory agencies to seek justice on behalf of victims of oil pollution, the onus has been on individuals and communities to seek redress either through negotiated settlements or through civil actions in court. The actual amounts of compensation for negotiated settlements are quite small (Fekumo 2001: 15); even so, only a few are successfully settled. However, the majority of unsettled cases do not proceed to litigation, owing to the severe difficulties faced by potential litigants. For instance, one study (Adewale 1989) showed that of 1,081 compensation claims made between 1981 and 1986, only 124 claims were settled, while only 24 of the remaining unsettled claims went to court. Another (Onyige 1979) found only six cases pending in courts out of 600 unsettled compensation claims in Rivers state. Some of the difficulties litigants face include poor knowledge of legal rights,[14] lack of proximity to courts with jurisdiction over oil pollution matters, and absence of legal aid for civil actions[15] or an established system whereby lawyers provide their services for a contingency fee, especially as most individuals and local communities do not have the financial resources required to sustain litigation against the much more powerful and rich oil multinational companies over long periods.

In the case of the few claims that do get to court, litigants face challenges at all stages of the process. The limited resources of such litigants mean that they are quite often unable to retain appropriate legal representation comparable to that of the oil companies, which clearly do not have any such limitations. This is further exacerbated by the very long delays in the judicial process.[16] Delays also mean that evidence, especially the availability and quality of oral testimony, may be compromised. The strict requirement to prove *locus standi* (sufficient interest)[17] as a precondition for instituting action also makes it difficult to institute public interest litigation to prevent environmental damage from the oil industry where direct harm to the individual has not occurred. In the Oronto Douglas case, the plaintiff was held not to have *locus standi* to enforce a breach of the requirements of the Environmental Impact Assessment Decree.

Also, in the absence of effective legislation on oil pollution, litigants rely mainly on common law torts such as trespass, negligence and nuisance. The strict requirements of proof under some of these torts, and the limitations as to who can bring an action and when, are major challenges. For instance, individuals can bring actions only in private nuisance and not public nuisance (which can only be instituted by the Attorney General), except where they can prove that they have suffered injury over and above that suffered by the general public. This is quite restrictive as oil pollution damage, such as when a water body is polluted, usually affects everyone.[18] Even where litigants have overcome all these impediments and successfully proved their case, systemic biases such as the reluctance of courts to grant injunctions against operations of the industry,[19] and until recently the very low compensation awards,[20] make this a pyrrhic victory.

Moreover, both the oil companies and the government have not always abided by decisions. For instance, the federal government did not implement a decision by the African Commission on Human and Peoples' Rights indicting it of human rights abuses in the Ogoni crisis (*SERAC* v. *Nigeria*), nor did Shell or the government abide by a decision of the Federal High Court declaring gas flaring to be an abuse of human rights (*Gbemre* v. *Shell*).[21] Instead, companies usually embark on delay tactics and long appeals. While the companies can afford such long litigation, plaintiffs are not so well placed, and this contributes to creating frustration and further disaffection.

With this failure of the law and its institutions to provide effective means of accessing justice, eventual resort to alternative means of redress is inevitable. Ultimately this has degenerated into extralegal and violent self-help as more peaceful efforts proved to be unsuccessful. Such extralegal and violent acts by the aggrieved have been met with a violent response by the state through the powers and security forces available to it under the law.

The move towards activism as an alternative means of seeking justice

The peoples of the Niger Delta closely link the federal government's lack of interest in their situation with their ethnic minority status within Nigeria, which effectively excludes them from wielding political power at the centre. Feelings of injustice preceded the current crisis, with expressions of dissatisfaction dating back to the 1950s. For example, even before the independence of Nigeria, the problem was highlighted in the Willink Commission's report of 1958, which made various recommendations for allaying the fears of the minority groups (Willink Commission 1958). In 1966, Isaac Adaka Boro led a ragtag group of armed youth in a revolt that failed in its bid to create a Niger Delta republic in protest against the perceived marginalization of the peoples of the Niger Delta within Nigeria. Nevertheless, at the time, the use of force in this instance was a one-off, as until the 1990s various actions or initiatives by the Niger Delta peoples were generally peaceful and localized within particular communities.

However, the persistence of the demand for justice led to the emergence of the Movement for the Survival of Ogoni People (MOSOP), which effectively organized a non-violent campaign against the Nigerian state and Shell in the 1990s. In response the government unleashed the army on Ogoniland and arrested activists, including the MOSOP leadership, nine of whom were executed after a flawed judicial process, in November 1995 (Idowu 1999; Frynas 2000; Worika 2001). Far from the obvious expectations of government, this forceful and brutal reaction fuelled, rather than doused, the upsurge of popular resistance in the Niger Delta. Several other ethnic groups in the region came up with their own associations, such as the Movement for the Survival of the Ijaw Ethnic Nationality in the Niger Delta (MOSIEND), the Chikoko Movement and the Movement for Reparation to Ogbia (Oloibiri) (MORETO). Interestingly, the various instruments drawn up by these youth-led groups were very similar in content and style, adopting a rights-based approach to the management and allocation of resources in the Niger Delta (Frynas 2000: 47; Manby 1998: 129–31).

According to Osaghae et al. (2007: 11), '[T]he youths regarded the elites and elders as weak, fearful and ineffective in seeking access, dialogue and agreements with an insensitive and repressive state and exploitative and socially irresponsible MNCs. The youths decided to take their destinies in their hands by mobilizing, organizing and engaging the state and MNCs.' In the face of increasing coercive and repressive actions by the state, the transition from non-violent to violent struggle was not a difficult leap. Crucially, as violent conflicts escalated in the Niger Delta, the elders and the weakened traditional institutions were unable to play an active role in resolving the crisis. This is so even in the area of inter-communal clashes which should have been a forte of customary law institutions (Jike 2004: 696). According to Douglas (2004), '[R]espect for elders is becoming rare. Communal government institutions like the council of chiefs [...] are also no longer respected. [...] Oil, gas and politics have put a sharp knife in them and they are fallen apart.'

The government's response to the rise in activism

Far from learning from the Ogoni experience that military intimidation could no longer silence the agitation in the Niger Delta, the government attempted to crush opposition from youths. In the process, ordinary citizens were killed and entire communities destroyed. Once again, the instrument relied on was the law – the president's constitutional powers of command over state security agencies and the military. Arguably, this was an illegal or unjust use of constitutional powers, which the state turned on its own citizens, including the elderly, women and children. Notable among these military misadventures are the Umuechem massacre of 1991 (Manby 1998; Frynas 2000), killings following the Kaiama Declaration of 1998 (Human Rights Watch 1999a), the destruction of Odi in 2000 (The News 1999; Africa Action 1999), and quite recently the destruction of Agge (This Day Online 2008) and Gbaramatu kingdom in May 2009.

The ill-treatment through violent repression was acknowledged by the then minister of environment. He noted that, '[T]heir mild protests and agitations for compensation and better environmental management/accounting were rebuffed. Opinion leaders were jailed. A few were murdered, with the implicit support of the major operators who should have shown understanding of their plight' (Guardian 1999). In a system where the rule of law prevails, such open acknowledgement of serious crimes, including 'murder' by such a highly placed member of an elected government, would lead to an inquiry, indictment and prosecution of those involved. Yet, just as with the violation of environmental laws by the oil companies, none of these happened in the Niger Delta. This speaks of the lack of effective systems for ensuring justice, and the inherent incapacity of the citizenry to hold government accountable.

Rather, the law and justice system has been used selectively against only those involved in protest (violent or otherwise) against the state. It is therefore not a question of lack of capacity. Prosecutions of individuals involved in acts of protest and insurgency in the region have been successfully undertaken (including in the Ken Saro-Wiwa case). More recently, there have been prosecutions of high-profile accused persons such as Asari Dokubo of the Niger Delta Peoples Volunteer Force (NDPVF), and Henry Okah of MEND, although these were discontinued. The use of the law and justice system is also very powerful symbolically in the labelling of activities of militia groups as criminal, without a corresponding labelling of other actors whose acts have a negative impact on the people of the region (see Zalik, this volume). Such arrests have therefore become reasons for the escalation of violence from militia groups such as MEND, owing to what they perceive as injustice against individuals considered leaders in the fight for justice for the peoples of the Niger Delta (Tell 2008a).

The other main government response in the region has been the use of selective financial payments/inducements as a means of pacifying insurgents and kidnappers. Rather than resolving the crisis, such payments fuel a rentier culture in the Niger Delta and encourage the growth of self-serving militia groups intent on getting their slice of the 'national cake'. This has resulted in a blurring of the line between violence and disruption in furtherance of genuine and legitimate struggle, and purely criminal activity. The use of negotiation to secure the release of hostages is not unique to Nigeria. However, by politicizing and commoditizing the process of negotiating with kidnappers in the Niger Delta, the government has arguably recognized the lack of strong legitimate institutions for securing justice, while rewarding criminal acts by some militia warlords.

The government has set up panels at various times to look into the Niger Delta question. The Report of the Technical Committee on the Niger Delta, under Ledum Mitee, gives a comprehensive overview of these (TCND 2008: 15–36). However, no official white papers have been issued, nor have any recommendations been implemented holistically. Rather, the government has resorted to piecemeal reforms and acts of tokenism. These include the establishment of the Niger Delta Development Commission (NDDC) in 2000, ostensibly to address the region's environmental and infrastructure problems. Previous experiments, however, had shown that these types of agencies (such as the Niger Delta Development Board in 1961 and the Oil Mineral Producing Areas Development Commission, OMPADEC, in 1992) are doomed to fail because of factors such as their very broad mandates, unclear objectives, inadequate funding, politicization of contract award processes and corruption (Frynas 2000). Almost a decade after the NDDC was established, no significant development has taken place in the Niger Delta. A new Ministry of Niger Delta Affairs was created in September 2008, with no clear division of responsibilities with the NDDC. It is already mired in controversy over the nature of projects, the high proportion of funds going to technical appraisal, and poor completion rates (Next 2009).

Conclusion

This chapter demonstrates that while the violence in the Niger Delta has reached very dangerous proportions the crisis is rooted in the failure of the state to provide effective access to justice through the legal or justice system to address the legitimate grievances of the people of the region. A solution to the violence in the region can therefore not be formulated outside of a genuine, holistic and concerted effort to address these perceived injustices alongside contradictions in the Nigerian political system. A holistic solution engendering lasting peace requires the government to engage in genuine dialogue with the local people. Such a process will ensure legitimacy and acceptability for any agreements that will ensue. Lessons can be drawn from other regions, such as South Africa and Northern Ireland, where seemingly intractable problems were resolved through dialogue. A long-term view has to be taken of a complete resolution of the issues, albeit with an implementation plan which has clear, achievable benchmarks and goals. This is one of the strong points of the Report of the Niger Delta Technical Committee, which sets out timescales for achieving specific goals. Unfortunately, the government is once again indulging in piecemeal implementation of the report.

The foregoing demonstrates the implications of the overarching governance and accountability deficits for the rule of law and access to justice in the region. Also of note is the nature of politics and inequitable power relations between the state and the people of the Niger Delta. Thus while law reform is crucial and should be pursued in the short term, policies must be developed and mechanisms put in place to ensure that the tenets of the rule of law, transparency and democratic accountability in government are nurtured in the Nigerian state. In the short term, the National Assembly must address various areas of glaring injustice in the region. Unjust laws and legal instruments, such as the 1999 federal constitution and the 1979 Land Use Act, need to be repealed as a matter of urgency. Second, easier access to the courts should be facilitated by ensuring that jurisdiction is clearly granted to courts that can be more easily accessed by the people. The effective regulation of the legal system is necessary, so that financial constraints do not deter aggrieved parties from seeking redress when their rights are infringed or when they seek justice. This can be done through effective legal aid provision and regulation of arrangements for representation on the basis of a contingency fee. This cannot, however, take the place of government regulatory agencies effectively undertaking their legal duty to enforce the relevant laws where they are violated by the oil companies. At the local level, and to ensure easy access, there should be establishment of private sector ombudsmen (grievance officers) to whom local people can complain, in order to help facilitate the process of resolving disputes.

Ultimately, one must look beyond specifics and indeed the law. True access to justice can be addressed only when the broader concerns of social equity, transparency and accountability of government and its agencies to citizens, as well as the inequities embedded in the political economy of oil in the Nigerian state, are justly addressed.

5 | The Ijaw National Congress and conflict resolution in the Niger Delta

Ibaba Samuel Ibaba

Introduction

The Ijaw National Congress (INC) is one of the many ethnic minority identity organizations that emerged in the oil-rich Niger Delta in the 1990s (Ikelegbe 2001). Its goals include the articulation of the demands, interests and grievances of the Ijaw – the largest of the ethnic minorities in the Niger Delta. The INC was formed in the context of economic crisis and reform, military rule and a 'guided' political transition programme, where political space was limited, and ethnic minority elites sought to centralize their identity-driven groups and politics to better propagate their campaign for states creation, fair compensation for oil pollution, and a greater and fairer share of oil revenues/benefits.

These demands were addressed to the federal government and the oil companies operating in the region. The INC was similar to other organizations in the delta, such as the Movement for the Survival of Ogoni People (MOSOP), the Isoko Development Union (IDU), the Urhobo Progressive Union (UPU), the Egbema National Congress (ENC) and the Movement for the Survival of Itsekiri Ethnic Nationality (MOSIEN).

Resource control and self-determination have been key demands of these organizations, as reflected in their various resolutions and declarations. Examples include: the Aklaka Declaration (1999); the Bill of Rights of the Oron People (1999); the Ogoni Bill of Rights (1990); the resolutions of the First Urhobo Economic Summit (1998); the Warri Accord (1999); the Kaiama Declaration by Ijaw youth (1998); and the resolutions of the INC–First Pan Ijaw Congress (2003).

The politics of these organizations was later to become a key factor in the conflicts that subsequently bedevilled the region and the subsequent quest for conflict resolution and sustainable peace. Joshua Fumudoh, a former president of the INC (1994–2000), characterized the position of the INC thus:

> The Niger Delta crisis has brought to the fore [...] the fundamental issues of resource ownership and control in a supposed federation of ethnic nationalities with divergent histories, interests and aspirations. The only Panacea for continued peaceful co-existence in this country is for each ethnic nationality to have meaningful control over its own environment and resources, and to use them for

self-development in accordance with each nationality's aspirations and desire. (INC 1999)

In the INC's view, Nigeria's centralized federalism has skewed powers and resources in favour of the federal government, which is controlled by the majority ethnic groups in Nigeria, to the exclusion and marginalization of Niger Delta ethnic minorities, whose region produces the oil (see Ako, Emeseh, Ukeje, and Ukiwo, this volume). This injustice and marginalization are regarded as the fundamental causes of the conflict. To address these fundamental injustices, the INC insists on resource control and self-determination to enable the Ijaw and other ethnic groups in the Niger Delta to control their resources, including oil and access to oil revenues, as a guarantee of their rights to use such resources for their own development and the benefit of their people.

However, it should be noted that the position of the INC regarding the struggle for equitable distribution and control of oil resonates with the Ijaw people. But this narrative often overlooks some of the contradictions that are embedded in the campaign for resource control and local autonomy. A key point is the role of corruption in the outbreak of conflicts, and as an obstacle to the resolution of conflicts (Peel 2005; Enweremadu 2008; Human Rights Watch 2007a, b). Although inequality and violence are interconnected (Billon 2003; Cramer 2005; Nafziger 2006), the neglect of corruption has created some gaps, limiting the effectiveness of the INC, and its capacity to act as an agent for sustainable grassroots conflict resolution in the Niger Delta. In this regard, this chapter addresses the following questions. Can the INC's agenda of resource ownership/control resolve the conflicts in the Niger Delta? What is the relationship of the INC with other Ijaw groups adopting different strategies in the struggle for resource control and self-determination? What has the INC done to tackle the challenges of insurgent violence, militarization and corruption in the Niger Delta, and has it been effective with regard to conflict resolution?

Ijaws and the Niger Delta

The Niger Delta extends from the Benin river in the west to the Imo river in the east (ANEEJ 2004; UNDP 2006: 19). Some geographical explanations emphasize a four-state structure (Tamuno 2000: 11–12, 2008: 3). But from a geopolitical perspective, the dominant view is that the Niger Delta is made up of six states (Akwa-Ibom, Bayelsa, Cross River, Delta, Edo and Rivers) of the Nigerian federation. This six-state structure of the Niger Delta is derived from the area defined by the Niger Delta Development Board Act of 1960 (Etekpe 2007b). However, it is important to note that the NDDC Act of 2007 expanded the geopolitical space of the region to cover nine states (by adding Abia, Imo and Ondo). Thus, by actions such as state creation, boundary adjustments and oil politics, some Niger Delta communities may be located within states outside the widely accepted six Niger Delta states, just as non-Niger Delta communities may be located in the area.

Over 28 million Nigerians live in the Niger Delta (UNDP 2006: 25). It is made up of about 20 ethnic minority groups, 800 communities (Okoko and Ibaba 1997: 57) and 7,717 settlements (UNDP 2006: 23). The ethnic groups in the region have settled there over many millennia. The Ijaws, the predominant ethnic group (Willink Commission 1958: 34), have lived in the region for over seven thousand years, while other ethnic groups have lived there for about a thousand years (Alagoa, cited in Survival 1999: 8). In 2003, the INC estimated the Ijaw population to be over fifteen million (INC 2003).This may be disputed, but the fact that the Ijaws are the fourth-largest ethnic group in the country (Ukeje and Adebanwi 2008; Ukiwo 2007) supports the claims of Ijaw dominance in the Niger Delta. Other ethnic groups in the Niger Delta include the Ogoni, Etche, Urhobo, Efik, Ibibio, Ikwerre, Abua, Isoko, Itsekiri and Ndokwa.

The Ijaws are the main settlers of the creeks and the riverine and swampy areas of the region (Preboye 2005), and are spread over six states: Akwa-Ibom, Bayelsa, Delta, Edo, Rivers and Ondo. The Niger Delta is central to the survival of Nigeria (Obi 1997a: 8–9), and this makes the Ijaws, the major group in the region, essential to the peace, security and development of the country. Most of the country's oil is produced in the Niger Delta, with the areas inhabited by the Ijaw nation accounting for about 75 per cent of oil production. About 90 per cent of offshore oil is also produced within proximity of littoral Ijaw communities in Akwa-Ibom, Rivers, Delta, Edo and Ondo states (Amakiri 2003: 32–3).

Paradoxically, the Ijaw areas are among the most neglected parts of the Niger Delta. This assertion is predicated on the fact that the Ijaw areas are among the least developed in the region. Under the Nigerian regional federal structure, the Ijaws were split into the Eastern and Western regions, where they constituted the minorities. In 1963, the western Ijaws were placed in the Mid-Western region, which did not change their minority status in the three southern regions. Because of the domination of these regions by larger ethnic groups and the ethnicization of resource distribution, the Ijaws, who lacked both numbers and political power, were short-changed (Tamuno 2005). Presently, the Ijaws are minorities in five of the Niger Delta states (Akwa-Ibom, Delta, Edo, Ondo and Rivers) where they are located, a fact that speaks to the state of their marginalization in spite of their demographic size.

The neglect of Ijaws, occasioned by their being split among many states where they are minorities, informs the INC demand for homogenous Ijaw states as a means of promoting development and conflict resolution. But this position appears to be contradicted in the case of Bayelsa state, which though predominantly populated by ethnic Ijaw lacks development, and is characterized by violence, despite being governed by Ijaw elites. The explanation for this situation is twofold. First, it is partly due to long years of neglect as a result of an 'urban bias' in resource allocation in the 'old' Rivers state. Before its creation in October 1996, Bayelsa state was part of the rural areas of Rivers state, and because of its location in the interior swamp, it suffered neglect in the allocation of social infrastructure and services. Figure 5.1 demonstrates this, illustrating projects executed by the presidential committee established in 1988 to manage the 1.5 per cent oil-producing areas development fund.

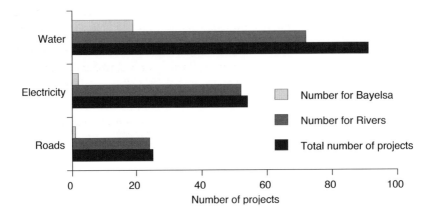

FIGURE 5.1 Projects of the presidential committee on the disbursement of the 1.5 per cent oil-producing areas development fund, indicating projects allocated to old Rivers state and the share of Bayelsa state (*source*: OMPADEC 1993)

When it was created in 1996, Bayelsa state had a population of 1,327,488 and 495 communities and settlements, but only 8 hospitals, 132 health centres, 9 pre-primary schools, 399 primary schools, 87 secondary schools, 1 technical college, 4 craft development centres and 1 teacher training college (Mangete et al. 1999: 335; Nwideeduh 1999: 329; Ibaba 2004: 20). The state had only one single-lane road in the capital, Yenagoa, had no tertiary institution, and was not connected to the national electricity grid.

Bayelsa state was highly underdeveloped at the time of its creation, and it needed a leadership with the capacity to pursue the public good. Unfortunately, this has not been the case since its inception, as the elites that control political power in the state have continued to pursue their selfish interests. This relates to the second factor explaining the violence in the state, namely, corruption. For example, in August 2009 the Economic and Financial Crimes Commission (EFCC), Nigeria's anti-graft agency, returned the sum of 10.2 billion naira (N) to the Bayelsa state government, as part of funds and value of assets confiscated from the former governor of the state, Chief D. S. P. Alameiyeseigha (Bayelsa State Government 2009). The former governor was arrested in London in 2005 for money-laundering, mysteriously escaped to Nigeria, but was later arrested, tried and convicted by a high court in Lagos in 2007 (see Ako, this volume). In

2009, the state government carried out a biometric exercise to determine its actual workforce, and reported a monthly loss of N300 million over three years to fraudulent civil servants who placed 'ghost workers' on the payroll (news item, Radio Bayelsa, 2010).

Bayelsa citizens have been alienated from the wealth of the state as corrupt officials divert funds meant for development, and only a fraction of the state's resources trickles down to the people. For example, a survey has shown that less than 5 per cent of the rural population has access to clean water (BMCAA 2009). The harsh realities resulting from this lack of development have created the abject poverty in the midst of plenty that has contributed to the tensions and grievances underpinning conflicts in the state. Corruption has also contributed to the use of violence in politics and the spread of a culture of 'easy money' and impunity within both the elite and the armed youth, which has contributed to the use of force in place of dialogue, often at the expense of peace and development in the state.

Ijaw nationalism and the formation of the INC

One of the significant outcomes of colonial rule in Nigeria was the emergence of ethnic consciousness and identity politics. Nnoli (1978), Coleman (1986), Dappa-Biriye (1995), Ademoyega (1981) and Tamuno (2005) attribute this to a number of factors. First is the divide-and-rule politics of the colonial government. Second is the tripartite structure of government and the resultant intersegmental imbalances.

The third point was inequality and the competition for scarce socio-economic resources among the different ethnic nationalities that had settled in the urban areas. Furthermore, ethnicity was politicized through the factionalization of the privileged class and inter-ethnic struggle for political power. The nationalist movement became ethnicized and ethnic associations of the major ethnic groups emerged to lead the process that led to the formation of ethnicity-based political parties such as the Action Group (AG) and the Northern Peoples' Congress (NPC).

The struggle for power by the major groups resulted in the minority groups joining in the politicization of ethnicity in an attempt to protect their interests in the respective regions. This resulted in the formation of Ijaw groups such as the Ijaw Rivers Peoples League (1942), the Ijaw Union (1952), the Rivers State Congress (1955), the Rivers Chiefs and Peoples Conference (1956) and the Niger Delta Congress (1959) (Etekpe 2005; Dappa-Biriye 1995).

At independence, the intra-ethnic struggle for state power and the resultant ethnicity-based politics strengthened the relevance of ethnic cleavages, expressed by the ethnic unions. By the mid-1960s oil politics had become a rallying point for ethnic mobilization, and noted as the root of Ijaw nationalism by Ukeje and Adebanwi (2008: 581). The Ijaw demand for a separate state, as documented by the Willink Commission, and the goals of the Adaka Boro rebellion support this assertion.

The history of the INC

The INC was established in 1991 to promote Ijaw consciousness, highlight the problems of Ijaw in Nigeria, sensitize Ijaw people to their problems, and centralize efforts to find solutions to the plight of the Ijaw (INC 1996: 2–3; INC 2008). Before the formation of the INC, there had existed a variety of Ijaw associations, such as the Ijaw Peoples League, the Ijaw People's Association and the Ijaw State Union. But these organizations were not effective in promoting a pan-Ijaw agenda of survival owing to the lack of a central body to coordinate their activities. The recognition of this gap in Ijaw nationalism triggered the establishment of the INC. The founding fathers, Chief H. J. R. Dappa-Biriye, Chief A. Weikezi and Chief F. H. E. Brisibe, convened meetings in Lagos under the auspices of the Ijaw People's Union on 25, 29 and 30 October 1991. The resolutions of these meetings led to the formation of the INC (Etekpe 2005).

The INC's quest for Ijaw development has led it to address issues of Ijaw rights, welfare, conflict resolution and peace-building in the Niger Delta. The INC has taken steps to support the resolution of the conflict in the Niger Delta, and has been involved in the resolution of communal conflicts and oil-company–community conflicts. Examples include the Ke and Bille inter-community conflict in Rivers state (2000) and the conflict between the Gbarain clan in Bayelsa state and the Shell Petroleum Development Company (SPDC) in 2007 and 2008 over issues concerning the establishment of a gas-gathering project. In 1998, the INC commissioned a study on oil companies' and host communities' relations and developed the policy of 'mutually stable expectations' for trial by the federal government and the oil companies. It was a win-win policy that sought to exploit the convergent interests of the companies and the communities.

On 29 June 1998, the INC wrote to then head of state, General Abdulsalami Abubakar, requesting an audience with him to discuss the plight of the Ijaw. Similarly, on 2 July 1998, and again on 24 July 1998, the INC wrote to the National Security Adviser, Major-General Abdulsalam Muhammed (retired), on the need for a dialogue on security matters in the Niger Delta. But he replied that the Ijaw complaints were receiving attention. Again, on 10 August 1998, the INC wrote to the Chief of General Staff, Admiral Mike Akhigbe, requesting a meeting to discuss the security situation in the Niger Delta. None of these requests was granted. In September 1998 the INC attempted to convene a meeting with all oil MNCs to negotiate on issues associated with oil-company–community conflicts. Only the Nigerian Agip Oil Company (NAOC) responded. The INC has continued to engage the oil MNCs in dialogue, whenever the opportunity has presented itself (INC 2003; Williams 2005: 110–49; INC 1999). However, the INC boycotted the 1995 constitutional conference organized by the Abacha military regime, citing the undemocratic and authoritarian character of the government, but actively participated in the 2005 political reforms conference convened by the Obasanjo democratic government. Table 5.1 below highlights the engagement approaches of the Congress and its demands on the state and oil companies.

TABLE 5.1 INC engagement approaches and demands

Engagement approaches	Demands on the state	Demands on oil MNCs
Advertorials	Development	Community development
Press releases	Resource control	Employment
Dialogue with state officials	Federal restructuring	Environmental protection
Coordination of Ijaw struggle	Demilitarization	
Organization of conference/ summit		

Source: Ikelegbe (2001: 444, 454, 456)

It is clear from its engagement strategies that the INC is a non-violent organization, but its demands have pitched it against the federal government and oil MNCs. The INC is a member of Ethnic Nationalities of the Niger Delta (ENND), a pan-ethnic association that coordinates and integrates the struggles of all the ethnic nationalities in the Niger Delta. Under this umbrella, it collaborates and consults with other nationality groups in its conflict resolution efforts. Its agenda for conflict resolution is discussed in the section that follows.

The INC's agenda for conflict resolution in the Niger Delta

Resource control and self-determination The Congress attributes the conflict in the Niger Delta to the country's centralized federal system and the resultant inequitable fiscal relations between the federal and state governments, which has not only subordinated the states to the federal government, but has also impeded development in the states (Okoko 2003). This position, which is in sync with the dominant resource control narrative in the Niger Delta, argues that Nigerian federalism is characterized by federal–regional structural imbalances and asymmetrical power relations, a situation blamed on its colonial origin and made worse by military rule and ethnic politics (Ikporukpo 1996, 2003 and 2004; Naanen 1995; Ikein 1991; Aaron 2006; Ikelegbe 2001; Etekpe 2007b; Orobator et al. 2005; Tamuno 1998).

The inequity in resource allocation by which oil-producing states get less, while the federal level retains most of the oil revenue, has fuelled grievances, uneven development and instability in the Niger Delta. The manipulation of the derivation principle of revenue allocation by dominant federal elites (believed to come mainly from non-oil-producing ethnic majorities) is seen to be central to the conflict. The derivation principle, which allocated a percentage of revenue to the federating units on the basis of wealth generated in each federating unit, had been the dominant criterion for revenue allocation in the country.

At independence in 1960, derivation was 50 per cent, as provided in Section 134(1) and Section 140(1) of the 1960 and 1963 constitutions. This was reduced to 45 per cent in 1970, and later to 1.5 per cent in the following decade. Because this reduction coincided with the displacement of agriculture by petroleum, as the mainstay of the nation's economy (Mbanefoh and Egwaikhide 1998), the INC blames ethnic politics for the manner in which the ethnic majority have centralized federalism to control national (oil) revenues, in spite of the fact that their regions contribute little or nothing to them. This explains the INC's position and preference for resource control, self-determination and the convoking of a sovereign national conference to renegotiate a just and fairer basis for Ijaws' relationship with the Nigerian federation as the solution to the conflict in the region (Okoko 2003).

The Niger Delta (Ijaw) demand for resource control implies that the ethnic minorities of the Niger Delta will have the right to legislate on the production and development of oil and gas, conservation and management of the environment and its resources, and the right to grant permission for the exploitation of its resources (see Ako, this volume). Two crucial expectations underlie this demand. First, that the oil wealth will be retained to fund development. Second, that the people will have proprietary interests in environmental protection and also firm control over the use of the environment, thus being able to adequately protect it from pollution and unsustainable exploitation. While the INC believes that this would enhance development and end the grievances that triggered the conflict, it is imperative to note that it depends on making votes count in elections, ensuring democracy, accountability and transparency in governance.

The INC, militias and the federal government's amnesty programme As noted earlier, the conflict in the Niger Delta has led to the emergence of militia groups in the region, with MEND as the most prominent (Watts 2007; Joab-Peterside 2005; Okonta 2006). The foundation for militia movements in Ijaw land, largely dominated by youths, was laid by inter-ethnic conflicts, the formation of vigilantes to secure lives and property, the commodification of violence in the electoral process (Joab-Peterside 2005) and piracy.

The objectives of some of these groups, which include true federalism and self-determination, an end to injustice and neglect (Ikelegbe 2006b: 96; Agbu 2004), are in sync with those of the INC. Probably because of this convergence of interests, a former president of the INC, Professor Kimse Okoko (who served between 2000 and 2008), describes these groups as freedom fighters. This explains the warm relationship between the INC and these groups. But he has also expressed some concern about the infiltration of the ranks of militia groups by criminals (Tell 2008b: 32).

This concern pertains mainly to the attacks on oil installations, oil theft, and kidnapping/hostage-taking for the sake of pecuniary gain. In spite of some convergence of interest between the militant resistance groups and the INC, the high levels of social disintegration in the region and the loss of control over the youths imply that the Congress has found it difficult to deal effectively with insurgent violence. Although the social crisis in the Delta can be partly linked to the impact of the oil industry (Ikporukpo 2003: 21–2), the situation has also been worsened by a culture of impunity, flowing from the erosion of ethical and moral values, which has undermined individual and social responsibility towards the state and society. This social decay of values has also impeded the effectiveness of the INC in terms of control over its membership.

The INC supports the 2009 amnesty programme, and took part in the processes that led to the surrender of arms and key militia group leaders. But the Congress has insisted that the amnesty can be meaningful only if the fundamental issues that triggered the conflict are resolved. For the INC, amnesty is only a step towards the resolution of the conflict, not an end (communication with Dr Ambily Etekpe, INC Central Zone Secretary, and Chief Peter Wikimor, member of the INC Eastern Zone Representative Council, 14 August 2009).

The INC, interventionist agencies and the Niger Delta conflict The INC does not see interventionist agencies as viable options for the resolution of the conflict, and has therefore not mobilized support for them. A number of reasons account for this perception. First, it insists that the establishment of these agencies does not meet the demand for the resource control and self-determination that are fundamental to the resolution of the conflict. Second, it notes that they are not adequately funded, and, third, they are vulnerable to the manipulations of ethnic chauvinists (see Ako, this volume). Thus, to make the NDDC useful to the peace-building process in the Niger Delta, the INC calls for increased funding to enable the Commission to intervene adequately in infrastructure development. Furthermore, it has suggested its restructuring to remove the agency from the grip of the federal government (INC 2003).

Interrogating the INC's agenda for resource control, conflict resolution and peace-building in the Niger Delta

As mentioned earlier, corruption in governance and inefficient management of resources pose a major challenge to the realization of the INC's agenda for resource control, conflict resolution and peace in the Niger Delta. The INC argues that the oil wealth is taken away from the Niger Delta through the politics of revenue allocation, leading to inadequate development funds and the resultant development plight of the region. But the huge revenues that have flowed into the region from the Federation Account since 2000, following the implementation of the 13 per cent derivation fund, appear not to have led to radical transformation or development (see Ukiwo, Ako, this volume). It is noteworthy that the six Niger Delta states (South-South) received over N3 trillion between January 2000 and November 2008 (www.fmf.gov.ng). Analysis of the revenue allocation data shows that the Niger Delta states have received far more revenue from the Federation Account than all the other states on account of the 13 per cent derivation fund. Figure 5.2 demonstrates this with the 2008 allocations.

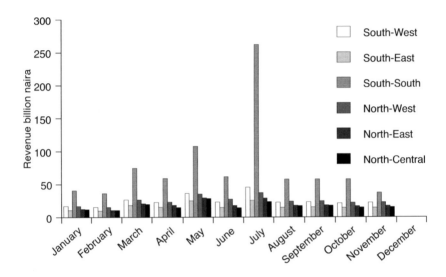

FIGURE 5.2 Comparison of revenue allocation to six geopolitical zones of Nigeria (naira, 2008 only) (*source*: www.fmf.gov.ng)

Although it was expected that the inflow of these huge revenues would lead to a reduction in the violent conflict, what occurred was the escalation of the conflict into a full-blown insurgency marked by acts of sabotage targeting oil installations, oil personnel and pipelines, and the Nigerian military operating in the region. For example, the SPDC recorded 1,243 oil spill incidences between 2003 and 2007, out of which 832, representing 66.2 per cent, were reportedly caused by sabotage (SPDC 2008: 18–19). Watts (2007: 639) has also noted that oil pipeline leakages due to sabotage rose from 497 in 1999 to 895 in 2004. Data provided by the Nigerian National Petroleum Corporation (NNPC) also indicates increases in pipeline vandalism. It shows that in 1999 497 incidents were recorded, but this rose to 984 in 2000. In 2001 the number dropped to 461 but rose to 516 in 2002. In 2003 a total of 779 cases were recorded; the total rose to 895 in 2004, 2,237 in 2005, 3,674 in 2006 and 3,224 in 2007 (TCND 2008: 114).

Corruption has led to the diversion of monies meant for the provision of social infrastructure and services, human capital development and the enhancement of production capabilities, poverty reduction and healthcare. Budgetary allocations neglect the provision of basic social amenities, while huge funds are allocated to corruption-prone white-elephant projects such as airports, and the wages and allowances of political office-holders. For example, the United Nations Educational, Scientific and Cultural Organization (UNESCO) stipulates a 26 per cent budgetary share for education. But an examination of the 2008 budget for some of the Niger Delta states shows wide gaps. The share of education in the budget was 12.05 per cent for Akwa-Ibom state; 5.61 per cent for Bayelsa state; 2.49 per cent for Delta state; and 6.39 per cent for Rivers state. But the allocations to Government House and the legislature were 26.8 per cent for Akwa-Ibom, 8.6 per cent for Bayelsa, 5.4 per cent for Delta and 7.6 per cent for Rivers (Niger Delta Standard 2009: 28). Consequently, the huge revenues benefit the elites who are the custodians of power at the federal, state and local government levels, but hardly get to the people.

Unfortunately, the INC has not been able to do much to address the issue of corruption, despite the ways it is feeding into the conflict in the region. At the first Pan Ijaw Conference in 2003, the INC noted that Niger Delta leaders were corrupt and had misappropriated the resources of the region. Accordingly, the Congress demanded that the states in the region should publish their monthly revenue receipts to ensure transparency. But this has not happened, and so far the INC has not taken any concrete steps to ensure this. Professor Kimse Okoko, former INC president (2000–08), blames the inaction of the INC on the inability of the people to vote out corrupt leaders owing to the subversion of the electoral process by corrupt politicians, backed by armed groups in the Niger Delta (Tell 2008a: 82). But corruption in the Delta does not occur within government circles alone. Oil MNCs have also been implicated in acts of corruption that have fuelled the conflict in the region. The sabotage of oil installations and oil theft, which is facilitated by corruption, has encouraged the proliferation of armed youth gangs and militia groups, and has thus exacerbated the conflict (Human Rights Watch 2005a; see also Zalik, Duquet, Ukiwo, Bøås, this volume).

Conclusion

This chapter has demonstrated that the INC has been engaged in the struggle for Ijaw rights, resource control, conflict resolution and peace in the Niger Delta. Through its engagement with governments at the state level, oil MNCs, and other ethnic associations, it has sought to advance the Ijaw cause using non-violent methods. The INC has also been involved in mediating communal conflicts in the region. It has resolved communal conflicts involving Ijaw communities on the one hand, and Ijaw communities and oil MNCs on the other. In a similar manner, it has encouraged communities to resolve conflicts with the oil companies through adjudication, in cases that involve the breach of existing laws. Similarly, in September 1998 the INC attempted to convene a meeting with all oil companies operating in the Niger Delta with the aim of negotiating various options, and finding solutions to issues such as youth unemployment, which had generated oil-company–community conflicts in several instances. This initiative largely failed as only the NAOC attended the meeting.

Also in 1998, the INC, in three separate requests to the then head of state, General Abdulsalami Abubakar, the National Security Adviser, Major-General Abdulsalam Mohammed (retired), and the Chief of General Staff, Admiral Mike Akhigbe, asked for dialogue to resolve youth restiveness and insecurity in the region. However, these requests were rebuffed. The INC agenda for conflict resolution and peace-building in the Niger Delta faces several challenges. These include the attitude of government and oil companies towards the INC, the violent context in which it operates, the corruption and opportunism of some Niger Delta elites, and the recent turn to criminality among some of the armed groups in the region.

These have created gaps and complications in the INC's responses to conflict. But given its non-violent nature, legitimacy and the fact that it has a substantial membership among the Ijaw elite, the INC is bound to continue to play an important role in the politics of conflict resolution, peace and development in the Niger Delta. A lot will depend on the ability of the INC's leadership to adequately respond to these gaps and challenges in a democratic, transparent, just and inclusive manner.

6 | Changing the paradigm of pacification: oil and militarization in Nigeria's Delta region[1]

Charles Ukeje

Introduction

This chapter analyses the factors driving and exacerbating the militarization of virtually all aspects of oil production activities in the Niger Delta and its connections to violent resistance. The Nigerian state's militarized response to community agitation is evident from the heavy presence of soldiers, naval officers and ratings, mobile policemen and a plethora of security agents deployed in and around the vicinity of oil installations to safeguard personnel and facilities. Since the 1990s heavy military deployment and presence has become one of the state's main responses to rising community protests and resistance against oil multinationals, making the Niger Delta the most militarized region in Nigeria. State repression of protests is evident from military campaigns against places such as Umuechem and Ogoni, Odi, Gbaramatu, in Rivers, Bayelsa and Delta states (Naanen 1995; Osaghae 1995; Obi 1997b; Ukeje 2001b; ERA/FoEN 2009).

The main argument of this chapter is that there are elements of continuity in the paradigms of state-led pacification in the Niger Delta, from pre-colonial to contemporary times. 'Pacification', in this context, refers to actions taken by the state or its agencies, often coercive in character, to suppress protests and defeat or destroy resistance or insurgencies (Ukeje 2009). What is particularly instructive is that under the prevailing atmosphere of militarization, the Nigerian state seems to be revealing its inability to exercise non-coercive and legitimized authority to address the festering crisis in the Delta region. In the context of the 'delegitimization' of state power, the state's response to the crises of authority and governance facing it is to pursue 'hard' instead of 'soft' power.[2] A plethora of factors is responsible for the growing inability of the state to exercise effective authority in the Niger Delta. What factors, for instance, explain the resort to military force? What is the relationship between state security agencies and the different oil-producing communities in the context of the militarization of the region, with what impact? Finally, what policy responses are likely to adequately address the profound dilemmas facing the Nigerian state with regard to the resolution of the festering crisis in the Niger Delta?

An important factor that assumes much salience in the militarization of the Delta region is the transnational character of oil, particularly the complexity of international energy security and strategic considerations. In a sense, oil may be what the former Venezuelan oil minister, Juan Pablo Perez Alfonzo, perceptively described as the 'devil's excrement', but it continues to define the context and pattern of global accumulation in a manner that is unprecedented in scale and intensity. Since 9/11, established and emerging powers such as the United States, Britain, France, China, India and Brazil have been locked in what has been described as the 'new scramble' to gain access to and secure a firm footing in oil-producing African countries. By accounting for the transnational character and impacts of oil, and its links to the energy security interests of established and emerging powers and their multinational or state oil companies, this analysis sheds light on the 'securitization' of oil, and how it reinforces the militarization of Nigeria's oil region, and the wider Gulf of Guinea.

The militarization of the Niger Delta has had a long and complicated history. It has structured and continues to shape the following relationships: between oil states and oil communities, between oil companies and host communities, between oil companies and host states, and finally between oil-producing and oil-importing/consuming countries. This chapter focuses on the Nigerian state and its militarization, and analyses how the paradigm of the pacification of the oil-rich Niger Delta is constituted and deployed. It also examines the role of multinational oil companies and their home governments in the militarization of the Niger Delta, and makes some suggestions for resolving the crisis, while examining the prospects for the future.

The evolution of an unending crisis

Many scholars have inadvertently hinged their narratives of the multifaceted crises facing the Niger Delta either at the point when the British colonial administration made laws at the beginning of the twentieth century, reserving oil concessions for 'British or British-allied capital' (Obi 2008a), or when crude oil was first discovered in commercial quantities in 1956, after which production and exports began in 1958. Such analyses mostly offer only a partial and incomplete explanation that can only be remedied by historicizing the changing political economy of the region from the 1450s onwards. It was from then that inhabitants of the region began to engage with a succession of European explorers, missionaries, slavers, colonial mandarins and post-independence state authorities, to produce the unique blend of social and political relationships that is evident to date.

Under the different regimes of transatlantic commerce, from slave to 'legitimate' palm-oil produce trade, the coastal peoples of the Oil Rivers, as they were known in colonial accounts, forged relationships among themselves, between themselves and societies in the hinterland, and finally with Europeans with commercial and colonial interests, whom they prevented from gaining access to the interior for almost four hundred years.

Although they constituted a demographic minority vis-à-vis other groups in colonial Nigeria, coastal communities of the oil delta region exploited their 'early-bird' contact and relationship with Europeans throughout the long trans-atlantic trade in slaves and palm oil to subjugate larger groups in the hinterlands. In 'Political minorities and historically dominant minorities in Nigerian history and politics', Ekeh (1996) interrogated several strands and implications of the majority–minority relations 'complex' as they affected the coastal delta com-munities vis-à-vis other groups, showing how they used the superior weapons and firearms acquired from European merchants to dominate others.

Paradoxically, the coastal delta experienced mixed fortunes with the discovery of crude oil in commercial quantities from 1956 onwards; but the minority status of its inhabitants remained intact as the political configuration that developed after the country's independence tilted power and authority in favour of the three biggest ethno-regional groupings: the Hausa-Fulani in the north, the Yoruba in the west and the Igbo in the east. Until much later, also, oil was not an issue in the quest for self-determination by minority groups in the Niger Delta, as exemplified by the grievances they brought before Henry Willink's Commission of Inquiry into the Fears of Minorities in 1958.[3] Since then, however, when oil became the fiscal basis of the Nigerian state from the 1970s, the grievances have assumed more vociferous and dangerous dimensions, particularly with regard to the need to correct the lopsided revenue allocation in favour of the federal government and/or the debate on resource control.[4]

Today, Delta oil communities harbour deep-seated resentment against gov-ernment, and multinational oil companies, aggravated by the curious irony that they host vast oil and gas reserves but still live, for the most part, in abject poverty, acute unemployment and poor health (Lindsay 2005). Invariably, conflict began to brew and escalate during the 1990s, against the backdrop of past failed promises, growing marginalization and frustration that reliance on non-bellicose community-based actions to draw attention to their plight had yielded little, if any, positive result. The groundswell of new community- and grass-roots-based protests began to grow during the late 1980s, exacerbated by the biting effects of the IMF/World Bank-imposed Structural Adjustment Programme (SAP). At the same time, nascent grassroots protests sprouted in the context of domestic and post-Cold War global discourses on human, environmental and minority rights, the former deriving from a nationwide clamour for a quick return to civilian rule, and the latter to do with attempts to bring about the empowerment of minority and environmentally challenged groups around the world.

Unfortunately, the popular belief that the return to civilian rule from 1999 would substantially open up the political space to accommodate previously aggrieved and disenfranchised groups and interests turned out to be misplaced. Instead, new forms of violent contestation, such as kidnapping for ransom, and violent protests and attacks by militants and armed cult groups, have compounded existing intra- and inter-communal conflicts. Indeed, given the trend of events in recent times – the spate of gang wars, cult activities, kidnappings and hostage-taking, arson and attacks on oil personnel and infrastructure – there is a disturbing but growing consensus that the Delta region has become the 'ground zero' of a putative security conundrum in Nigeria, with the potential to spill over into the adjacent West African sub-region.

The Niger Delta conflict has been described as 'the product of human self-interest rather than of some atavistic, visceral rivalry of the type that some outsiders lazily and insultingly describe as the sources of conflicts in African countries' (Peel 2005: 3). It is also the product of structural deficiencies inherent in the Nigerian state, and systemic anomalies within its society (Idemudia and Ite 2006a: 402). Events in the region have also revealed that the poor handling of previously minuscule pockets of community grievances over the inequitable distribution of oil wealth could cause a degeneration into full-blown insurgencies. Indeed, a vicious logic of brute force is feeding on a convoluted system of oil-based accumulation in Nigeria that can only be sustained, ironically, with the deployment of greater coercion and unbridled militarization.

Oil, militarization and the banality of state power

A 'potent cocktail of poverty, crime and corruption is fuelling a militant threat to Nigeria's reliability as a major oil producer' (International Crisis Group 2006c: 36). To comprehend the factors underpinning the militarization of the Niger Delta, it is important to examine the character of the colonial state, and its post-colonial reincarnation. Historically, the Oil Rivers (the name previously given to the Niger Delta) had been central to the enterprise that eventually became Nigeria, and the region has remained so to date in the context of the country's overwhelming dependence on crude oil.

Three overlapping epochs are central to the construction of British colonial hegemony in Nigeria. The earliest took place before 1807, when the transatlantic trade was abolished; the second from 1807, when legitimate trade in palm oil commenced; and the third from 1885, when the major European powers met in Berlin to partition Africa into de facto spheres of influence, and set about imposing formal colonial rule. Significantly, each of them coincided with different regimes of foreign capital accumulation based on slave, palm oil or crude oil production, and each produced, in varying scales and intensities, the mobilization of different administrative powers by the British. Throughout the long duration of the transatlantic slave trade, and the subsequent transition to palm-oil (legitimate) trade, the political economies of the Delta region experienced severe instabilities. In the scramble to gain access to, and control of, palm-oil markets, for instance, trade rivalries and wars frequently broke out throughout the nineteenth century (Kalu 1980: 16; Jones 1963).

By January 1891, an effective government for the Oil Rivers Protectorate was formed, followed two years later by the inauguration of the Niger Coast Protectorate.[5] From the early nineteenth century, when its naval squadrons became prominent along the coastal seaboard, much like the US Navy on the same waters today, the contours that British pacification of the Delta using gunboats would take had already started manifesting. British colonial incursions and the establishment of formal rule rode on the back of the pacification of the region (Afigbo 2003: 15) because it pitched the British against notable kings and merchant princes of the Niger Delta city-states (Dike 1956; Ikime 1968; Cookey 1974).

For the most part, then, whether it was aimed at expanding British trade or promoting Pax Britannica, colonial Britain never wavered in forcefully asserting its authority (Tamuno 1978: 47). These encounters invariably turned the rivers of the Delta into ferocious arenas of anarchy, and they have remained so in the context of the festering governance and security problems currently facing the region. For the British colonial authorities, the use of force was inevitable in order to maintain peace; after all, it was simply impossible to make an omelette without breaking eggs (Asiegbu 1984).[6]

The governance and security structures deployed by the post-colonial Nigerian state were exactly the same as those inherited from the departing British colonial authorities and used throughout the colonial period (Jackson 2007). Indeed, out of the myriad institutional relics adopted wholesale by the successor post-colonial state, the most notorious were the police and the army. For the most part, both derived their existence, mandate and also notoriety from the same stencil of power and authority designed by, and deployed under, colonial rule. Specifically, they were instruments of state coercion, subjugation and exploitation, sustained by some of the most obnoxious and arbitrary colonial ordinances, retaining intact, or only slightly tinkered with, to date.[7] As mentioned previously, the early British penetration into the Delta was facilitated by the ruthless deployment of gunboats. Beyond that period – except, of course, for graver situations – routine administration of justice and the enforcement of law and order relied on constabularies such as the Glover Irregulars, the Royal Niger Constabulary and the Oil Rivers Irregulars.

Unfortunately, in terms of training, orientation and doctrine, the constabularies – much like the police in post-colonial Nigeria – were programmed to secure and advance the narrow interests of the ruling elite, and by extension those of the colonial state against colonial subjects, including women (Mamdani 1996; Ukeje 2004). Although they had superiority of firepower vis-à-vis the coastal communities, they never had a monopoly of this important instrument of coercion and repression owing to lax controls on the importation of weapons and ammunition and the cover provided by the dense network of uncharted rivers and waterways for smuggling to thrive. The proliferation of weapons, in turn, became a constant source of irritation to the British colonial authorities as the interdiction and arrest of smugglers and 'miscreants' that threatened the colonial authorities proved difficult to contain (Jones 1963; Isichei 1973).

It is important to note, though, that the police were never properly administered or funded. It is particularly instructive that virtually all the visiting colonial police advisers on fact-finding missions to the Delta region at various times documented their concern about these inherent limitations, and how this shortcoming was partly at the root of the pervasive and persistent grievances among police personnel, officers and rank-and-file, respectively.[8] How the unenviable origins and unpleasant conditions of service of the police go to the roots of the crisis of legitimacy that continues to dog the institution in the post-independence era is already well documented. Studies have shown that the police force was ruthless, corrupt, dishonest and prone to brutalizing the colonized peoples and vandalizing their property (Alemika 1993: 187). The police were key in the ruthless suppression of dissent; for instance, during the anti-tax riots of 1929/30 in Warri province and other parts of the Eastern region, and in the suppression of the Egba women's demonstration against the arbitrary indulgences of their king, the Alake, in 1948 (Ukeje 2004).

Significantly, there is a striking parallel between the behaviour of the police, army and other security agencies during the colonial era and now. Like the police, the inherited army was also an instrument for the enforcement of the will of the state, not the protection of the people. Quite revealing, then, is the frame of mind of an apparently senior official in the Office of Secretary of State for Colonies in London, who inscribed a handwritten note on one of the ordinances held at the Public Record Office that troops on pacification missions should strive to minimize the burden of peacekeeping 'by living' off the restive community. Except, perhaps, for the brief civil war years, when federal troops fought ferociously to liberate the region from the occupying Biafran army, the current ruthless disposition of the police and military personnel across the length and breadth of the Niger Delta incontrovertibly shows that very little has changed in the character of policing in that region.

Since the 1990s, there has been a clear upsurge in the number and frequency of confrontations between government and multinational oil companies, on the one hand, and host oil communities, on the other. *The Price of Oil* is one of the most compelling accounts of how the corporate behaviour and actions of multinational oil companies fuel flagrant human rights abuses in the Niger Delta (Human Rights Watch 1999b). According to this report, some of the documented cases included excessively punitive reprisals in the form of raids on and the burning down of entire villages, the brutal killing of innocent people for acts ranging from the seizure of boats and employees of oil companies to kidnapping of oil workers and public figures, and occasionally the killing of security personnel. If the heavy-handed military assault on the Ogoni between 1990 and 1995 marked a notoriously distinctive phase in the militarization of the Niger Delta, another began in the aftermath of the Kaiama Declaration (KD), in which the Ijaws asked oil companies to vacate their territory by January 1999. The Declaration promptly provided the subtext for government to order massive deployments of troops not just in and around oil installations but throughout the region (Ukeje 2001b). Unsurprisingly, this type of massive militarization has become a major source of irritation in the day-to-day activities of the communities, especially as troops stay long enough to engage in a range of activities that pitch them against communities.

A pervasive but ill-conceived notion is that every threat to law and order in the contemporary Niger Delta is viewed as another attempt to undermine oil production and state security. This mindset – which permeates and drives government's response – continues to raise the threat level attached to even the most routine, daily disagreement across the Delta region. Principally owing to its obsession with oil, and the persistent threat arising from violent threats to security and stability, the Nigerian state is increasingly and readily disposed to the most unusual securitization of virtually every aspect of society and politics in the oil region. Omeje (2004: 429–30) conceptualized the different trajectories of conflict developing in that region without a compelling oil connection as 'extra-oil frontiers of conflict'. What the state does, according to him, is to 'oilify' such conflicts, by distorting and reconstituting an extra-oil threat or conflict to justify military action. In other words, 'within the context of oil conflicts, oilification helps protagonists and the state officials to justify the securitisation of non-oil threats and issues, including ill-motivated vendettas'.

In response to the frequent breaches of the peace, however, it is obvious that the Nigerian state underplays the obvious distinction between the activities of criminal elements and those involved in genuine community protests to draw attention to their plight and demands. One of the most important implications of such blanket securitization of protests is that conventional military responses often inflict disproportionate punishment on entire communities instead of fishing out and punishing the few elements responsible. This reliance on collective guilt and collective punishment, even in cases where the culprits are well known, has turned policing and soldiering in the Delta region into a vicious cycle of state brutality and military repression. There are several recent examples, but still by far the most ruthless was the razing of the entire village of Odi, an Ijaw community located in Bayelsa state, on Christmas Eve of 1999, in retaliation for the killing of some policemen on routine patrol. Instructively, reports at that time had indicated that the same band of hooligans that brutally murdered the policemen had also been terrorizing the villagers for months, and that their atrocities had become sufficiently disturbing to force the Odi community leaders to formally solicit the assistance of the police (Ukeje 2001b, 2004).

There is no standard manual stipulating what operational procedures security forces deployed in the Delta region should follow, beyond the mandate to protect oil infrastructure and personnel, and ensure unhindered oil production, by every means necessary. During the earlier pacification of the Ogoni and the Movement for the Survival of Ogoni People (MOSOP), a secret memo by the Rivers state commissioner for police in 1994, entitled 'Operation Order No. 4/94 – Restoration of Law and Order in Ogoniland', called for extensive and combined military operations involving the navy, air force, army and the police in Ogoniland (Human Rights Watch 1995). Another leaked memo dated 12 May 1994, by the notorious Rivers State Internal Security Task Force, then led by Major Paul Okutimo, identified specific strategies for achieving this; noting that the police in Ogoni had remained 'ineffective since 1993', it went on to state: 'Shell operations still impossible unless ruthless military operations are undertaken for smooth economic activities to commence.'

Instructively, Major Okutimo recommended mounting 'wasting operations [...] making constant military presence justifiable', heavy deployment of military personnel (officers and men), the erection of new security checkpoints along roads, and 'psychological tactics of displacement'. The memo also requested press censorship, including the 'restriction of unauthorized visitors especially those from Europe to the Ogoni', along with 'high level authority for the Task Force effectiveness', and recommending 'ruthless operations' and 'direct supervision by MILAD [military administrators] to avoid unruly interference by other superior officers'. Finally, it suggested an ECOWAS Monitoring Group (ECOMOG) allowance rate and 'pressure on oil companies for prompt and regular inputs as discussed'. To date, the pattern has remained strikingly similar: what typically happens is that – sometimes in joint operation with the notorious anti-riot police – soldiers of other ethnic origins (outside the Delta), who are unlikely to identify with and be sympathetic to the cause of restive oil communities, are deployed. This pattern, as noted earlier, is actually a throwback to the colonial era, when the colonial army mobilized mostly Hausa, Yoruba and non-Nigerians in seeking the consummation of British pacification projects in the coastal delta.

The foregoing is particularly obvious in the Niger Delta, and less so in other parts of the country, where the need to deploy police and soldiers to quell civil disturbances becomes important. The trend, for the most part, is degenerating into a treacherous and vicious cycle of violence, which, in turn, is blurring the fundamental separation between policing and soldiering. There are several implications, including that the paradigm of pacification currently in vogue is inescapably leading the state into thinking less of the police – and more of the military – as more appropriate in managing protracted law-and-order problems in the region. Implicit here is the notion that the crises in the Delta threaten unfettered oil revenue and accumulation from which the survival of the Nigerian state necessarily derives, and that only the military – not the routine deployment of police – can effectively resolve the problem. Thus, except in major towns and cities, the kind of police presence and facility that should exist is either thin or non-existent, as they have been replaced by soldiers and naval personnel, or the notoriously controversial hybrid force, the Joint Task Force (JTF).

Where police presence is visible, often they are poorly equipped and the morale of personnel is abysmal. The realities on the ground often do not support the claim by the police authorities that they are capable of responding to the changing demands of policing. The Special Security Committee on Oil Producing Areas set up by government under the chairmanship of then Chief of Army Staff, Lieutenant General Ogomudia, in 2001, was more forthcoming regarding some of the inherent and environmental constraints facing police operations in that region.

Although security falls within the administrative purview of the federal centre, state governments often augment it by offering financial support to strengthen policing within their domains. Unfortunately, such contributions fail to achieve the desired result in the face of excessive bureaucracy and corruption. This was what reportedly happened with regard to the donation of N557 million (over £2 million) by the Bayelsa state government towards the procurement of arms and ammunition for the police. By March 2008, several months after the money had been lodged with the police authorities in Abuja, the Federal Capital Territory, there was an allegation in a substantive petition that the money had sunk into the bottomless pit of a highly corrupt police and state bureaucracy.[9] A corollary to this, of course, is that those who derive incentives from such corrupt practices are not likely to spearhead or support the quest for an effective solution to the lingering crisis. In any analysis of resource-linked violent conflicts, therefore, the private interests of the military and police should be specifically identified as one of the drivers of the conflict.

Since the 1990s, when the Rivers state government set up the notorious Rivers State Task Force on Internal Security (RSTFIS) under Major Paul Okutimo, virtually all other state governments in the region have established similar military task forces, drawing their membership from the army, navy and, to a lesser extent, the mobile police unit. In the aftermath of the prolonged violent crisis in Warri, Delta state, in 2003, the federal government also created the JTF and launched a military campaign code-named 'Operation Restore Hope',[10] whose activities have been the subject of public controversy and criticism for the high-handed manner in which the JTF has been carrying out its mission, further threatening peace and stability in the region (Barret 2008).

Given the topography of the Niger Delta, and the sheer lawlessness perpetrated by state and non-state armed groups on the creeks and waterways, a vibrant and more functional marine unit within the police force with effective coastguard capability would do a better job than the Nigerian Navy (NN), whose mandate is to protect the country's territorial waters and maritime boundaries from external threats. In the absence of any functional marine or coastguard unit, however, the capability of the NN to effectively deliver on policing duties along the sprawling creeks and waterways is significantly undermined.

In the first place, it is a daunting task to patrol such a vast and poorly charted area with a maritime zone stretching 200 nautical miles offshore and covering about 286,000 square kilometres of water – almost one third of the total land surface of Nigeria (Ogbu 2008). The Eastern Naval Command alone controls 196 nautical miles of coastline, out of which 70 miles is within Rivers state – the remaining 126 is shared by Bayelsa, Akwa Ibom and Cross River states respectively.[11] The other point is that even though it maintains naval bases in all the Delta coastal states, except in Bayelsa, its presence is still not sufficiently felt. In Bayelsa state, which is both the epicentre of oil production and the hotbed of Ijaw militancy, for instance, the NN has only one forward operation base (FOB), located at Egweama.[12]

The implication of this lean presence was brought home in June 2008 when the withdrawal of the Eastern Naval Command's fleet of warships to commence three days of naval sea training, 'Exercise Sentry',[13] provided the Movement for the Emancipation of the Niger Delta (MEND) with an opportunity to attack the Bonga offshore oilfields.[14] This attack, coming barely three days after the presidency pledged to grant amnesty to militants ready to lay down their arms, reportedly shut in about 200,000 barrels of oil per day.[15] In response to the breach, the federal government deployed two small frigates – NNS *Nwamba* and NNS *Ologbo* – mounted with 30mm canons and a crew of about fifty, on patrol around the field.[16] Also, Shell and the NN quickly responded to protect Sea Eagle, another new-generation floating oil terminal moored 15 kilometres off the western Delta shorelines, with the capacity to process 170,000 barrels of crude oil per day and 100 million cubic feet of natural gas simultaneously (Global Policy Forum 2003). During the same period, two of the controversial warships (refitted 180-foot Second World War patrol boats) donated by the US government were also deployed.

The Nigerian Senate Committee on the Navy recently drew attention to the enormity of challenges facing the NN, given that it is poorly equipped to deal with the festering crisis in the Delta region. According to the chairman of that committee, Senator Bode Olajumoke, given 'the stark reality [...] that militants are using more sophisticated weapons to fight the regular arms being applied by our Armed Forces', official consideration was being given to a significant increase in annual subventions to the navy to 'enhance optimum result in the naval operations and services' (Ojeifo 2008).

Specifically, the committee proposed that funds be released for the construction of five FOBs, and for the purchase of platforms and boats. It also recommended that the Senate should promptly pass into law the Armed Forces Act Supplementary Provisions Bill 2008 to provide statutory powers for the NN to control and deal with illegal oil bunkering in Nigerian territorial waters and other related matters. Other sections of the armed forces have also, from time to time, bemoaned the state of disrepair that their different services have sunk into.[17]

Placing all of these in a broader perspective offer fresh insights into how the unfolding paradigm of pacification is inescapably leading the state towards the articulation of 'security' in an overtly militaristic sense. Ibeanu (2000: 24–5) has shown how conflicts might arise out of this type of 'contradiction of securities', and how the Nigerian state is characteristically unable to manage its fallout. This 'contradiction of securities', according to him, hinges on 'the opposition between perceptions and conditions of security advanced by local communities and those advanced by state officials and *petrobusiness*'. In the former case, security is construed in terms of recognizing that 'mindless exploitation of crude oil and the resultant ecological damage threaten resource flows and livelihoods', while the latter perceives security as consisting of an 'unencumbered production of crude oil at competitive (read: cheap) costs'. If the state is unable to 'mediate these opposing relations and conditions of security', it will continue to find itself drawn and locked into the conflict as a key protagonist against a range of armed non-state groups (ibid.: 25).

Several scenarios are likely to develop. First and foremost, social relations are inescapably assuming a format that is inherently conflict-inducing as the state and multinational oil companies increasingly become the target of the armed groups involved. Second, state violence resulting from excessive militarization becomes a principal variable in social conflicts. Third, since the Nigerian state has become a repository of violence against specific groups, instead of advancing broader, nationalistic interests, the kind of violence it produces comes at a huge social cost. Finally, according to Ibeanu, state violence makes conflict resolution very difficult and costly.

It is clear that the state – which ideally should be at the forefront of mediating oil conflict – is itself a major actor in, or 'fueller' of, violent conflicts and insecurity in the region. Also, what is becoming evident is that conflicts resulting from contestations over resource control are now closely tied to the inability of the state to deliver even on the most basic developmental expectations of the people. The disposition of the state is more a reflection of the vacuity of power and legitimate authority that it is struggling at all costs to gain and retain. Rather than respond to the legitimate demands of the people, the state has adopted a 'carrot and stick policy', in which the 'stick' appears to be the preferred option. Hence, the routine deployment of force by the state to contain opposition and exercise its authority is increasingly tenuous (Anugwom 2005: 109–10).

Multinational oil companies and the militarization of extraction

The sheer scale of oil industry operations in the Niger Delta is overwhelming.[18] Regrettably, given the unending controversies arising from the way the

93

industry is pursuing its operational goals and community relationships (see Zalik, Idemudia, Duquet, this volume), it might be difficult, if not impossible, to find any oil community without a minor or substantial grievance against an oil company; and, by extension, the government. Either directly or otherwise, multinational oil companies – including some indigenous ones – have contributed to the militarization of the Delta region. There are several explanations for their deep involvement. The first has to do with the fact that multinational and local oil companies and the Nigerian state are locked in a complex, opaque and very often incestuous relationship in which each party looks to the other to sustain and advance mutual interests.

A second explanation is that in the context of the weakening or eroding commitment of the state towards oil communities in the Niger Delta, oil companies have become the 'government' that the communities see and relate to on a daily basis. Still, as communities become increasingly vociferous, oil companies are quickly turning to, and relying on, the state for assistance and protection. The cumulative effect of state repression is that protests have turned violent, amid increased hostility towards multinational oil companies making it very difficult for them to engage in oil exploration and production activities without elaborate security protection from the state.

Thus, oil companies operating in Nigeria have had a long history of close relations with the police, military and other state security services. They all maintain a corps of reasonably paid supernumerary policemen (see Duquet, this volume) to secure administrative, operational and residential facilities. The oil companies all make ad hoc or routine payments to state security agencies (supplemented by the hiring of private security contractors) for a range of security-related duties, including when they are called upon to provide escort and other important military support services. While there is a widespread pattern of partial or piecemeal disclosure, and of non-disclosure, by oil companies on the depth of their relationship with the police and military in Nigeria, as elsewhere, what is incontrovertible is the manner in which they have engaged security forces that 'have a popular reputation for brutality and impunity' (Peel 2005: 5).

Omeje (2006b: 486–9) has identified at least three major consequences of the transnational oil companies' threat-management strategies, which fuel militarization and insecurity in the Niger Delta, manifesting in terms of: (1) 'security communitization', a term describing 'the contractual engagement of members and youth groups of the local oil communities to provide security for oil installations and operations within their localities'; (2) 'security privatization', as witnessed by the 'surge of specialized security companies/organizations and private military corporations' offering non-combatant-related security services that have 'a considerable measure of professionalization'; and (3) the 'corporatization of security', or corporate militarism, whereby some large businesses are allowed to operate their own security outfits or to have a detachment of the state's defence forces assigned to protect the corporation's personnel and property.[19]

The dynamics of securitization are assuming greater salience with the proliferation of private security outfits, or private military contractors (Dunning and Wirpsa 2004; Abrahamsen and Williams 2008). Whereas private security firms have been in existence in Nigeria for much of the country's post-independence era, they are assuming greater salience and relevance in the Delta region (where they are mostly engaged in the protection of oil installations and oil workers in remote locations where state presence is weak) and across the country where threats to law and order are on the rise. What is also particularly revealing about them is that some of the same elements that played or are still playing an active role in state and civil society militarization (especially the growing ranks of retired military, police and naval officers) are also the key operators of local private security companies, some in undefined partnerships with transnational security companies.[20]

Oil companies such as Shell have recently launched a framework to encourage host communities to set up security outfits and receive security contracts.[21] Some state agencies also routinely pay protection fees to some militant groups: a controversial development that officially came into the open when then group managing director of the state-owned Nigerian National Petroleum Corporation (NNPC), Engineer Yar'Adua, informed the House of Representatives panel probing government revenue and remittance to the Federation Account that the Corporation had to pay $12 million in two months to militants as a pay-off to protect oil pipelines and expatriate oil workers, because it was losing $81 million as a result of incessant attacks on Chanomi pipelines in Delta state.[22]

The foregoing underscores certain opaque standard practices among multinational oil companies operating in developing countries, especially where they partner authoritarian governments that have few or no qualms about ensuring their own survival at all costs in the face of mounting local opposition (Frynas and Wood 2001: 600–601). Often, oil companies rationalize their complicit response, or blame their collusion in militarization and human rights abuses as being mostly driven by the increasing inability of the state to adequately protect people and property.

However, given the threshold that has been reached in the Niger Delta,[23] it is difficult for oil companies to sustain the argument that they are not responsible for the way state security personnel behave once they have been deployed. Even if they are obliged to involve state security forces from time to time, as they have always claimed, doing so places the responsibility on oil companies to outline the rules and limits of engagement for the use of force, which is not the case in the region. Human Rights Watch drew attention to this point almost a decade ago by noting that a multinational oil company – in that case, Chevron – did not have 'internal written guidelines relating to security at its facilities and the response of company staff or contractors to security incidents, and [...] there is no written agreement with the Nigerian government relating to the provision of government security at its facilities' (Human Rights Watch 1999b: 4). The trend has continued to date, for the most part, as virtually all exploration and production activities – including protection of oil personnel – are carried out with high levels of state security presence.

The more things change ...? Oil and the future of the Niger Delta

On 20 June 2008, MEND claimed responsibility for the attacks on Bonga offshore oilfields, operated by a consortium of firms led by Shell. Taking place about 120 nautical miles offshore, in the Atlantic Ocean, that attack was perhaps the most daring to date given the enormity of logistic and practical challenges the militants had to overcome to reach this target. It was significant in demonstrating the capacity of militants to strike at targets offshore, previously considered as being beyond their reach. It also showed that they could go so far as to undermine the security of neighbouring countries in the Central and West African regions.[24] The attack on Bonga drove home the point about the need for a fundamental, urgent and well-informed shift in the manner in which the Nigerian government, multinational companies and the international community should be responding to the festering crisis in the Delta region.

The first major step towards sustainable peace is to repudiate the paradigm of military pacification, and pursue a comprehensive project of demilitarization, peace and sustainable development of the Niger Delta. To achieve this, key actors – the state, oil companies and local communities – must come to terms with the fact that their dispositions and actions have contributed in significant measure to the spectres of militarization and insecurity evident across the region. Apart from armed 'militant' groups that are generally seen as beneficiaries and spoilers, a retinue of serving and retired government officials and politicians, high-ranking military, naval and police officials, traditional rulers, business elites and oil company executives who benefit from the current dispensation are unlikely to embrace genuine and sustainable changes.[25]

Change and sincerity must therefore start with the highest political leadership, at the federal, state and local levels. Government and political elites must muster the political will to accept the blame for the failure of previous developmental interventions and focus more on finding genuine non-military, locally rooted political solutions to the endemic crises in the region. As events unravel in the region, however, the unspoken truth is that the state may find itself increasingly unable to exercise credible and effective control and management of the festering crises.

There is also the need for sustained 'strategic' engagement by the international community, especially Nigeria's key development partners, to help the country grapple effectively with the persistence of crises in the Niger Delta. To date, the principal concern of Nigeria's major external partners has been more with gaining access to the country's oil resources than any genuine commitment towards its stability and development. This outlook is evident in the choice that Western countries make between fraternizing with a ruthless but stable authoritarian regime/state and an unstable democracy. In most cases, such countries have demonstrated enthusiastic preference for the former as the best guarantee of unrestrained access to cheap oil.[26] In a broad sense, this is partly the central logic subtly driving the geostrategic calculations of major Western countries, and that of major oil-consuming nations such as China and India, vis-à-vis key oil producers in Africa.

Two other external factors are shaping Nigeria's relations with key importers of its oil. These are the increasing volatility of global prices of crude oil and the quest for a robust response to global terrorism, especially in the aftermath of 9/11. The location of the Niger Delta in the Gulf of Guinea, which holds 5–7 per cent of the world's proven petroleum reserves and supplies 15 per cent of US imports, defines it as strategic to US national interest (Oliveira 2007: 3).[27] From 2002, when President George W. Bush indicated that Washington would be willing to risk a war to protect strategic African oil, the United States has scaled up its military presence in the Gulf of Guinea (Volman 2003: 574; Ukeje 2009). Given the increasing visibility of the US Navy in the region, and the establishment of African Command (AFRICOM), it is no longer a secret that the convergence of US and Western energy and security interests in the Gulf, especially in Nigeria's oil, is already creating discomfort in the region. For Nigeria, this growing nexus between the energy and security interests of the USA and other countries is likely to raise the stakes of pacification in the Niger Delta rather than de-escalate the situation (Ukeje 2008).

Already, the disposition of key Western governments is towards helping Nigeria and other Gulf of Guinea countries strengthen their security sectors through the sale of arms, helping to build their military and naval capabilities, and maintaining a visible presence in the region as a possible deterrence (Volman 2003: 577).[28] Some of the 'incentives' arising from the presence of the US naval fleet include extending training support services to NN personnel and their counterparts in the other arms of the military on night surveillance, coastal patrolling and rapid response to small insurgencies, as well as donations of military hardware.[29]

Such offers tend to be merely cosmetic, coming from virtually every country with strategic interests in Nigeria (Akpuru-Aja 2003).[30] Unfortunately, they mostly come with little or no guarantees as they are driven purely by the enlightened self-interest of the benefactor rather than any genuine commitment to the country. Over the years, key donor agencies such as the World Bank, the European Union (EU) and the United Nations Development Programme (UNDP) have been keen to support a range of social, economic, technical, environmental and capacity-building intervention programmes for the Niger Delta. Desirable as such interventions might be on paper, they have proved to be insufficient and poorly implemented palliatives, such that their overall impacts have been only minuscule. Hence, there is need for a change of focus and strategy on the part of key Western countries, specifically focusing on nudging oil-rich but poorly governed African countries to do more by way of bringing a human face to public policy and governance in their countries.

This is partly why the push for greater transparency and accountability in the activities of multinational oil companies operating in the country under the Nigeria Extractive Industry Transparency Initiative (NEITI)[31] is timely and essential. The key thrust of the policy, sponsored by the United Kingdom, is to substitute greater transparency and accountability for opaque transactions in government dealings with multinational oil companies, and vice versa. Beyond this, key Western countries ought to commit themselves to issues such as greater support for the rule of law, qualitative capacity- and institution-building, main-streaming and the empowerment of civil society, as well as discouraging state (and institutional) impunity. The expectation is also that the West, in particular, should be in a position to hold to account those who undermine governance, support freedom of the press, and assist in the retraining and repositioning of the security services to make them answerable, ultimately, to civil authority. In the final analysis, the dire prospects facing the region can be stymied only by taming the myriad drivers of militarization within the state, and civil society. How quickly the festering issues at the heart of the Niger Delta crisis are attended to and resolved satisfactorily will shape the future of Nigeria, for good or bad.

7 | Nigeria's oil diplomacy and the management of the Niger Delta crisis

Kayode Soremekun

Introduction

Oil has been the central issue in the evolving discourse on the crises in the Niger Delta and the various perspectives to their possible resolution. This discourse – given oil's centrality to Nigeria's political economy and its strategic importance to the energy security and the hegemony of the world's established and emerging powers – implies that the Niger Delta is defined both as a source of a precious commodity defining Nigeria's power (or its lack of it) and its place in 'international relations'. These two factors have some relevance to the interrelated issues of Nigeria's oil diplomacy and the management of the Niger Delta crisis.

Nigeria's oil diplomacy lies at the interface between the domestic and the external environments. Since oil became the dominant national revenue-earner in the wake of the quadrupling of global oil prices in the 1970s, it has remained a crucial element in defining national power and the robust regional and pan-Africanist thrust in the country's foreign policy. Looking back to the 'golden age' of Nigeria's diplomacy in the 1970s, when Nigeria played a leading role in West African integration, and in providing material and moral support to the liberation movements in southern Africa, it could be noted that the country's foreign policy received a boost from 'oil power' (Mustapha 2008: 369). This aspect of oil diplomacy was played out between Nigeria and Britain, when the former decided to nationalize the assets of British Petroleum (BP) in the context of Nigeria's support for the liberation struggle in southern Africa. In this respect, what Nigeria did was to use oil as a basis to redefine the relationship between itself and this extra-Africa power. In a similar vein, Bassey Ate argued that, owing largely to oil revenues, Nigeria challenged the United States as regards African issues (Ate 1987). Such African affairs can be located in various contexts, such as Gowon's unyielding resistance to the Nixon administration, General Murtala Mohammed's historic challenge to President Ford over Angola, and General Obasanjo's progressive partnership with Jimmy Carter as regards the liquidation of Ian Smith's settler-colonial regime in Zimbabwe (Soremekun 1984).

However, the decline in global oil prices in the context of the global economic recession of the 1980s, which was refracted into Nigeria as a full-blown economic crisis, also had adverse (constraining) consequences on the country's 'activist' foreign policy, thus confirming that Nigeria's internal and external fortunes are tied to oil. On the domestic front, shrinking oil revenues and the adoption of a socially harsh Structural Adjustment Programme (SAP) based on market reforms (Soremekun and Obi 1993) deepened oil politics, as more people were excluded from the distribution of public goods. This also led to intensified struggles for control of access to shrinking oil revenues. The collapse of the economy worsened the situation in the Niger Delta, and contributed to the emergence of identity movements seeking restitution for decades of oil exploitation, impoverishment and environmental degradation by the oil industry, paving the way for the internationalization of the conflict in the 1990s, and its current insurgent phase.

However, given the evolving post-Cold War global context marked by increased demand and a new scramble for Africa's oil (Obi 2009b), Nigeria as the continent's largest producer is at the cusp of a resurgent oil-fuelled foreign policy consistent with its regional and continental leadership aspirations. But the insurgency in its oil region, which has led to disruptions in supply and cuts in revenue and growing concerns on the part of international oil companies (IOCs) and oil-import-dependent powers, poses great challenges to the country's foreign policy.

This chapter critically explores the nature of oil as a paradox in Nigeria's diplomacy. Oil, which happened to be the basis of Nigeria's visible standing in global diplomacy, particularly in the seventies, was to subsequently become the nemesis of the Nigerian state. Indeed, it is because of this paradox that Nigeria has been described in an oxymoronic way as 'a failed successful state' (Oliveira 2007). The chapter examines the relationship between three actors: the Nigerian state, other countries (Western and developing) in the international system, and the multinational oil companies, and how such relations have enhanced or constrained Nigeria's foreign policy.

Second, it explores a new dimension in Nigeria's foreign policy based on the fact that non-state forces – local and transnational, below and above the state, particularly in the Niger Delta – are now involved in the crisis-ridden relationship between the Nigerian state and the international system (Soremekun and Obi 1993; Okonta 2008a, 2005; Obi 2009c). The site of this complex struggle is the Niger Delta. And the crisis spawned by this intermingling of, and contestations between forces is what has added a complex dimension to what is often referred to as the Niger Delta crisis. While the Delta is a site connecting the local to the global, the ramifications of the conflict and crises are not limited to it, but rather span transnationalized territorial space(s).

What is glibly referred to as the Niger Delta crisis is in fact a series of crises. Perhaps the most obvious of these crises has to do with environmental degradation and the virtual absence of the state in a positive and wholesome way in the local communities. What is perhaps less well known and appreciated is that this and other aspects of the Niger Delta crisis are due to the rather interesting but dismal relationship with the oil companies on one hand and the Nigerian state on the other. It is this seemingly productive but uneven relationship which lies at the centre of the other dimensions of the crises in the Niger Delta.

Oil multinationals and the Nigerian state: more than a partnership of convenience?

The relationship between the Nigerian state and oil multinationals (MNCs) has passed through various phases. These phases include: the concession era and various forms of participation such as the joint venture agreements (JVAs), production-sharing agreements (PSAs) and the risk service contracts (RSCs) (Soremekun and Obi 1993). Despite the changing phases of the relationship between the (oil-dependent) Nigerian state and the multinationals, the persisting outcomes have been the hegemony of the oil companies and their parent governments. And the hegemony is such that the Nigerian state is locked in a relationship of dependence on the oil companies. Over 80 per cent of Nigerian oil production is accounted for by oil MNCs, operating in partnership with the state. But this is only one side of the picture. A comprehensive insight reveals that despite this dependence, the state has still been able to accumulate vast and providential oil revenues (ibid. 1993).

The vast, unearned wealth accruing to both the state and the oil MNCs constitutes an important element in defining the mutual interests that bind them and their role in the Niger Delta crises. The oil MNCs direct the production of the oil that 'fuels' the state and the ruling elite, and the state protects oil MNCs when their predatory activities are resisted by the people of the Niger Delta. For in the context of the political economy of oil, the oil MNCs are wedded to the Nigerian state, and anyone who resists the exploitative activities of oil MNCs necessarily invites the wrath of a state keen to protect its valued partner and an immense source of petro-dollars. Even when the ability of the state to protect its partner becomes a concern to the international community, in the wake of the escalating insurgency and insecurity characterized by acts of sabotage and kidnapping of foreign oil workers, corruption and oil theft by criminal gangs working with highly placed officials linked to transnational criminal networks, the tendency has been for the international community to seek to strengthen the capacity of the state to better protect its partners – the oil MNCs (see Ukeje, this volume).

The partnership between the Nigerian state and IOCs is embedded in the early internationalization of the oil industry in the context of Nigerian colonial history. As noted elsewhere (Soremekun and Obi 1993), the oil industry had its origins in a policy of the British colonial state which granted exclusive oil exploratory rights in Nigeria to 'British or British-allied capital'. It was in accordance with the legislation that the Nigerian Bitumen Company (German) and the British Colonial Petroleum Company started to search for oil in 1908, but without commercial success. Later Shell D'Arcy (Dutch and British) was granted an oil concession spanning the entire Nigeria mainland in 1938.

It was Shell-BP which identified the most promising areas, and first struck oil in commercial quantities in Oloibiri in 1956, commencing exports in 1958. Shell's success attracted other oil MNCs and defined the early character of the Nigerian oil industry in which IOCs were clearly dominant. Thus, from its onset, the logic of the Nigerian oil industry was driven by external extractive interests. With the advantage of its head start in the industry, Shell has remained Nigeria's largest oil producer from 1956 to the present day, currently accounting for almost half of Nigeria's daily oil production. Nigeria's oil industry has essentially remained an 'enclave industry' for the local production of oil for the external/ global market in spite of several policies to diversify the industry and encourage real local participation. In this way the early foundation has largely continued to define the character of the industry, and the intervention of oil in Nigerian economics and politics. It also influenced the early oil diplomacy in terms of the efforts of the state to create favourable conditions for investments by IOCs.

Indigenous participation in the oil industry was minimal until the 1970s, when Nigerian oil bureaucrats, driven by nationalist and class interests and riding on the crest of the 'OPEC revolution', pushed for the indigenization or Nigerianization of the oil industry. This took the form of vesting the ownership and control of oil in the federal military government and the holding of majority government equity stakes (usually 60 per cent) in JVAs signed with oil MNCs. It also involved the appointment of Nigerians to top management positions on the boards of IOCs operating in Nigeria as a strategy for ostensibly representing and protecting Nigerian interests in the decision-making levels of the companies. This also reflected the fact that, given its oil clout riding on 'OPEC power' in the 1970s, Nigeria was in a position to make IOCs cede space to Nigerian participation in an oil industry from which it had hitherto been marginalized.

It was believed that, through Nigerianization, the formal control of oil would pass from oil MNCs to the Nigerian state and its national elite, but in reality it merely cemented the partnership between oil MNCs and the state, based on the inclusion of the Nigerian ruling elite, not at the level of production, but rather in the distribution of the profits from oil production and exports. It also integrated Nigerian appointees to the management and boards of IOCs into the transnational petro-elite, whose interests transcended, but drew legitimacy from, the 'national'. In this way, oil became an important element in elite formation and reproduction in post-civil-war Nigeria, as well as a modality for integrating the Nigerian oil elite into the transnational or global 'scheme of things'.

This meant that oil became indispensable to the elite project of controlling an oil-rich state that was dependent on the oil MNCs that produced the oil. This, in turn, fed into state power, the fortunes of the ruling elite, and the country's foreign policy. It also meant, rather unfortunately, that the loyalty of the trans-nationally integrated Nigerian oil elite was not necessarily to the Nigerian people. Oil diplomacy in this regard had domestic and external linkages. It had to do with how the state and ruling class managed its relations with oil MNCs and their home governments in the context of the extractive, degrading and disruptive impacts of their operations in the oil-rich but impoverished Niger Delta. It also had to do with the ways in which an oil-fuelled foreign policy enabled the state to pursue its regional and pan-African leadership aspirations on a global stage. Beyond this, it also shaped the response of the state elite to changes at the international level. Of particular note was the state's initially incoherent response to the 'globalized' resistance to the predatory and repressive activities of the state–IOC alliance in the Niger Delta, where ethnic minority civic activism framed in the global discourse of rights, democracy and good governance had gained ascendancy in the 1990s.

Thus, the relationship between state and oil goes beyond a mere partnership to one of enmeshment and complex intimate connections. It is this which explains the revolving-door relationship between oil MNCs and the state oil bureaucracy (Obi 2007). Okonta (2008b: 122) gives examples of several Nigerians who have moved between state and oil company positions. These include Philip Asiodu, a top oil bureaucrat in the 1970s who subsequently became a director of Chevron, before returning as a chief economic adviser to President Obasanjo in 1999; Godwin Omene, who moved from the position of deputy CEO of the Shell Petroleum Development Company (SPDC) to that of the managing director of the Niger Delta Development Commission (NDDC) in 2000; and Edmund Daukoru, who moved from the position of Executive Director for Exploration and Deep Water of SPDC to become the oil adviser and then minister under President Obasanjo. President Obasanjo also appointed another top SPDC official, Tony Chukwueke, director and CEO of the Department of Petroleum Resources (DPR), the oil industry's regulatory body. In 2010, the former Head of External Relations and the first female executive director of SPDC, Diezani Allison-Madueke, was appointed Nigeria's oil minister in continuation of a revolving-door tradition between the Nigerian state, its ruling elites and the oil MNCs.

Oil MNCs and their home governments

Oil companies do not act alone (Turner 1978). Several writers on the subject emphasize the implicit and explicit alliance of interests between oil MNCs and their home governments. In other words, entities like ExxonMobil, British Petroleum, Shell, Chevron-Texaco and Total can be fully appreciated only in a context that respectively takes on board countries like the United States of America, Britain and France. A detailed and empirical version of what has been sketched above can be observed as early as the sixties in the heat of the Nigerian civil war. At that point in time, there was an altercation between Nigeria, Shell-BP and the then breakaway Biafra (ibid.). In the end Nigeria forcefully asserted its claim to the oilfields of the Niger Delta. It was also in recognition of this linkage of oil to foreign policy that Nigeria nationalized the assets of BP in the country as a way of pressuring the UK not to lift sanctions against the racist minority regime in what was then Rhodesia in the context of Nigeria's support for the liberation of the country.

It is not difficult to fathom the strong influence oil MNCs wield over their home governments. As noted by Obi (2007: 97), they are 'guarantors of steady supplies of cheap energy, employment for their citizens, profits for shareholders and revenue for their home governments'. Apart from this, they 'contribute funds to major political parties in Europe and the United States'; while some top-level government officials have their roots in the oil industry. However, in the context of oil diplomacy, the highest stakes revolve around the importance of IOCs 'to the energy security and global influence of established and emerging powers'. In this connection, these powers provide support to those IOCs operating in oil-exporting countries, most of which are located in the global South.

It is, however, apposite to note that oil MNCs are also global players in their own right. This is due to the central role they play in globally integrated oil operations, which are crucial to capitalist globalization. Given the global scope of their operations and their massive turnovers, which sometimes make them 'richer than some of the petro states with which they do business' (ibid.: 97), oil MNCs, given their enormous clout, dwarf and pose a major challenge to petro-states, some of which are subordinated to transnational and elite interests defined by oil capital.

What this implies is that oil MNCs, backed by their home states, have considerable leverage over petro-states, which in some cases offer an ambiguous response, depending on their dominant and exigent interests. While on the one hand they seek 'national' space for indigenous or state capital to compete against the global oil giants, they also value their partnership and the support of their home governments in ensuring the steady supply of petro-dollars and international support for the ruling petro-elites. As gatekeepers of a highly strategic commodity, oil, petro-elites in oil-rich countries tend to navigate between complicity with oil MNCs and using oil as an instrument of foreign policy, part of which is, of necessity, oil-dependent. It is the oil-dependent nature of Nigeria's foreign policy since the 1970s which defines both its direct link to the Niger Delta and the ways in which the crises in the region impact on Nigeria's oil diplomacy.

Government strategies for managing the Niger Delta crisis

The Nigerian government has adopted a mix of methods, which range from coercion through co-option to the establishment of various commissions in managing the Niger Delta crises (Ahonsi, this volume). Since the 1990s, when protests became pronounced in Ogoniland and other troubled areas of the Niger Delta, thousands of regular and mobile policemen, complemented by battalions of soldiers and plainclothes security agents, have been deployed to the region (see the chapter by Ukeje, this volume).

There was also, however, a less militaristic attempt at solving the problem against the background of the increased protests in the early 1990s. This can be observed in the creation of agencies like the Oil Mineral Producing Areas Development Commission (OMPADEC), the Petroleum (Special) Trust Fund (PTF) and the Niger Delta Development Commission (NDDC). OMPADEC was established in 1992, by the Babangida administration. The Commission was charged, among other things, with the responsibility of:

- rehabilitating and developing the oil-producing areas;
- tackling ecological problems that have arisen from the exploration of oil minerals;
- liaising with the various oil companies on matters of pollution control.

However, by 1999, it was dissolved. According to reports, by the time its pioneering chairman was removed from office, billions of naira had been sunk into either white-elephant or non-existent projects. For his own part, General Sani Abacha established the PTF, headed by Major-General Muhammadu Buhari (a former oil minister and military head of state). The PTF, as it turned out, largely confined its activities to the northern part of the country. This in itself was ironic, since the Niger Delta, where the oil came from, was in more need of development. Thus, by 1998, the Niger Delta had become a volatile zone, characterized by protests, agitation and communal conflicts – a reaction against perceived neglect and insensitivity by government. At the same time the social movements of the ethnic minorities put more pressure on the IOCs operating in the region.

Following the failure of the earlier interventionist bodies, President Obasanjo's government established the NDDC in 2000. The main objective of the Commission is to formulate and implement programmes for the development of the region in the areas of transportation, health, education, industrialization, agriculture, housing, telecommunications, etc. The funding of the NDDC derives from various sources, such as: the federal government; oil and gas companies; the Ecological Fund; and proceeds from other NDDC assets. In collaboration with the various stakeholders, such as the oil companies, development agencies and civil society, the NDDC facilitated the production of the Niger Delta Regional Development Master Plan. A Partner for Sustainable Development (PSD) forum was also established to implement the Master Plan.

It remains to be seen, however, whether the NDDC will be able to deliver, and thus hopefully end this particular nightmare of the Nigerian state. The NDDC is bedevilled by problems of poor funding, and accusations of corruption. In September 2008, the Niger Delta Ministry was created by the Yar'Adua administration to address the youth and environmental problems in the context of a state response to the Niger Delta crisis. The creation of the ministry with two ministers (both from the Niger Delta) is the most recent institutional response to the Niger Delta crisis.

Another way in which attempts have been made to manage the Niger Delta problem is through the policy of co-optation. Co-optation involves a situation in which individuals as strategic social forces from within the Niger Delta elite are given top positions in the political life of the country, or offered 'juicy' contracts by the state or IOCs. It is arguable that co-optation appears to have reached its zenith with the selection of Dr Goodluck Jonathan as the vice-president (and later president) of Nigeria, ensuring a situation in which, probably for the first time in the history of Nigeria, there is ensconced in the presidency or Aso Rock (the official residence of the Nigerian president in Abuja, the Nigerian capital) an important politician and a number of aides who come from the Niger Delta.

This co-optation seems to be paying off in that the vice-president visited the various militants in their camps at Okerenkoko, Oporoza and other communities in the Niger Delta after being sworn into office in 2007. Moreover, he chaired the federal government committee that entered into negotiations with the leaders of militant groups in the region. As a result, the vice-president played an important part in the establishment of the Technical Committee on the Niger Delta in 2008, and the granting of a presidential amnesty to Niger Delta militants in 2009. Some of his efforts have been integral to the amnesty, the buying off of some militia 'generals' and a reduction in the level of violence in the region since the third quarter of 2009, even if the roots of the conflict remain unaddressed in any fundamental manner.

We will now turn, if only briefly, to how the Nigerian state, through legislation and policy organs, has attempted to contain the environmental hazards spawned by the oil industry.

Regulatory agencies like the Department of Petroleum Resources (DPR) and the Petroleum Inspectorate Commission (PIC) lack both the autonomy and the resources needed to regulate the very sophisticated operations in the oil industry. As far as the Nigerian state and other sub-national forces are concerned, money – or, better still, cash – has been the main preoccupation of the jostling and politics around oil. And this may well explain why the Nigerian state, in managing the crisis of the Niger Delta, has also attempted to use the policy of increased funding and the creation of several institutions with overlapping functions partly as a strategy for distributing patronage among the colluding Niger Delta elite and their various allies in the communities and creeks – including the militia 'generals'.

Two different observations seem to validate the view that the funding which has gone into the Niger Delta has merely been frittered away by the various status quo forces in the region (see Ukiwo, Ako, Ibaba, this volume). The first was a study conducted by the Port Harcourt-based Centre for Advanced Social Science (CASS). In this illuminating study, it was revealed that the increased funding to the Niger Delta has been characterized by features like plunder, financial recklessness and a monumental misplacement of priorities. Other sources have reached similar conclusions regarding the ways in which the Niger Delta state governors and political class have wasted enhanced revenues resulting from the increase in the oil derivation allocation principle in 2000.

The international dimension to government's management of the Niger Delta crisis

Although the Niger Delta crisis pre-dated the age of oil and was embedded in ethnic minority agitation for self-determination (see Ukeje, this volume), oil added a volatile dimension to it. An early sign of things to come was Isaac Adaka Boro's 'twelve-day revolution', which was eventually crushed by federal troops. It is instructive to note that Boro had initially made overtures to the international community, seeking support for his cause from the Cuban embassy in a neighbouring country, but was rebuffed.

However, the struggle of the ethnic minorities of the Niger Delta resurged in the early 1990s, when the Movement for the Survival of Ogoni People (MOSOP) successfully linked up with transnational rights advocacy organizations such as Greenpeace, Amnesty International, Friends of the Earth, the Unrepresented Nations and Peoples Organization (UNPO) and a pro-human-rights company, the Body Shop, which supported its international campaign against the government and Shell (Saro-Wiwa 1995).

The MOSOP campaign was largely anchored on Saro-Wiwa's reading of the 'relevance of global discourses and transnational networking as a way of challenging economic injustice, environmental degradation and political marginalization, based on the right to self-determination of ethnic minorities' (Obi 2009c: 474). Saro-Wiwa went on to tap into this discourse by framing the Ogoni 'issue' in the context of environmental problems caused by Shell in a local community in Nigeria (ibid.: 476).

By targeting Shell, the leading oil producer, as being complicit with the state in exploiting Ogoni resources, and violating the human and environmental rights of its people, MOSOP, as a non-state actor working with global NGOs, rights groups and media, became a potent counter-hegemonic actor in 'Nigeria's' external relations. Apart from this, MOSOP's protests and international campaign hurt both Shell and the state, with the latter having to deal with a challenge from within and from outside. Government's initial response was to ignore MOSOP, but when it became clear that its international campaign was effective, the response changed from ambivalent indifference to the military repression of Ogoni protests.

Thus, when nine Ogoni leaders, including the MOSOP president, Ken Saro-Wiwa, were hanged on the orders of a special court and the military ruling council in November 1995, in spite of international appeals for clemency, leading the summit of the Commonwealth heads of state to suspend Nigeria from the body, the country's oil diplomacy was in crisis. A lot of resources went into laundering Nigeria's image and managing the diplomatic furore that followed the crisis.

On the one hand the Nigerian state had come down hard on its own citizens protesting against the exploitative and environmentally destructive practices of an oil MNC with which it was wedded in partnership, but on the other it had suffered condemnation internationally, to which it had to respond, at a price. As Okonta notes (2008b: 123), this situation reduced the ability of Nigeria to 'scarcely look beyond its borders to participate effectively in the game of international power politics amidst this domestic turmoil'.

The foregoing is a scenario that has largely haunted Nigeria's oil diplomacy since the Niger Delta resistance became globalized in the 1990s. The morphing of resistance from non-violent to violent and insurgent proportions contributed to the situation in which Nigeria's oil production dropped by a third between 2006 and 2008.

This was due to disruptions in oil production and exports as a result of acts of sabotage, attacks on oil installations and the kidnapping of oil company expatriate workers for ransom by armed groups and militias seeking to attract international attention to their cause. The resultant shortfalls in state revenues, company profits and oil exports in an already tight global oil market contributed to further insecurity and the internationalization of the Niger Delta conflict. Reduced oil meant that the capacity to pursue an activist foreign policy was somewhat curtailed, but beyond that it also suggested that the strategic importance of the oil supplies from the Niger Delta made the security of the region itself a key object of Nigeria's oil diplomacy (see Ukeje, this volume).

The global securitization of the Niger Delta: emerging challenges for Nigeria's oil diplomacy

The context of the securitization of the Niger Delta lies in the definition of the oil in the region as being vital to the energy security of the United States and the Western powers that are the main importers and consumers of Nigeria's sweet crude. The threats posed to Western interests in the restive Delta have been compounded by the recent entry of Chinese and Indian state oil companies, which are aggressively seeking a toehold in the region to meet growing domestic demand and diversify their sources of supply (Obi 2009a; Klare and Volman 2006).

The new scramble for oil not only underlines the high strategic stakes of US interests in Africa's oil, including that in the Niger Delta, but also shows the interest of other established and emerging powers, particularly the BRIC countries: Brazil, Russia, India and China. However, the reality that the Nigerian oil sector is dominated by Western IOCs has ensured that the USA has been in the lead in securitizing the Niger Delta in the context of the need to remove potential threats to an important source of US energy supplies in a post-9/11 world.

The emergent paradigm has meant that ethnic minorities' militias have been increasingly seen through the lenses of 'criminal' or 'terrorist' threats to be removed by any means, including military force. It is in this context that MEND has been labelled a 'terrorist' organization targeting Western oil interests in the Niger Delta (Pham 2007). In real terms this has meant the militarization of an aspect of Nigeria's oil diplomacy in which the Nigerian government has received help from Western militaries – specialized training, arms supplies and information-sharing (Keenan 2008a; Obi 2008b, 2009b: 20; Watts 2007: 644; Klare 2004). Nigeria, which in the 1970s was at the forefront of pan-Africanist activism against Western powers, is now under pressure from, and receives support from, the same powers to deal with insecurity in the Niger Delta. At the same time, Nigeria has had to cut back on some of its regional peacekeeping activities in the context of reduced 'oil muscle' and the need to direct its focus internally towards ensuring stability within the country.

The activities of non-state actors on both sides, within and outside Nigeria, also mean that the formal diplomatic tools are not adequate in handling these actors, further constricting the scope for Nigeria's oil diplomacy. Of note are the activities of MEND, which attacks oil and security targets and taps into global media to 'propagate its war' against the Nigerian state and IOCs. Also, there is the issue of international NGOs that have kept the spotlight on the violations of rights in the Niger Delta and the reportedly high levels of oil-related corruption in the country. There are other challenges posed by other international and local NGOs that are working in the areas of development and conflict mediation across the Niger Delta, playing state-like roles, but not connecting to state policies and agencies at various levels.

Either way, the ability of the Nigerian state to act internally and project itself externally is subjected to critical interrogation, even as oil-dependent friendly powers provide support. This partly explains the presence of various military partnership programmes between these powers and the Nigerian government, and the presence of the US-African Command (AFRICOM) in the Gulf of Guinea (Keenan 2009; Klare and Volman 2006). Although Nigeria joined other African states in refusing to host AFRICOM on African soil, its oil diplomacy has been weak and remained pragmatic, focusing on common interests, rather than competing ones. What is clear, however, is that Nigeria's capacity to deploy the oil weapon as a tool of diplomacy has remained on the wane, partly as a result of the Niger Delta crisis.

Conclusion

The foregoing speaks to the deadly impasse that is currently the lot of the Niger Delta and Nigeria's oil diplomacy. It is therefore logical to posit that the resolution of the Niger Delta crisis lies at the heart of overcoming one of the most potent challenges facing Nigeria's oil diplomacy. And here, one calls for some deeper reflection on the view expressed in a speech by Nigeria's then vice-president, Goodluck Jonathan, when inaugurating the Technical Committee on the Niger Delta, to the effect that 'the resolution of the crises in the Niger Delta cannot be done outside the Niger Delta and its people'.

It is necessary to point out that the Niger Delta is no longer just about Nigeria, it is about the world, and the domestication and extractive operations of some of the world's most powerful multinationals in the country's oil-rich region. Can the Nigerian state in the face of a globally backed securitization of the oil-rich region find non-violent, democratically inclusive ways of addressing the deep-seated grievances and rights of the people of the region? Will the IOCs, the colluding elites – including those from the Niger Delta, and the various merchants of violence milking the region of its natural wealth – buy into a higher logic hinged upon transformed equitable social relations of oil production as a foundation for reinvigorating Nigeria's oil diplomacy?

Answers have to be sought in the will of the state and its partners, the oil MNCs, to change from their old ways, or the ability of the state to transform itself from its current rentier nature, which underlines its unequal partnership with the oil MNCs, and also leads to a situation in which the windfalls from oil exports have been largely misspent, stolen or exported, without translating into real national development and international clout. Nigeria can learn a lot from successful oil-rich countries like Norway, where a strong developmental and democratic state used its oil wealth to build an effective public bureaucracy and institutions, as well as a viable welfare basis for development, and also insulated the socio-economic system from the rather volatile and corruptive effects of oil revenues (Karl 1997). A key aspect of this is the de facto national control of oil technology and the oil business in the form of a globally competitive national oil industry, as opposed to the Nigerian industry now, which is a globally subordinated one.

For Nigeria's oil diplomacy to connect a project of national development and a robust pan-Africanist foreign policy, the leadership of the country will have to comprehensively address the Niger Delta in the context of the larger Nigerian crisis of state and society. It will also have to take another look at how to balance the interests of its own citizens with the energy security calculations and profit motives of hegemonic global players in the complex politics of oil. If it does not respond to the challenges from below in the Niger Delta in a socially just and environmentally sustainable manner, Nigeria will remain a victim of the paradox in which its oil diplomacy is currently enmeshed, with consequences that may not bode well for the country in the long run.

PART TWO

Conflict actors' dynamics

8 | 'Mend Me': the Movement for the Emancipation of the Niger Delta and the empowerment of violence

Morten Bøås

Introduction

The description by the Willink Commission in 1958 that the Niger Delta is 'poor, backward and neglected' is still an accurate presentation of the conditions in this part of Nigeria. The Niger Delta is, despite the recent amnesty offer by the Nigerian government (see BBC 2009), still a dangerous witches' brew of poverty, marginalization and underemployment, combined with environmental problems, crime, corruption and local communities that see few benefits from oil production. This has fuelled a militant uprising that threatens not only Nigeria's oil production, but also the country's fragile democracy. During the last few years, different insurgent groups have fought against the army, destroyed oil installations, and taken oil workers hostage. There is, however, also little doubt that connections exist between militia groups and local political elites in the Delta (see Eberlein 2006).

The aim of this chapter is therefore to unpack the contradictions of the armed insurgencies in the Niger Delta – their relationships of attachment, as well as opposition and resistance, to the various manifestations of the Nigerian state – and thereby suggest some alternative frames for understanding the conflict and the situation prevailing in the Niger Delta.

Attempts to explain conflicts such as the one in the Niger Delta commonly emphasize the problem of state recession, combined with the emergence of warlords and warlordism (see Thomas et al. 2005; Lezhnev 2005; Green and Ward 2004; Mackinlay 2002; Rashid 2001; Shawcross 2000; Rich 1999; Reno 1998). Much less examined are the behaviour and actions of the non-state armed groups fighting these conflicts, and how these tend to change over time.[1] Why do movements that began as a social – albeit violent – rebellion against an authoritarian and deeply corrupted state end up as a perverted mirror-image of the state they originally set out to destroy? Greed and increased access to resources provide one explanation for the mutability of armed groups' behaviour over time (Keen 2000) and a greed-based approach may capture groups' increased reliance on resource extraction and marketing over the lifetime of the conflict. However, the profit motive does not itself explain why or to what extent groups turn away from their original political agendas – and why many end up replicating certain pathologies of the states they contest.

Thus, in this chapter, it is suggested that the process by which rebel groups forsake political agendas to become profit-seeking, market-based entities may best be understood using a dual analysis. The first aspect of this analysis is to contextualize the insurgency with regard to the pre-conflict levels of structural and actual violence in society. The analysis in this chapter is therefore in line with Richards's (2005: 1) contention that the violent character of these movements needs 'to be understood in relation to patterns of violence already embedded in society'.

The second aspect builds outwards from the first. It centres on the question: did the state structures – specifically, the particular logic of dysfunctional neopatrimonialism – place insurgencies in the affected countries on a path-dependent track to a violent profit-seeking warlordism? More specifically, the question this chapter seeks to explore is to what extent militia structures in the Niger Delta are grounded in meta-narratives that reflect and expound collective experiences of corruption, abuse of power and position, and poverty (see Bøås 2004).

Thus, the chapter will discuss how situations of marginalization and exclusion, in a neopatrimonial society such as the Niger Delta with the possibility of natural resource extraction, seem to lead to a rebellion characterized by the same features as the society against which the original grievances were targeted. The argument is not that this is bound to happen, but rather that a certain path dependency exists, and that the strength of this dynamic depends on local, national and international responses to the conflict.

Thus, the extent to which an armed movement with an agenda of social and political change can sustain, and act consistently with, that vision arguably depends to some degree on how the group is treated by the system and society it is rebelling against. Currently, dispatches from the Niger Delta tend to downplay the very real social causes that the armed groups put forth, and focus on the piracy tactics they employ. This is worryingly evident in the Nigerian state's approach, which officially treats the armed youth as bandits that can legitimately be crushed using the full force of the state. Their only alternative is to hand in their arms and accept the government's offer of amnesty.

Neopatrimonialism as social practice

Neopatrimonialism is usually seen as a system of rule in which bureaucratic and patrimonial norms coexist (Médard 1991, 1996; Braathen et al. 2000). If such a system of rule exists on a nationwide scale, the outcome is a state able to extract and redistribute resources. However, this extraction and redistribution is privatized. This circumstance is not unique to the Niger Delta and Nigeria, or even to sub-Saharan Africa: neopatrimonial aspects can be found in political systems worldwide. Yet there are important distinctions between systems, both in the degree to which the neopatrimonial logic has penetrated the political system in question, and in its functionality.

In essence, neopatrimonialism is a system of rule like any other: it lays the foundation for the political game of distribution and redistribution and, as illustrated by the longevity of many African regimes, can provide both stability and order. Yet neopatrimonial systems are also prone to extreme vulnerability. For example, Mobutu's regime in Zaire shows how rapidly state fragmentation occurs once the system can no longer reproduce itself. Dysfunctional neo-patrimonialism follows the same logic as before, but without the same ability to deliver.

Even when functioning, however, a primary consequence of this kind of rule is that the various patrimonial paths of redistribution divide the population along regional, ethnic and, at times, even family lines. This has obvious impli-cations for the regime, state institutions and competing elites, but is equally important for the population as a whole. Thus, for the purpose of this chapter, the questions that arise are: what are the conditions for resistance within and against such a system?; to what degree is it possible to design an alternative political organization when such logic is embedded, not just in the state and its macro-institutions, but also in people's daily life – when it has become the *order of things*, the main principle of socio-economic interactions at all levels of society? It is the social system which all are implicated in and part of, willingly or not; it forms the fabric of daily life and practices even for those far removed from the spoils.

Thus, instead of seeing neopatrimonialism only as a variant of Weber's (1947) typology of rule, it is perhaps more fruitful to interpret it as an iterated social practice that creates an informal institutional structure, which is not easily broken or bent. The argument is not that resistance is useless and change impossible. Yet in examining why projects for change morph into distorted agents of the status quo, one explanation is that pervasive and increasingly dysfunctional neopatrimonial systems have created a machine-like character of African politics. This machine-like character may re-create itself in various armed insurgencies, particularly those that are long-lasting and occurring in an environment where resource extraction is possible, and victory (in any mean-ingful sense of the word) more and more unlikely. The consequence is that resistance in the broad sense is possible only within and between the nexus of crime and politics: turning militia structures into some sort of social banditry (see Crummey 1986); operating along the lines of Corsica's venerable *bandits honorables* – men forced into a life beyond the law, stealing from the state ('bleeding Satan'), but also at the same time preying on the very population they come from – thus taking us back to the ambiguous relationships between armed insurgencies and local host communities introduced above.

Social banditry and neopatrimonial structures

If we accept that there is a relationship between pre-war state structures and the character of the armed insurgency, we must then ask: what kind of social norms are internalized, and what kind of mindsets and cosmologies developed, under such circumstances as those described above?

The case of the Niger Delta rebellion vividly illustrates this point: all social relations between groups and interests in the Delta region revolve around oil and oil revenue. Nonetheless, despite mismanagement of oil resources, corruption, poverty and marginalization, some sort of order still prevails in the Delta (International Crisis Group 2006a, b, c). This order enables oil production, but at a cost. Oil companies conduct their business in an uneasy cohabitation (or cooperation) with a range of actors, including rebel movements like the Movement for the Emancipation of the Niger Delta (MEND); other armed factions; bandits; local politicians; private security companies; the Nigerian army; and national politicians (Yates 2006; International Crisis Group 2006a, b, c). Yet local communities that receive few benefits from oil production – and struggle under the weight of poverty, underemployment, environmental problems, crime and corruption – have fuelled a militant uprising that threatens both Nigeria's oil production and the country's fragile democratic transition (see Omeje 2006a; Kaldor and Said 2007).

Prior to the global economic meltdown in 2009, this was easily observed in world market prices. As a consequence of attacks on oil pipelines in Isaka and Abonema in Rivers state in April 2008, oil prices exceeded $117 a barrel for the first time (see Reuters 2008).[2] Nigeria is Africa's largest oil exporter and the eighth-largest oil-producing country in the world, but since early 2006 rebel activity in the Niger Delta has reduced the output by as much as 25 per cent.[3] Barely hours after the aforementioned April 2008 attacks, the main insurgency group, MEND, put out a statement claiming that since they had been pushed into the background after the Nigerian elections in 2003,[4] they had nothing to lose or protect and would fight to destroy all oil facilities until their demands were met.

According to MEND, the new series of attacks (which they named Operation Cyclone) was the insurgency's answer to the illegal government of President Umaru Yar'Adua, dispelling the impression that the government had tried to create – that peace and security had been restored in the Delta – and to protest against the detention and secret trial of Henry Okah (the alleged MEND leader arrested in Angola).[5] Moreover, as a comment on the increased military cooperation between Abuja and Washington, MEND said that this was their way of welcoming the USS *Swift* to the Gulf of Guinea. Clearly aware of the increased attention paid by both US policy-makers and American oil companies to Nigerian and West African oil, MEND expressed its readiness to fight US forces if they tried to intervene, while simultaneously asking for peace talks to be led by former president Jimmy Carter.[6]

The nature of the insurgency

There is clearly a tendency, both in international media as well as on the part of oil companies, to downplay the socio-economic causes behind MEND's actions and focus instead on the piracy tactics that the insurgency employs, and the terrorist card, which, if not played yet, could be played imminently. This is, however, not a conflict that can be solved by military means alone, and foreign involvement under the banner of the 'war on terror' could have disastrous effects (see also Bøås 2009).

After a wave of hostage-taking in August 2006, President Olusegun Obasanjo threatened to crush the so-called 'criminal elements' in the Niger Delta. However, the most tangible result was the razing of hundreds of slum houses in Port Harcourt, close to where a soldier had been killed during the kidnapping of foreign oil workers (BBC 2006a). These heavy-handed tactics have been tried in the past: they did not produce the desired outcome then, nor is there reason to expect they will be effective now (Lindsay 2006). The growth of militias, whether defined as armed factions with a political agenda, bandits or something in between (for example, social bandits), is a consequence of local grievances that must be addressed.

Two aspects of the situation in the Niger Delta are particularly noteworthy. First, there is little doubt that connections exist between militia groups and local political elites in the Delta. The second notable aspect of the Niger Delta rebellion is the degree to which the young armed men wear different hats (BBC 2006b).

Militia groups and political elites The link between militia groups and political elites was amply illustrated in the conduct of the 2003 and 2007 elections. The 'convergence of militancy and politics' (International Crisis Group 2006c: 21) is not foreign to Nigerian elections in general, but in the Delta this has reached extreme proportions. Here, previous elections have featured the harassment of candidates and their supporters by armed groups, mainly consisting of young men, in the service of another candidate; and clashes between armed groups controlled by different political opponents. This type of political behaviour started to emerge after the death of Sani Abacha, and in the Delta it exploded around the time of the 2003 election.

The starting point was Rivers state, and its capital Port Harcourt, which is also the hub of the oil industry, making this state in theory the wealthiest in Nigeria.[7] Here state governor Peter Odili spearheaded a strategy of violent vote-rigging in favour of the People's Democratic Party (PDP) with the help of Asari Dokubo's Niger Delta People's Volunteer Force (NDPVF) and Ateke Tom's Niger Delta Vigilante (NDV).[8] Election violence therefore became widespread in Rivers, but was also successful for those that had initiated it as this strategy saw Odili receive 98 per cent of the popular vote in 2003.

However, as soon as the elections were won, Odili – along with other 'patrons of violence' – tried to distance himself from the most prominent gunmen that he had hired for his campaign. Some militiamen and their leaders accepted this 'remarginalization' as a fact of life in the Delta, but others reacted with anger, threatening violence and rebellion against their former masters. These included Asari Dokubo and the majority of his NDPVF fighters. The result was that Asari and the NDPVF were suddenly out of favour, and as they threatened to resume the violence of the election campaign, their former political sponsors responded by attempting a strategy of 'divide and rule' by encouraging Ateke Tom's group, which had remained loyal, to subdue Asari's men by force.

This had two immediate consequences. First, it started a 'small civil war' in and around Port Harcourt as rolling battles – in the streets as well as in the creeks and the local communities – killed not only militia members but also local civilians, and created large-scale displacement. The second consequence was a general proliferation of guns, gangs and violence in the period between 2003 and 2007 as the original insurgents fragmented into new groups.

In this period, various gangs and militias therefore acquired wealth through a series of violent activities, such as illegal 'oil bunkering', bank robberies and kidnappings, turning some of their leaders into figures of real authority in the Delta. Some of these groups were new, others old, but both old and new alike were related to the Nigerian 'cult' phenomenon.[9]

This is a phenomenon worth considering in some detail as its very existence reveals the embedded history of co-optation between elites and marginalized youths. The term 'cult' refers in the Nigerian context not to specific religious practices, but to the criminal gangs that originally appeared as fraternity organizations among students at university campuses. However, since the establishment of the first 'cult' at the University of Ibadan in 1952, such groups have not only multiplied, but also morphed into violent and highly sophisticated criminal organizations, sowing terror on university campuses and beyond, particularly in the southern part of the country. Membership of the cults is open only to students on the campuses where the groups operate, but most cults have formed 'street wings' by recruiting off-campus members. As most leading politicians are university graduates it also means that many of them belonged (or even still belong) to cults, suggesting that the relationships they cultivate with militias today is not a novelty for them, but in fact a continuation of an intimate relationship between politics and violence that they internalized in the formative campus years of their life.[10]

Conversely, many prominent militia leaders therefore started their careers as the off-campus hired thugs of these soon-to-be political and economic leaders. Some later rebelled – or at least partially, as experiences of betrayal led to the development of political grievances – whereas others by and large returned to the service of their original masters when called for (during elections and at other times when their services were in demand). When not operating under 'command', the latter groups were 'allowed' to cater for their own needs as they saw fit with the tools at their disposal (guns and the readiness to use them) as long as their actions did not interfere too much with the business of the elite.

The very same period and the events within it therefore also indirectly constitute the birth of MEND as the betrayal that many militia members and leaders felt, which events after the 2003 election exposed them to, led some – obviously not all – to develop political grievances against their former political sponsors, whom they saw as having refused to fulfil promises of money, employment and education. Local communities and civilians also felt betrayed, but they could be ignored, whereas this was not as easy with the effective 'insurgency machines' that the politicians had created in order to win the 2003 elections. Having first acquired the tools of violence such groups are not too easily subdued into a position of obedient patronage, as violence can not only kill, it may also empower. Groups like the NDPVF and men like Asari therefore have a past as violent supporters of the regime that they would later claim to be rebelling against, but that does not in itself make the grievances they articulate any less real.

This may sound strange, but there is nothing particularly unusual about this (another example is Côte d'Ivoire's Jeunes Patriotes), and the alliances and what happened later can be seen as first a marriage of convenience and later as a result of the failure of the elite to control the 'monster' they had created – owing either to unwillingness or inability to provide sufficient spoils or because the young men they initially hired and organized as a militia later developed agendas and interests of their own.

One obvious example in this regard is again Asari, who started off as a gang leader, but ended up charged with treason on the basis of the allegation that he declared that the Delta should secede from the rest of Nigeria. In this regard there is also another line of continuity from Asari's NDPVF to MEND, which first emerged in 2005. The latter is just as much an idea as it is an amalgam of several groups operating across the Delta. It is much less a cohesive force than a brand for large groups of insurgents, militias and gangs (see Eberlein 2009), and owing to its networked and fragmented nature also very hard to crush with one decisive military blow.

Given that many militiamen undoubtedly had grievances owing to the betrayal they felt exposed to after the 2003 elections, the pattern of 2003 repeated itself in the 2007 elections. The 2007 polls were universally condemned by foreign and domestic monitors as completely lacking credibility. More than three hundred died in election-related violence, and election day itself saw gangs of thugs hired by the ruling PDP stealing ballot boxes, chasing off voters and fabricating results – official results even indicated massive turnout figures in areas where no voting took place at all. Nowhere was this more evident that in the Niger

Delta states. The history of 2003 repeated itself not only in the 2007 elections, but also in the violence that followed.

In 2005, a large group of the 'Icelanders' led by Soboma George broke away from Ateke Tom's leadership, forming their own militia, the 'Outlaws'. Swiftly, the Outlaws under George's leadership managed to establish themselves as the preferred 'thugs' of high-ranking government and PDP officials, doing such a large amount of the dirty work needed during the 2007 elections that they seemed almost to have acquired a monopoly on government patronage and state-sponsored violence. Among other things, it was reported that George had been given control of a busy filling station owned by the Nigerian National Petroleum Corporation (NNPC), whose daily revenue therefore went directly into George's and the Outlaws' pockets.[11]

The consequence was the formation of an alliance between other gangs and militias which saw their income drop as George and the Outlaws monopolized the networks of state patronage. Thus, under the leadership of Ateke Tom, a diverse range of cults and gangs – including Axemen, Klansmen, Deebam and the Bush Boys – started to attack both the Outlaws' members and areas perceived to be under the control of that group. The consequence was both deliberate and random violence in the form of 'turf wars' that created havoc, death and destruction in Port Harcourt, as well as neighbouring communities. Several dozen civilians were killed and at least 150 more shot and wounded, and this situation was allowed to continue for over a month before the Joint Task Force (JTF) intervened on 12 August 2007.[12] The JFT operation restored a nominal form of order in and around Port Harcourt, but apart from killing some militiamen and also some civilians caught in the crossfire, the only thing this operation accomplished was to increase the bitter grievances of young men with militia connections who once more realized that after the dirty business of elections was completed the political and economic elite had little if any concern for them. The result was therefore not less sabotage, but renewed attacks on oil installations and the infrastructure in the Delta under the banner of MEND.

The many faces of MEND The violence of the Niger Delta is therefore not only some sort of crude resource war between different political and illicit elites; between the 'cults' and the 'boys in the creeks'. The very same young men involved in this 'war' also use the banner of MEND to attack oil installations and take oil workers as hostages in order to put forward political demands for increased regional autonomy (such as 'true federalism') and control of oil revenues ('resource control').[13]

In addition, the same people also sometimes deploy as the armed wing in sup-port of the grievances of local communities – taking hostages for local commun-ities, as a means of addressing – or at least highlighting – local company-specific grievances. This was for instance the case with four sailors taken hostage in

August 2006. The hostages were taken by a group of armed young men, who then handed them over to a local community that had grievances against a Nigerian oil company, Peak Petroleum.[14] Both the original kidnapping and the subsequent hostage situation leading to negotiations, although different in type and nature, could be considered political acts, stemming from legitimate grievances and demands. This is the same group of men who also take hostages purely for ransom, with no political pretence, and who work – as we have seen – as hired thugs for local strongmen and politicians, especially during election campaigns.

Thus roles and activities overlap. They are conducting an armed political insurgency, but also operating as bandits, and in the latter role are actively co-opted by the very elite they are rebelling against. As one role does not seem to exclude the other, the question is what logic will come to dominate the situation in the Niger Delta: the political logic of MEND or the personal economic logic of men like Ateke Tom and Soboma George?

MEND is sophistication – of argument and operation: a rebellion in which the gun is mightier than the pen, but the latter still not completely dysfunctional as MEND also pays a great deal of attention to its verbal communication with the world. Typical in this regard was the language of mockery it used to denounce the Nigerian offer of amnesty in the spring of 2009. In its verbal response MEND wrote:

> We call on political thugs, armed robbers, kidnappers, pirates etc., from other states in Nigeria to take advantage of the government's offer by travelling to one of the centres in Niger Delta and trade their weapons for amnesty. Come with the whole gang and get rehabilitated with gains of free education, money to start legitimate businesses etc. This is a unique opportunity in a country where so many graduates cannot find jobs and girls no longer marry for love.

The statement is not only making fun of the government; the last sentence also vividly captures a perception of marginalization well known to Nigerian youth. The only way to make sense of the rebellion in the Niger Delta is therefore to approach it as a combination of efforts based on tactical as well as strategic agency (see Honwana 2006): the insurgency is thus an attempt to address social injustice (a strategy) as well as a mode of production and a way to make a living (a tactic).

Whether the Niger Delta rebellion will continue to have a social profile or deteriorate solely into criminality remains to be seen. However, the way in which its participants are embedded in patrimonial clientelistic relationships with local strongmen, and the quantity of oil money and multitude of actors in the region, implies that those rebelling walk a very fine line between 'greed' and 'grievances'. If they overstep this boundary, they may turn what is still a legitimate rebellion into a market-based entity operating in a downward-spiralling, dysfunctional patrimonial order.

The amnesty offer made by the Nigerian government in June 2009 and MEND's unilateral ceasefire around the same time may constitute a political dialogue in its very infancy. However, a meaningful dialogue is possible only if the various elements of the insurgency and its connections with the state it is rebelling against are sorted out. The question is not how to bring the insurgency under political control, as it was the very control by the political elite which created the context for the rebellion in the first place, but rather to facilitate the creation of autonomous spaces for dialogue as well as legitimate political resistance against the dysfunctional structures of the neopatrimonialism that informs politics in the Delta. MEND undoubtedly has many faces, but not only are all of them shaped by the political economy of oil in the Delta, some are also more legitimate than others.

Conclusion

Based on the discussion above, it is not inevitable that MEND will take the path of a total collapse into fatalistic violence, random killing and profit-seeking warlordism. MEND has put forward legitimate political claims that should be taken seriously, including their suggestion for negotiations on the distribution of oil revenues, under the supervision of a neutral third party.

If these claims are ignored or denied, there is, however, every likelihood that the patrimonial politics in which the armed youth of MEND are implicated will come to dominate the movement – and it will thus end up as another perverted facsimile of the society it rebelled against. It is immensely difficult to predict what the immediate future will bring for the Niger Delta.

However, it should be clear that international efforts focusing solely on increasing the military capacity of the Nigerian army are counterproductive, suggesting that external stakeholders should place more emphasis on dialogue and the establishment of a 'respectable' face for MEND than on offering military support to the government, as facilitating the transformation of an insurgency such as MEND into a more genuine and legitimate political force and less a vehicle for violent patrimonialism is in the interests of both the population of the Delta and those of stakeholders seeking to secure the long-term sustainability of the area's oil production. If not, there is every reason to believe that the lessons in 'violence as empowerment' that the young insurgents have learned will continue to be passed on to new generations of marginalized young men.

9 | Popular and criminal violence as instruments of struggle in the Niger Delta region

Augustine Ikelegbe

Introduction

This chapter examines the complex forms of popular and criminal violence in the Niger Delta and the factors that drive the appropriation of violence as an instrument of popular struggle, and crime. It also analyses the factors responsible for blurring the boundaries between militancy-as-resistance and criminal violence, and the roles played by the Nigerian state, the military, oil MNCs, the region's elites and youth organizations, and the relations of power spawned by the oil economy in the transition from popular to criminal violence.

Conceptual and analytical notes

Violence is essentially the use of force, intimidation and psychosocial and physical injury in the context of personal or social relations, or in the pursuit of set goals. It can be social, popular, statist or criminal. Social violence is the threat, or actual use, of force deployed in the construction or subversion of 'some relations of power, force and dominance' (Abbink 2000). It is an instrument of social construction or deconstruction of power relations in terms of inequity or equity, hegemony or counter-hegemony, representation or exclusion and incorporation or opposition.

Popular violence is a variant of social violence, deployed in the course of expressing grievances or making demands, and as a form of popular resistance, such as protests against exclusion or inequities. It is usually a response to state violence or oppression, driven by a quest to seek freedom from, or redress for, perceived injustices or domination. State violence is the excessive deployment of coercive power against the citizenry in the form of repression, often justified in the name of maintaining 'law and order', and can even be perpetrated through non-formal institutions such as militias/vigilantes or through sponsorship of attacks by rival communities and groups (Allen 1999: 371). It is not unusual for the state to criminalize popular dissent or popular forms of violence.

There is a problem of perception in the characterization of violence. Abbink (2000) has rightly stated that the meaning, interpretation and communicative messages are situational and context-dependent. Popular violence, for example, may be seen as heroic and justified by some, while state actors would brand it as sheer sabotage, treason and crime. In addition, generational differences and frustrations over conflict outcomes could underpin perceptions of protests and violence as brave and heroic, while the more moderate, accommodationist and dialogic methods are denigrated as weak, laggardly, incorporationist or compromised.

In relation to determining which forms of violence and crime constitute popular violence and which constitute criminal violence, the critical questions are: what are the objectives of the actions?; who has undertaken the actions, what interests do they represent?; and what is their level of control over the instruments of violence? Violence in situations of agitation and social struggles could be a deliberate violation of existing law and order. It could also be an act of rejection of particular laws, policies and power relations perceived as being unjust, alienating and oppressive. Such crime could then be situated in a wider context, underpinned by some form of socio-political consciousness or propelled by socio-political discontent and objectives (Crummey 1986: 3–4). In this way, crime could be an instrument of, or spin-off from, resistance. However, it has to be noted that the resistance–crime nexus is complex, and great care should be taken to nuance this. While some crimes may be committed in the course of violent popular struggles, they are not the same as violence motivated solely by criminal intent and self-interest – and completely unrelated to the broader social struggle.

Admittedly the lines between criminal and popular violence may appear blurred, and each case should be closely studied, and its complex dynamics understood. This is because struggles that start out on the basis of popular violence could over time descend into pure criminality and banditry (Mkandawire 2002: 208; see also Bøås, this volume). Beyond the clarification of our central concepts is the critical question of what underpins the appropriation of popular and criminal violence as instruments of struggle and the descent from popular to criminal violence.

We identify three categories of variables as important to our analysis. The first category comprises structural variables: state weakness, corporate misgovernance and the (fluid) organizational character of resistance movements. The second comprises social variables: marginalized groups, women and youths, and the elite. The third category comprises socio-economic variables: inequitable resource distribution, poverty and arms proliferation.

A motley crowd of unemployed, frustrated and desperate youths, with poor social incentives and blocked aspirations, undergirds much of the popular and criminal violence associated with uprisings, protests and rebel movements in Africa (Abdullah and Muana 1998). In the Niger Delta and elsewhere in Nigeria, militias and armed groups are largely made up of school dropouts and unemployed youth, as well as a sprinkling of the underclass and artisans (Human Rights Watch 2005a; Ikelegbe 2006b; Guichaoua 2006). Youth involvement in militias, armed gangs and cults suggests that violence can be a form of 'empowerment', the outcome of the search for new forms of identity and integration, a form of employment and an opportunity for looting and accumulation (Allen 1999: 372). It is an opportunity to 'reach the benefits of modernization and a clothing with social power and arrogance' (Doom and Vlassenroot 2001). Rebellion, arms and violence offer a 'new system of social incentives' to the youth, albeit a negative one (McIntyre et al. 2002: 13). The proliferation and easy availability of arms is another factor in the horrendous violence and crime among youth militias and insurgent movements (Nzongola-Ntalaja 1999: 37; Agbu 2004: 12). Small arms can be a status symbol and a weapon of power which attracts young persons (Nzongola-Ntalaja 1999: 37). But it should be noted that the youth still remain in a subordinate position in the dominant power relations, which both appropriate and constrain the 'agency' of the youth, giving them a sense of power that is both illusory and expedient.

Organizational incoherence, poor discipline, factional conflicts and poor coordination often characterize armed groups and make the task of organizing popular violence difficult. Indeed, the task of shaping or taming the diverse elements and frustrated youths into a coherent and disciplined movement is usually a Herculean task (Mkandawire 2002: 204–5). Furthermore, inter- and intra-elite power and resource struggles are sometimes conducted through infiltration, manipulation, funding and arming of youth and armed groups (ibid.: 192; Ellis 2003: 461).

The oil economy and the emergence of militant agitation in the Niger Delta

By the late 1990s the crushing of the leadership of the Movement for the Survival of Ogoni People (MOSOP) resistance and the violent repression of the Ijaw Youth Council (IYC)-led campaign for resource control by government forces paved the way for a discourse that clearly expressed frustration with the failure of non-violent protest to gain the attention of the government and oil companies and get them to respond to the demands of the people. This, coupled with Nigeria's return to democracy in 1999, and the emergence of a Niger Delta political class intent on consolidating its local power base, gave vent to, and provided resources for, more militant forms of resistance. In the decade that followed, protests and resistance assumed violent and insurgent proportions in spite of the presence of the Nigerian military. Youth activism emerged as the vanguard of a new phase of more intensive and extensive resistance actions and volatile demands in the late 1990s.

The proliferation of the fighting arms of some ethnic minority groups and communities in the Niger Delta marked a shift from peaceful engagement and demands (Ikelegbe 2005a, 2006b). Within the Ijaw ethnic group, the largest ethnic minority group in the region, the militant movements that emerged include: the Movement for the Survival of the Ijaw Ethnic Nationality (MOSIEND), the Federated Niger Delta Ijaw Communities (FNDIC) and the Niger Delta Resistance Movement (NDRM). Others include: the Egbema Youth Movement, Membutu Boys and the Itsekiri Youth Movement, operating in the western part of the region. The Bush Boys, the Niger Delta Vigilante Service (NDVS) and the Niger Delta People's Volunteer Force (NDPVF) operate in the eastern Delta. Smaller Ijaw armed groups include the Ijaw Freedom Fighters, the Niger Delta Freedom Fighters, the Atangbata Youths, Tombolo Boys and the Adaka Marine. However, the main groups involved in the ongoing insurgency are MEND, the Martyrs Brigade, the Coalition for Militant Action in the Niger Delta (COMA), the Iduwini Volunteer Force (IVF) and the Joint Revolutionary Council (JRC).

Youth militias in the Niger Delta: complexities and colorations

Attempting to make distinctions among the youth militias is fraught with serious problems. This is because, first, identifying which militias are genuine and which are criminal is becoming difficult as the criminal elements are crowding out the genuine militants (Ukiwo 2008b: 1175). Second, attempting a distinction raises the critical issue of whether criminal actions are undertaken in the name of the struggle, and therefore constitute popular violence conducted by insurgent militants, or are conducted by criminal elements for opportunistic and selfish gains. Third, the steady descent from insurgency to criminality occasioned by factionalization, the differences betwen leaders or co-optation by the political elite or oil companies complicates the task of distinguishing genuine militants from opportunists and criminals. However, an attempt is made here to categorize the armed groups into three types: the insurgent militia, the deviant insurgents and criminal gangs.

Insurgent militias evolved out of resistance against the state–oil partnership in the region, in terms of the struggle for ethnic minority rights against exploitation, marginalization and exclusion from the benefits of the immense oil wealth extracted from the region. The insurgent militias connect, and are fertilized by, the 'structural and historical causes' of the conflicts and the 'fundamental socio-economic conditions of the region' (ibid.). Second, insurgent militias have clear objectives hinged upon an ideology of self-determination for ethnic minorities' control, and a fair share of the oil produced from their ancestral lands and waters. They also engage the oil MNCs on issues relating to compensation for expropriation of land or losses suffered as a result of oil accidents, remediation for environmental damage, employment and provision of basic social amenities.

Third, insurgent militias have a broad membership mainly drawn from the local grass roots, but also supported by some members of diasporic groups. Within the Ijaw, insurgent militias have a membership, support and cooperation across the states and communities in the eastern and western Delta. The fourth characteristic of insurgent groups is their capacity to network, form partnerships and coalitions such as the IYC, the Supreme Egbesu Assembly (SEA) and the JRC. Furthermore, the insurgent groups have developed a sophisticated strategy for engaging local and global media, using information technology, resources and personal contacts to promote their cause internationally. They are very well armed and operate through loose decentralized units.

Deviant insurgent militias are often breakaway factions of mainstream militias organized around a 'powerful' individual linked to local power brokers, top people in the political and military establishment, or oil companies. They are often organized as warlord-based militias, community and clan militias, private militias, cult groups and violent street gangs.[1] Often, they represent a slippage from popular to criminal violence or a complex mix of both, depending on expedient calculations of gain, or the disposition of the 'warlord', 'commander' or 'general' at a given point in time. Lacking any clear ideology, they are driven by a mix of grievances (usually at the initial phase), opportunism and political mercenarism. The key characteristic of these groups is their immersion in a culture of violence as a mode of survival and accumulation, which causes them to swing from time to time between a popular and a criminal agenda. This makes it difficult to categorize them under one or the other tendency, or to predict what their next course of action will be, as they tend to 'change sides' rather quickly, depending on several factors or changes.

This explains why they are available to various sponsors to periodically intimidate opponents and neighbouring communities, fight security forces, act as enforcers, or engage in political thuggery during elections, and participate in transnational criminal networks involved in oil theft in the Niger Delta. In this regard, they either directly engage in illegal oil bunkering (they consider the oil their oil as it is produced from their land), offer protection to barges laden with stolen oil plying the creeks or levy tolls on barges passing through their 'territories'. Given their well-armed presence in the maze of creeks and swamps in the Niger Delta, it is hardly surprising that they also get into expedient, often covert relationships and protection deals with oil MNCs and some local politicians and 'rogue' security personnel (see Bøås, Ukeje, Zalik and Ukiwo, this volume).

Some oil MNCs are implicated in the violent behaviour of these groups. By deploying divide-and-rule tactics, and using military personnel to intimidate and molest innocent and defenceless communities, they fuel a culture of impunity and violence, which also fuels counter-attacks by militias and armed groups seeking to disrupt their oil production. By also making the cash payments to some armed and youth groups, often through the award of 'surveillance contracts', oil MNCs have tended to accentuate deviant youth participation in conflicts and violence, as well as provide funds for arms purchases (Human Rights Watch 2005a: 5–6; Davies 2009; Etim 2002; Bisina 2003: A6; SPDC 2003; see also Bøås, Duquet, Zalik, this volume).

Criminal gangs are mainly loose elements that may be associated with, or claim linkages to, insurgent and deviant insurgent militias. They are small, mobile and operate as criminal gangs. These gangs participate in and profit from illegal oil theft from pipelines or illegal oil bunkering, kidnapping for ransom, extortion from government and oil MNC officials and traditional elites, armed robbery and piracy (Human Rights Watch 2005a: 3). However, in the complex and slippery terrain of Niger Delta resistance, individuals from these criminal gangs sometimes network with insurgent militias or participate in insurgent actions.

A critical question that arises is: what is the nature of interconnections between these groups? It appears that expedient alliances are formed for operational purposes and in the event of intra- and inter-militia conflicts. Even the most powerful militia group at the moment – MEND – is actually a coordinated grouping of several militia leaders, with camps and groups across the western and eastern axis of the Delta. The networking is at the operational level but may not preclude the groups from independent and self-interested actions.

It should be noted, too, that criminal violence is rarely undertaken by community youths and the larger ethnic militia groupings. Insurgent acts relating to the attacks against, seizure or occupation of oil installations and stoppage of oil production are usually undertaken by alliances of ethnic minority militia groups. Even when they kidnap oil workers and attack oil installations and government targets/security forces, these are widely publicized and used as propaganda opportunities for their demands, framed in the rhetoric of ethnic/oil minority and communal resistance. The smaller groups, built around 'commanders' or 'generals', and which are outside the direct control of larger militia groups, tend to easily slide into deviance and criminality.

There could, therefore, be cross-transformations or shifts within and between groups and alliances, but the dynamics would depend on the nature and quality of leadership, the influence of politicians and ethnic entrepreneurs, the nature of the conflict at hand and the level of discipline and coherence of the militia group. Some of the more ideologically oriented groups within MEND tend to be more coherent, but it also includes loose elements that break off and commit crimes well outside the umbrella group's objectives. Even then, the larger insurgent groups may be involved in illegal oil bunkering and extortion from oil MNCs as a means of financing the struggle. What may be at issue, then, may just be the scale at which some groups are involved in certain activities, the reasons for which they are involved, and the prevalence of such deviant activities in the overall actions and operational framework.

From protesters to militias

Most of the early militia groups, such as the NDVS of 1966, the Egbesu Boys of Africa and related groups between 1998 and 2000, were clearly insurgent. Asari Dokubo's NDPVF was insurgent at one point, but several of its affiliates may have been deviant. A faction of MEND and its larger affiliates, such as the JRC and COMA, are clearly insurgent. Some of the smaller militia groups and the armed gangs have tended to be deviant sometimes, but this has not excluded them from collaborating with other militias in insurgent activities on a rather random basis.

One major factor that contributed to the adoption of violence by these groups was their co-optation by Niger Delta elites. This process took place during the build-up to elections in 1999, 2003 and 2007. Community and ethnic leaders 'recruited youth leaders and provided them with money and weapons' to facilitate the competition for leadership positions and the control of communities (Human Rights Watch 2005a: 5–6). A study by Osaghae, Ikelegbe, Olarinmoye and Okhonmina (2007) found that respondents believed that political leaders (42.6 per cent) and ethnic leaders (21.3 per cent) were the main sponsors of militant youths, while 31.9 per cent believed that they were self-sponsored. The situation of elite sponsorship is captured vividly by Edeogun (2008: 67): 'A significant percentage of these youth were trained, bankrolled, equipped with high calibre assault rifles and used to attain power; only to be abandoned thereafter without [being] disarmed. Some joined the rebellion, some constituted their own rebel groups; and others went into criminality, pure and simple.'

Political leaders in the region have also used the militant youths to create tensions and raise the tempo of the struggle for resource control. Such leaders, mostly in government, have mobilized some armed groups to raise tensions around the agitation for resource control, to justify the high opaque state expenditures on security, and create a false sense of performance in the control and handling of security-related threats resulting from militia activities.

At the root of most of the conflicts between cult groups and militias in Rivers state since 2003 are allegations of divide-and-rule tactics by governmental leaders between favoured or dumped cult and militant leaders (Human Rights Report 2005a: 1). Thus, elite patronage and manipulation of the militants, as well as their quest for profit, contracts, personal recognition, appointments, selfish ambitions and gains, have fuelled violent conflicts in the region.

The failure of the agitation to generate much-needed facilities, employment and improvement in the conditions and fortunes of the region has further deepened youth frustration and pushed it towards criminal violence. Poverty, unemployment, repression, economic misery and hopelessness have intensified. The ensuing frustration and aggression have made many youths take to the creeks and camps as a way of escaping poverty and hunger, an opportunity to fight against the source or causes of their predicament and, further, an opportunity to acquire some material gain. The numerous militia and camps in the creeks are therefore not short of recruits. The militia phenomenon is both a form of employment and a chance to survive the dire and deeply frustrating economic and social crises.

TABLE 9.1 Kidnapping/hostage-taking in Bayelsa state, 2004–07

	Date reported	Militants involved	Hostages/ victims	Reasons	Date released
1	03/03/04	32	13	Clashes between youth, security operatives and TNC	08/03/04
2	19/12/05	24	42	Impeachment of Speaker/governor	03/01/06
3	15/01/06	48	14 expatriates & one Nigerian	Arrest of militant leader	23/02/06
4	10/05/07	Faceless	16	Detention of Alamieseigha	23/05/07
5	25/05/07	40	Nine expatriates	Non-development of host communities	08/06/07
6	30/07/07	14	Child of member, state House of Assembly	Welfare of militants	04/08/07
7	08/08/07	11	Mother of Speaker, state House of Assembly	Welfare of militants	22/08/07
8	18/08/07	23	Mother of member, state House of Assembly	Welfare of militants	17/09/07
9	08/10/07	Commander, Pius Group	One Nigerian	Ransom	15/11/07
10	15/10/07	Unknown	One Nigerian	Ransom	15/10/07

Source: Police Crime Diary, Bayelsa State Command, in Eseduwo (2008)

Popular violence and the insurgency in the Niger Delta

Popular violence was until recently at the centre of the resistance and insurgency in the Niger Delta. Apart from the Adaka Boro-led insurgency of 1966, a new phase in the resistance struggle began in 1997 with the birth of militant and coordinated youth groups such as the Chikoko Movement (CM) and the IYC. Alongside these were the FNDIC, INYM and MOSIEND, which were more oriented towards militant resistance or militant Ijaw nationalism. These groups responded to political events or incidences such as the delay in the establishment of the NDDC, court judgments, and government policies in relation to the dichotomy between derivation-based revenues attributable to onshore and offshore oil production. Their actions were sometimes in retaliation against the military and the oil MNCs for attacks against protesting oil communities. These groups justified their actions as being driven by the historic struggles of the Niger Delta ethnic minorities for equity, justice and resource control.

The resistance of these groups to continued marginalization and neglect by the federal government and the oil MNCs paradoxically fed into more repression and patronage politics by the government, which continued to ignore their demands, paving the way for an escalation of militancy. The targeting of government and oil MNCs then moved into an insurgent phase in which the object was to forcibly stop or disrupt oil production, and force the government to address their demands.

Their involvement in bunkering was directed towards obtaining resources for the struggle,[2] while hostage-taking was adopted to compel companies to withdraw expatriate oil workers, and internationalize the struggle. Attacks on oil installations were directed at disrupting or stopping oil production. Initially, these actions adopted violence to indicate the seriousness of the demands and to compel a response from the state and the oil MNCs. By threatening the basis of state revenues and the profits of the oil MNCs, militants believed that the government would be forced to address the region's demands.

Criminal violence in the Niger Delta

Criminal violence in the region can be categorized in terms of: a deliberate instrument of struggle; excesses and fall-outs from the resistance; and under the pretext of the struggle. These all occur among actors in most conflict situations and may be attributable to the levels of discipline or control and the levels of coherence of operations. While criminal violence can be an instrument of struggle, it can also be perpetrated in the name of the struggle by fringe or rogue elements, fifth columnists and other opportunists. For example, some kidnapping for ransom until recently was a major crime committed in the name of the struggle, but its spread outside the core Niger Delta states has made Nigerians perceive it simply as the action of criminals.

Militias face problems of control and discipline within their ranks and factions. The broad nature of the alliance of insurgent militias and the porous boundaries between them and other groups allow for infiltration by various opportunistic and criminal elements. Since such elements are amenable to inducements and co-optation by various political elite and business interests, they have dragged the name of militias into different kinds of private schemes in the name of the struggle. Over time, the insurgent militia was increasingly infiltrated by these elements. It is necessary to reiterate that the core of the insurgent militia is quite different from the criminal elements using violence for personal ends. This kind of criminal violence is conducted by armed bands, syndicates and criminal gangs in the name of the struggle.

As Ikelegbe (2006a: 88) notes, criminals from within and outside the region have cashed in on the agitation and insecurity to perpetuate social and economic crimes. For example, the kidnapping for ransom since 2007 of parents and children of political leaders, the rich and traditional rulers in the Niger Delta states is a clear example of criminal violence in the name of the struggle (Tell 2008a). There have been numerous incidents since 1998 of kidnappings and ransom demands, particularly involving foreign staff of international oil companies (IOCs) and oil service companies (Table 9.1). It appears that there are kidnapping syndicates and warlords to which members of some militias belong. Such a syndicate was implicated in the kidnap of seven expatriate staff of an oil-servicing company (Bedero) along the Udu river in November 2003 (Omonobi and Okhomina 2003). The kidnapping and abduction for ransom of expatriates and Nigerian staff of non-oil companies such as Michelin in 2007 and Julius Berger in 2008 are clearly criminally bent, as these companies are not oil MNCs.

Piracy in the waterways, particularly the Rivers Nun and Forcados and the Tungbo creek, is another manifestation of criminal violence in the Niger Delta. In addition to piracy in the internal waterways there is piracy in the coastal and maritime waters. There were forty incidents of piracy involving attacks on twenty-seven vessels and five incidents of hijackings and abductions of crew members in 2008, while ten incidents of sea piracy took place in January 2009 in the Delta (International Crisis Group 2009: 5).

Conclusion

The current dynamics of the militia phenomenon and the transition in some segments from popular to criminal violence are quite complex. There are complex relations between patrons and militias, between ethnic minority petro-elites, oil MNCs and militias, between oil communities and militias, armed groups and gangs. Furthermore, there are complex relations between militia camps, their 'commanders' or 'generals' and state governors, top politicians, the military and oil MNCs. Even within the militia formations, there are complex relations and tensions within the alliance(s) and between the diverse groups, armed bands, cultists and pirates.

The tendency to criminal violence is traceable to state repression and serious democratic deficits, alongside weak organizational structures and poor control and cohesion within the insurgent militia. This situation has been compounded by elite infiltration, immense opportunities for self-enrichment by the few, in a context of high levels of poverty and youth unemployment, and the proliferation of arms (see chapter by Duquet, this volume). The tragedy is that what began as a genuine, insurgent struggle has been hijacked by the elite and oil theft syndicates who now manipulate and deploy some of the militias for the perpetration of diverse acts, most of which tarnish the image of the struggle.

Although emerging from a populist youth movement, some segments of the militia are now market-based, working for those that arm and pay them. While struggling against the Nigerian state, and its ruling class and political elite, who are the architects of the region's misfortune, some components of the militia have now become the agents and foot-soldiers of the political elite, ethnic entrepreneurs, government leaders and even political parties. As the core of genuine insurgents in the Niger Delta continues to shrink, these paradoxes denote the complexities and dynamics of the militia formation and local resistance. They also indicate that the forces driving the complex dimensions of the now ambivalent resistance and violence need to be reckoned with in the efforts to curtail criminality, resolve the conflict and build peace in the troubled oil-rich region.

10 | Swamped with weapons: the proliferation of illicit small arms and light weapons in the Niger Delta

Nils Duquet

Introduction

This chapter examines the proliferation of small arms and light weapons (SALW) – such as revolvers, assault rifles and machine guns[1] – in the Niger Delta and its impact on the armed conflict raging in the region. Researching the illicit possession and trade in SALW is not an easy task since these activities are of a covert nature. Reliable and detailed data on illegal arms transfers are not easily available. This study therefore relies primarily on published findings of field research undertaken by local and international researchers and advocacy organizations. First we provide an overview of the key causes of the proliferation of illicit SALW in Nigeria in general and the Delta region in particular. Afterwards we elaborate on different methods of illicit SALW acquisition by non-state actors. Finally the impact of the proliferation of SALW on the armed conflict in the Niger Delta is analysed.

The end of the Cold War has drawn a great deal of scholarly and policy attention to SALW, which have become the weapons most used in contemporary violent conflict (Wezeman 2003). SALW cause an estimated 60 to 90 per cent of all direct deaths in these conflicts (Small Arms Survey 2005). This is not surprising given that these weapons are especially attractive for use by non-state actors: they are lethal, relatively cheap, often relatively easily available, durable, simple to use and maintain, highly portable and easy to conceal (Boutwell and Klare 1999).[2] It is very difficult to estimate the total number of SALW circulating worldwide. Yet, despite their attractiveness to insurgents and other armed groups, only 0.2 per cent of all SALW worldwide are believed to be possessed by these non-state actors (Small Arms Survey 2009). In 2001, former secretary-general of the United Nations Kofi Annan stated:

> The world is flooded with small arms and light weapons numbering at least 500 million, enough for one of every 12 people on earth. Most of these are controlled by legal authorities, but when they fall into the hands of terrorists, criminals and irregular forces, small arms bring devastation. They exacerbate conflict, spark refugee flows, undermine the rule of law, and spawn a culture of violence

and impunity. In short, small arms are a threat to peace and development, to democracy and human rights. (Annan 2001)

One of the parts of the world in which the proliferation of SALW has been an important factor in armed conflict is West Africa. According to estimates of the United Nations Development Programme approximately eight million illicit SALW circulate in West Africa.[3] The widespread availability of these weapons poses an enormous threat to the stability of this volatile region as nearly every West African country has in the recent past witnessed endemic violence in which SALW were the weapons primarily used (Keili 2008). A significant proportion of these illicit SALW circulating in West Africa can be found in Nigeria. Ever since the development of the Nigerian oil industry as the country's main revenue-earner, the Niger Delta has been a site of increased ethnic minority agitation, followed by intense violence. In the mid-1990s, non-violent resistance to oil company operations by local communities transformed into low-intensity armed conflict. The violence in the Niger Delta does not reflect a 'typical' armed conflict but consists of a macro-level conflict – between larger armed groups, Nigerian security forces and oil companies – and a wide range of micro-level conflicts – between different communities, within communities or between communities and oil companies. Although the violence in the Niger Delta has taken numerous different forms, many analysts (e.g. Human Rights Watch 2005b) argue that the violence is essentially a battle for control over oil revenues and government resources. Although a number of heavily armed groups, such as MEND and NDPVF, use the rhetoric of long-standing political grievances, it is not always clear to what extent their actions reflect sincere political intentions (Iannaccone 2007).

The proliferation of small arms and light weapons

The most important stock of legally possessed SALW can be found among the Nigerian security forces, such as the armed forces, police, intelligence agencies and a number of specialized units within other security agencies. Owing to some reluctance on the part of the military to release information, very little is known about the size and content of the existing stockpiles of the military forces. The exact figure for SALW controlled by the Nigerian military is therefore unknown. Information about the holdings of the police forces, on the other hand, is more easily available: the Nigerian police possesses about 65,000 rifles, 8,500 pistols and more than one million rounds of ammunition. In addition to state stockpiles, a rather limited number of SALW are also legally possessed by civilians (Hazen and Horner 2007).

It is difficult to estimate the precise amount of illicit weapons circulating in Nigeria. However, at the UN Small Arms Convention in 2001 the Nigerian minister of defence stated that approximately one million SALW were possessed illegally in the country (Vines 2005). Other estimates place the number of SALW in Nigeria at roughly between one and three million, of which a majority are illegally possessed by non-state actors (Hazen and Horner 2007). In 2004, a police spokesman stated that the exact number of illicit firearms circulating in Nigeria is unknown, but is believed to outnumber the quantity of weapons in police armouries nationwide (Olori 2004). Data released by the inspector-general of the police on SALW seizures indicate that more than 8,500 arms were seized in Nigeria between 2000 and 2003 (Hazen and Horner 2007).

Yet the amount of weapons seized by the military, the police and customs officers is believed to be negligible compared to the number of SALW smuggled into the country on a daily basis. It is important to note that while illegal SALW are generally associated with militant activity, some analysts (e.g. Davies 2009) argue that the majority of illegally possessed weapons are owned by civilians in the villages. But this claim does not alter the fact that the great proliferation of illicit SALW in Nigeria since the end of military rule in the late 1990s is strongly related to the intensification of armed violence in the Niger Delta.

Analyses of the surrender of SALW during disarmament initiatives indicate that the armed groups operating in the Niger Delta use a wide range of SALW. In Rivers state, for example, the 2004 disarmament process revealed that armed groups use a wide variety of assault rifles, such as the infamous AK-47, the Czech-manufactured SA Vz. 58, the Heckler-Koch G3 assault rifle, and FAL and FNC rifles of the Belgian arms manufacturer FN Herstal. Interestingly, about three-quarters of the collected AK-47s in Rivers state had no butt stocks, which make them less balanced and accurate. This indicates that precision and accuracy are not of primary importance for these armed groups (Best and von Kemedi 2005). Besides these assault rifles, armed groups also use pistols, revolvers, hunting rifles, craft weapons, pump-action shotguns and (light) machine guns such as Beretta 12S and AR-70, MAT 49, Sten MK 2, Czech Model 26 and Model 59 (Rachot), MG 36, Tokarev TT and Marakov PM pistols (ibid.; Davies 2009).[4]

According to some sources, some of the armed groups operating in the Delta are even better equipped and trained than the Nigerian security forces (Hazen and Horner 2007). The disarmament aspect of the 2009 amnesty to Niger Delta militants (see chapter by Obi and Rustad, this volume) also provides some information on the arms returned by militants. These included weapons such as: the AK-47, general-purpose machine guns (GPMGs), rocket-propelled grenade launchers, FN rifles, sub-machine guns, pump-action guns, ammunition and explosives. However, the source of these weapons has been subject to some controversy as a faction of MEND denied their ownership by alleging that they were provided by government for publicity purposes (Houreld 2009).

Although not all armed groups rely primarily on SALW[5] the different armed groups in the Niger Delta have sufficient firepower to seriously face up to the state security forces (Davies 2009). Most of the armed groups operating in the region are relatively small in size, with between fifty and a few hundred members, and the amount and sophistication of weapons they hold vary markedly between these groups. Given the difficulty in obtaining information about armed groups in general and the fluidity that characterizes armed groups in the Niger Delta, little is known about the weapon arsenals of specific groups. At some points, leaders of certain groups have made public statements on their weapon arsenal. Asari, the leader of the NDPVF, for example, stated in 2004 that he owned sixty-seven boats – each armed with two light machine guns – and more than three thousand assault rifles. Others in his organization have even stated that the group has more than five thousand weapons including machine guns, self-loading rifles and AK-47s (Best and von Kemedi 2005).

Yet one needs to interpret these statements with the necessary precaution, given that militia leaders might exaggerate the size and nature of their own weapon stocks in order to artificially boost their military capacity. It has become clear that not all types of armed groups carry weapons to the same extent. Of all types of armed groups ethnic militias – paramilitary groups of youth who promote and protect the interests of a specific ethnic group – are the best trained, organized and armed (usually even with sophisticated weapons), while vigilante groups – which consist of community members providing protection from violence and criminality for their community – are not even always armed. Confraternities and 'cults' are generally smaller groups that originate in tertiary academic institutions and are usually territorially localized around these institutions (Bøås, Ikelegbe, this volume). Prospective members must prove their bravery and demonstrate their ability to handle weapons. Some analysts believe the small number of large armed groups, with a few thousand members, have only a relatively small arsenal of a few hundred weapons, which means that not every member can actually carry a weapon (Hazen and Horner 2007). Yet one does not need to possess a weapon in order to use it. In recent years, the day hire of SALW from military and police officers has become a common feature in the Niger Delta (Davies 2009).

The drivers behind the proliferation

Popular accounts often point to one principal cause for the proliferation of SALW in the Niger Delta. Yet it is impossible and undesirable to single out only one cause. The causes of the use of SALW in the Niger Delta are multilayered and have many drivers, such as chieftaincy disputes, criminal motivations, electoral violence and illegal oil bunkering (Isumonah et al. 2005). Surveys in Delta and Rivers states support this observation: in the perception of the local population a wide range of actors play an important role in the acquisition and proliferation of SALW (Abayomi et al. 2005; Nsirimovu 2005). The problem of SALW in Nigeria is largely demand-driven. While the Nigerian military and the police are increasing their legal stocks of weapons in an attempt to restore law and order in the country and to modernize their troops, non-state actors are acquiring weapons, often illicitly, to provide security for themselves and sometimes to reap more benefits from illegal activities (Hazen and Horner 2007). In the following section we will give an overview of the different dynamics underlying SALW proliferation in the Niger Delta.

It is important to note that SALW proliferation in the Niger Delta is partly the outcome of decades of military rule (1966–79 and 1984–98) and the culture of violence that accompanied it. Under military rule, the political space was completely militarized and violence was used systematically to target individual opponents and groups. In this way a culture of violence and militarism became entrenched, in which coercion is favoured over persuasion in order to achieve goals (Ebo 2005; Ibeanu 2005). In this culture, possession of SALW is of crucial importance. Youths in the Niger Delta have grown up believing that violence, especially if backed with weapons, is the way of gaining respect, power and material benefits (Nsirimovu 2005; Garuba 2007). Besides fostering a culture of violence, military rule also deepened feelings of 'negative communalism'.

In the absence of political and civil space, political mobilization was possible only under the realm of ethnic and communal groups.[6] Under the umbrella of communalism many groups found a means to pursue their own particular interests. By including some groups while excluding others, this situation was manipulated by the military regime and local political elites in order to strengthen their grip on power (Ibeanu 2005). Under military rule, ethnic and communal groups were largely kept under control, but with the return to civilian rule and the related expansion of political space in the late 1990s, ethnic-based armed groups blossomed and gradually started replacing state security structures (Ebo 2005). In an attempt to increase their access to oil company payments, several ethnic and communal groups were embroiled in violent clashes,[7] which fuelled arms proliferation in the Niger Delta (Isumonah et al. 2005).

Even though territorial disputes pre-date the discovery of oil deposits, and these disputes also take place in other regions in Nigeria, the presence of oil has undoubtedly exacerbated political disputes and conflicts within and between neighbouring communities in the Delta region. This is because the presence of oil installations, despite their potential negative effects on the environment and local population, also offers potential benefits for local host communities in the form of compensation payments and development projects. Hosting oil installations can thus be very lucrative, especially for traditional leaders, who generally mediate between the oil companies and local communities (Human Rights Watch 1999b). Under the guise of providing security, many communities in the Niger Delta have jointly raised the necessary financial resources to acquire weapons in support of local vigilante and community defence groups. These vigilante groups are generally well armed, especially with AK-47s (Isumonah et al. 2005; Florquin and Berman 2005; Naagbanton 2008). In addition, some traditional leaders have also supplied weapons to youth groups[8] in an attempt to seek protection from rival groups (Best and von Kemedi 2005).

The policy of oil company compensation payments to host communities also fuelled more violence within communities through the channelling of large sums of money to traditional leaders, many of whom did not share this money with their respective communities. This made traditional leadership positions very lucrative and intensified competition for these positions. Rival claimants hired youth groups and provided them with SALW in an attempt to capture lucrative leadership positions. Also, youth groups started challenging communal leadership power structures in order to become an 'official' partner in the negotiations with the oil companies and reap oil company compensation benefits (Human Rights Watch 2005b). The majority of the youth groups that were initially formed and hired to provide security for certain communities 'have transformed into what most of the original initiators could no longer control' (Abayomi et al. 2005). The fact that these groups received weapons from their original patrons but did not return them afterwards played an important role in this process. These youth groups did not restrict their use of SALW to intra- or inter-communal strife. The possession of SALW boosted their power and offered them plentiful opportunities for self-enrichment. Over time some groups started using their firepower to engage in criminal activities, such as hostage-taking, under the guise of 'resource-control' agitations. With the revenues from these activities, they procured more weapons to consolidate their power and expanded their enterprises by partnering up with elites involved in the oil bunkering business. This led to numerous incidents of armed violence between rival groups, resulting in the killing of dozens of people, especially in Rivers state (Akpode 2004).

Politicians also played a crucial role in SALW proliferation in the region. In a situation where contestants for political office are often motivated more by gaining access to public resources and personal wealth than in serving the people, political competition is often fiercely contested by illegitimate means, such as the recruiting of youth to intimidate opponents (Nsirimovu 2005). The 2003 elections offer a clear example of 'gunpowder politics'. Politicians provided these groups with cash, weapons, intoxicants (particularly alcohol) and immunity from arrest and prosecution by law enforcement in exchange for the manipulation of community leaders into favourable opinions and positions in the run-up to the elections and for the intimidation of voters and electoral officials at polling stations during the elections (WAC Global Services 2003). Allegedly the politicians paid unemployed youth up to N10,000 to participate in attacks and the intimidation of political opponents (Human Rights Watch 2003).

Other groups were given free rein to carry out their lucrative oil bunkering and other criminal activities in exchange for their participation in violence directed against political competitors (Human Rights Watch 2005b). Although political intimidation is not a new phenomenon in Nigeria, it became evident in the 2003 elections that the tools of political violence were shifting from more rudimentary weapons – such as machetes, clubs and knives – to SALW (Vines 2005). The creation of small private armies by politicians in the run-up to the 2003 elections led to an upsurge in the cross-border trafficking of SALW (IRIN 2002). Politicians made promises to the violent youth groups to ensure loyalty, but these promises were often not kept and rewards not forthcoming. As a consequence, many groups did not return the weapons they received from their patrons and instead turned them to other criminal purposes – such as large-scale oil theft, pillaging of villages or kidnapping – or deployed them in inter- and intra-communal conflicts (WAC Global Services 2003). Heavily armed and with their own access to financial resources, these groups became less dependent on their former patrons and started acting as well-armed independent purveyors of violence. In the urban areas of the Niger Delta, and especially in Port Harcourt, political godfathers still promote and use militias to widen their power and influence or to promote conflict as a smokescreen for their illegal activities such as oil bunkering (Davies 2009).

Another key driver behind the proliferation of SALW in the Niger Delta is the trade in stolen oil. Oil bunkering has become the most profitable illegal private business in Nigeria. With low capital costs the bunkering syndicates reap enormous profits (Human Rights Watch 2003). Oil bunkering is not a new phenomenon in the Niger Delta. Over the years it has evolved from a rather small-scale practice in which locals tapped small quantities of oil for personal use or for the local market into an extensive and sophisticated business involving transnational criminal networks. Especially since the late 1990s, oil bunkering activities have increased significantly. Large quantities of stolen oil are loaded into barges, and transported through the Delta waterways to ships and oil tankers waiting on the high seas. The market for this stolen oil is abroad: through a wide range of middlemen the stolen oil is either bought by neighbouring countries or sold to refineries in Africa, Europe, Asia and North America (Ikelegbe 2005b).

This practice is fostered by poverty, the large pool of unemployed youth in the Delta, the widespread feeling among the local population that they do not benefit from oil company operations, the detailed knowledge of local armed groups of the swampy terrain, the corrupt and ineffective law enforcement agencies, the voluntary or coerced cooperation of local communities, and patronage of oil bunkering groups by senior government officials and politicians (Vines 2005). Oil bunkering finances arms acquisition either directly as part of payment for the stolen oil or indirectly by payment for providing security services for oil bunkering operations (Davies 2009). It is very difficult to estimate the precise amount of oil that is stolen every day, and the figures fluctuate considerably, with periodic efforts on the part of the Nigerian security agencies to police the waterways more effectively (Human Rights Watch 2003). In 2008 an estimated volume of 150,000 barrels of oil was stolen each day, worth approximately US$6.3 billion (Davies 2009). Although the stolen crude oil is sold at below official market prices, the bunkering syndicates generate enormous revenues. With this money the syndicates have provided armed groups with the necessary funding to acquire more powerful weapons from external sources (Hazen and Horner 2007). In order to control the bunkering waterways against rival groups, weapons are needed. While these weapons were at first primarily provided by patrons, the armed groups gradually became more self-sufficient and started engaging in criminal activities and acquiring weapons themselves.[9] In this way a number of armed groups involved in oil bunkering became the prime customers of the growing black market of (primarily smuggled) SALW (Duquet 2009).

Other key players in the proliferation of SALW in the Niger Delta are the oil companies operating in the region. In their report, commissioned by Shell, WAC Global Services (2003) argue that incompetence in the implementation of company policy and the overall insecurity it creates in the operating environment are at the core of the conflict-promoting role of oil companies. Allegedly a number of small arms were transferred to the Niger Delta after the government decided that oil companies should be allowed to import weapons for the supernumerary police forces (SPY) protecting oil infrastructure (Hazen and Horner 2007).

In the mid-1990s Shell received much negative publicity internationally when it was disclosed that the company had imported handguns and ammunition for its 'unarmed' supernumerary or SPY police, responsible for providing internal security services, such as access, control and the protection of its premises, personnel and facilities.[10] Shell acknowledged negotiating the purchase of these guns, but refused to disclose the number of imported guns and their origin. Shell also stated that this practice was carried out by a wide range of companies operating in Nigeria (Duodu 1996; Human Rights Watch 1999b). Given the high levels of corruption within the Nigerian security forces, it is not unlikely that a number of these SALW eventually ended up in the hands of armed groups threatening to attack oil installations.

It is also reported that financial resources from oil companies have been used by the armed groups to acquire weapons (von Kemedi 2003; Best and von Kemedi 2005). The practice of oil companies awarding surveillance and security contracts has fuelled violence in the region, not only by providing militant groups with sufficient financial means to purchase weapons, but also by encouraging competition between rival groups for contracts. These contracts have also encouraged youths from other communities to actually start sabotaging infrastructure in order to receive similar 'stay-at-home payments' (Omeje 2006a). Paying ransom for kidnapped employees is another way oil companies have facilitated weapons procurement by armed groups. Over the years, members of staff of oil companies and their contractors have increasingly become the targets of kidnapping attempts (Nsirimovu 2005).

Since early 2006 there has been a spectacular escalation in the number of kidnappings in the Niger Delta (Concannon and Croft 2006). Armed groups have taken hostages for two primary reasons: political bargaining and direct economic gain. In most cases, ransom is paid to the kidnappers and the hostages are released unharmed within days or weeks of being captured (Hazen and Horner 2007). Over the years hostage-taking has become big business in the Niger Delta and an active ransom market has emerged, providing significant financial revenues for several groups (Iannaccone 2007; Garuba 2007). Part of the ransom paid by oil companies and their contractors is used by armed groups to acquire more weapons, although some analysts (e.g. WAC Global Services 2003) argue that these contributions can be considered insignificant in the broader context of supply.

Methods of sourcing small arms and light weapons

Weapons procurement by armed groups in West Africa is sometimes the result of recirculation of arms stocks already within the region (Florquin and Berman 2005). Although it is difficult to obtain details on arms transfers in the Niger Delta, several different methods of sourcing SALW can be discerned.

Domestic sources of small arms and light weapons A significant proportion of the SALW in Nigerian state stockpiles comes from the Defence Industry Corporation of Nigeria (DICON). This Kaduna-based and government-owned industrial arms manufacturer was established in 1964 to supply weapons and ammunition to meet Nigeria's immediate defence needs after gaining its independence. DICON is the only legally recognized manufacturer of SALW in Nigeria and produces rifles, pistols and ammunition exclusively for the Nigerian police and armed forces.

Over the years, however, the focus of the company has shifted from production to importation of weapons (Vines 2005). This shift is connected with decades of neglect by successive administrations. In 2006, for example, the company was operating at only 15 per cent of its installed capacity. Recent initiatives to upgrade DICON's production capacity seem to be paying off, with a reported increase in the production level of nearly 70 per cent. In 2007 the company announced it would soon start the mass production of OBJ-006, a Nigerian version of the AK-47. The ultimate goal of the refurbishment of DICON is to become self-sufficient in the procurement of SALW and ammunition, and if possible even export them to neighbouring countries (Oji 2007; Hazen and Horner 2007). Although armed groups do not acquire weapons from DICON directly, the risk exists that these locally produced weapons can end up in militants' hands through security-sector black-marketeering.

Government stockpiles are an important source of SALW circulating in conflict zones worldwide. Through theft, corruption, seizure, distribution and sales, weapons from these armouries end up in the hands of armed groups (Khakee et al. 2005). This type of procurement is a common occurrence in West Africa. Poorly controlled and managed stockpiles have contributed to the proliferation of illicit SALW in the region (Bah 2004). An analysis of arms acquisition patterns of armed groups in West Africa has demonstrated that the theft or seizure of government arms stockpiles is a primary source of armaments for these groups. Given the lack of transparency in stockpile management, it is, however, unclear which weapons have disappeared and exactly where to (Lombard et al. 2006). Small arms and light weapons from state stockpiles have also ended up in the hands of armed groups in Nigeria. Between 1996 and 2001, for example, the Nigerian police documented the loss of 1,554 weapons and types of ammunition. In reality, the number of weapons that disappeared from security officials and state armouries into the hands of armed groups in Nigeria is likely to be much higher (Bah 2004). In 2002, President Obasanjo recognized this problem and stated that the bulk of ammunition circulating illegally in the country emanated from state security agencies (Agboton-Johnson et al. 2004).

A significant proportion of the SALW circulating illegally in the Niger Delta was transferred from state stockpiles to civilians with the deliberate aid of Nigerian security officials (Davies 2009). Security officials are reportedly complicit in the theft and seizures of state stockpiles by members of armed groups. A survey among non-state agents in Bayelsa state indicates that security officials are an important source of SALW for armed groups. According to this survey approximately 70 per cent of SALW were distributed to armed groups by members of the police (30 per cent), the military (25 per cent) and the mobile police (15 per cent). These security officials sell weapons they claim are 'lost' or 'stolen' while on duty. These small-scale transfers can go unnoticed since it is very difficult to verify their claims. Security officials are also implicated in smuggling schemes by accepting bribes (Isumonah et al. 2005).

There are also reports of Nigerian soldiers selling weapons they brought back from Economic Community of West African States Cease-fire Monitoring Group (ECOMOG) missions in Sierra Leone and Liberia, either directly to the militants or through local arms dealers (Bah 2004; Best and von Kemedi 2005).[11] Besides distributing SALW or facilitating their acquisition, there are also reports of serving and retired security officials providing military training to armed groups (Hazen and Horner 2007). In 2008 several Nigerian soldiers were court-martialled for selling large quantities of weapons of different specifications to MEND.[12] Not only have Nigerian soldiers provided weapons to the armed groups: Cameroon soldiers stationed in the Bakassi peninsula – its jurisdiction was long disputed between Cameroon and Nigeria, but it is currently ruled by Cameroon, following a judgment by the International Court of Justice[13] – have reportedly lost or sold weapons to these groups (Best and von Kemedi 2005).

In Nigeria, blacksmiths have traditionally been an important source of SALW for local hunters and security providers. Locally crafted SALW are commonly used by armed groups in the Niger Delta (Abayomi et al. 2005). The previously mentioned survey among armed group members in Bayelsa state (Isumonah et al. 2005) indicated that approximately 20 per cent of the weapons they possessed were locally crafted weapons. One of the advantages of these locally manufactured weapons is that they are generally substantially cheaper than imported weapons sold on the black market. Over the years, Nigerian craft weapons production has grown exponentially, with increased patronage from criminal elements, ethnic militias and vigilante groups (Ebo 2005). There are even reports that gunsmiths from Ghana, known in West Africa for its vibrant craft arms production,[14] have travelled to Nigeria to teach and train local blacksmiths in the art of gun-making (Best and von Kemedi 2005).

The local fabrication of SALW demands a high level of organization and confidentiality in order not to compromise collaborators who often include security officials and loyal kinsmen. The identities and locations of the local fabricators in this underground network are therefore covered in secrecy. It is believed the fabrication is basically carried out by blacksmiths and by trained fitters (Abayomi et al. 2005). The techniques used for the craft production of weapons are rudimentary and materials are sourced locally (Hazen and Horner 2007). Awka, the capital of Anambra state, appears to be the most important centre of craft arms production in Nigeria (Best and von Kemedi 2005). Locally manufactured guns are therefore often called Awka in local parlance (Naagbanton 2008). Awka has been an important centre for the craft production of weapons since the outbreak of the Biafran war, when explosives were produced in the town.[15] Ever since, the expertise and know-how for local production has been passed down through the generations within families (Hazen and Horner 2007). Onitsha, an important commercial city in Anambra state, is also believed to be a hub of illegal market operations and local fabrication of SALW (Abayomi et al. 2005).

External sources of small arms and light weapons Despite the lack of clear data on the quantity of weapons smuggled into the Niger Delta, most observers believe that the majority of SALW used by armed groups are smuggled into the country (Adejo 2005).[16] Border control in West Africa is generally poor or inadequate owing to a lack of technical infrastructure and human resources, the nature of the terrain and the often extremely long borders (Fall 2005). Nigeria, with more than 36,450 kilometres of land and maritime borders,[17] is no exception to this observation. Its long and porous borders make the smuggling of SALW a relatively easy endeavour since these borders are not effectively patrolled by Nigerian security officials, who lack manpower, vehicles and resources (Adejo 2005). Weapons are smuggled into Nigeria by land or sea from Benin in significant quantities (with weapons originating in Ghana, Togo and Burkina Faso). In an attempt to halt these illicit imports, Nigeria unilaterally closed its border with Benin in August 2003 for a short period. Weapons are also smuggled into Nigeria from the northern borders with Cameroon, Chad and Niger (IRIN 2002; Florquin and Berman 2005; Olori 2004; Vines 2005).

Although not a neighbouring country, Togo is also an important transit point for illegal arms smuggling into Nigeria. Craft weapons purchased by Nigerian arms traffickers in Ghana and Benin are often smuggled into Nigeria via Togo (Florquin and Berman 2005). Over the last several years, SALW have been smuggled into the country from each of these entry points, but the three most notorious arms-smuggling frontiers are Warri (Delta state), the south-west (Idi-Iroko in Ogun state and Seme in Lagos state) and the north-eastern border with Niger and Cameroon (Adamawa, Borno and Yobe states) (Ebo 2005). Warri especially is widely recognized as a major arms-trafficking and distribution hub. Smugglers from neighbouring countries use speedboats to transport purchased SALW from ships anchored on the high seas and then sell these to various communities in Warri. From there, the weapons are trafficked to surrounding towns (Ojudu 2004; Best and von Kemedi 2005; Hazen and Horner 2007).

The flow of SALW in the Niger Delta is facilitated by a labyrinthine network of creeks and rivers in the region (Garuba 2007). Primary distribution points can be found all across the Niger Delta, and a number of towns and cities are known for the availability of weapons, including Port Harcourt, Asaba, Benin City, Aba, Owerri and Awka (Hazen and Horner 2007). Weapons that enter Nigeria through the Niger Delta are generally acquired by armed groups through more direct means, such as cash payments, or exchanged for stolen oil, while weapons that enter the country through border areas or the south-east generally end up in the hands of armed groups after passing through a number of dealers in different primary and secondary distribution points. Despite the high demand for SALW in the Niger Delta, not all weapons that enter the country via the Delta region also stay there. Some of the weapons that enter through the southern borders are transported up north (ibid.).

Recently, an important evolution has taken place with regard to the nature of illegal SALW importation: over the years armed groups started relying increasingly on imported weapons, which in turn increased the quality and sophistication of the weapons. Before 2003 most illicit weapons circulating in the Niger Delta were older weapons, often of poor quality. These weapons were generally war surplus, sourced from other conflict zones in West Africa such as Liberia and Chad, weapons used in previous communal conflicts, or weapons obtained from the police or army through theft or diversion. In the lead-up to the 2003 elections the supply of illegal weapons, often procured through international networks, expanded.

In 2003/04, the practice of illegal oil bunkering boosted the acquisition of arms. It provided the armed groups with increased financial means and better networks, in turn enabling them to acquire not only more weapons but also more sophisticated and better-quality weapons. The increasing reliability of illegal weapons supply generated a growing preference for new weapons; and this resulted in an escalation in prices. With the 2004 Peace Accord the demand for SALW fell, and during the attendant disarmament process around three thousand small arms were destroyed. Yet during this disarmament process the money received for the surrendered weapons was used to place orders for better-quality weapons, and in 2005 a new wave of rearmament took place. As a result of major orders to international arms dealers to supply rebel groups from conflict zones all across West Africa with AK-47s, the prices of these weapons fell dramatically by mid-2005.[18]

The new wave of militancy that arose in the Niger Delta in late 2005 in turn boosted SALW proliferation. The fracturing of former groups and the spectacular emergence of MEND led to growing demand, which was met by the international illegal SALW market (Davies 2009). As in several other conflict zones, armed groups in the Niger Delta generally prefer SALW from external sources to domestically sourced weapons. Yet not everybody has access to these external sources. Smaller criminal groups, for example, such as petty criminal cartels in their embryonic stages, are often forced to rely on the locally crafted guns (Naagbanton 2008). These groups generally lack the necessary financial resources and networks to acquire SALW from abroad. The oil bunkering groups generally have more financial resources and contacts with international arms dealing networks; therefore, they have more acquisition options than other groups. This has enabled a number of these groups to acquire more and better-quality weapons, which has enabled them to overpower rival groups and use them as proxies (Duquet 2009).

The devastating impact of small arms and light weapons

The foregoing sections have demonstrated that the proliferation of SALW in the Niger Delta is not a new phenomenon and is partly rooted in the decades of military rule in Nigeria. Yet with the return to civilian rule in 1999, the problem of proliferation did not just vanish into thin air. In the last decade, several key factors – such as inter- and intra-communal conflict, ill-considered oil company behaviour, the large-scale trade in stolen oil, and political manipulation – have intensified the illicit trade in and possession of SALW in the conflict-ridden Delta region. The proliferation of SALW has considerably increased the level of destruction and the number of casualties of violence in the Niger Delta.

The presence of weapons alone, however, is not sufficient to cause, prolong or intensify armed conflict. The problem of proliferation in the Niger Delta is chiefly driven by demand. Demand is the key to understanding the dynamics of SALW proliferation since a symbiotic relationship exists between insecurity and proliferation: as long as insecurity persists and there are political, social or economic opportunities to use SALW, there will be a demand for these weapons, which in turn increase the insecurity and the related opportunities. In order to halt the proliferation of illicit SALW in the Niger Delta, one needs to address the core issues underlying the demand for these deadly weapons, such as high unemployment, social disintegration, unequal revenue distribution, political manipulation and corruption. Yet more short-term issues related to the supply of these preferred tools of violence also need to be addressed, since their prolonged presence has an important impact on the prospects for peace and justice in the Delta region, and thus finally for the demand for SALW. Not only does the presence of these weapons pose an important threat to law and order, but 'prolonged exposure to criminal activities [...] fuels social disintegration and creates a growing cadre of "irretrievable" youths who are likely to become important drivers of violent conflict in years to come' (WAC Global Services 2003: 43).

Every day that arms proliferation continues, the risk of a further criminalization of the conflict increases and the prospect of a lasting peaceful resolution to the political issues in the Niger Delta becomes more remote. And even if the violence in the Niger Delta were to cease, the widespread availability of SALW might have serious consequences for other parts of Nigeria, as these weapons might end up in the wrong hands in other places across the country or even in neighbouring countries, a process that accounts for a large proportion of the weapons that are currently used in the Niger Delta. What is needed, therefore, in any attempt to resolve the Niger Delta crisis, is a well-thought-out programme for disarmament.[19] The disarmament, demobilization and reintegration (DDR) process accompanying the amnesty and post-amnesty programmes needs a comprehensive and sustainable development strategy that addresses the root causes of the conflict. Otherwise the self-reinforcing cycle of arms proliferation and violence will continue. At the same time, the international community needs to adhere to strict arms export control and implement an effective juridical framework capable of halting illegal arms brokering.

11 | Women's protests in the Niger Delta region

Oluwatoyin Oluwaniyi

Introduction

This chapter explores Niger Delta women's protests in the context of the ongoing violence in the region from two perspectives. The first relates to the exclusion of women from the benefits of the oil economy, state repression of their protests, and the ways in which oil production threatens the environmental basis of their subsistence: land and water. The second relates to the ways in which dominant patriarchal relations marginalize and subordinate women to men, and how this is expressed in women's protests and politics.

Women in the Niger Delta struggle simultaneously against the state–oil partnership as well as oppressive gender relations. This partly finds expression in the collaboration between the local male elites, the state and oil MNCs, which conspire to exclude women from the distribution of the benefits of the oil industry, resulting in their impoverishment and disempowerment. Human Rights Watch (2002, 2005b and 2007c) perceives Niger Delta women as the poorest of the poor. A UNDP (2006: 125) study also shows that out of the 30.4 per cent of women who cited lack of money as a barrier to accessing healthcare in Nigeria, 47.1 per cent were from the Niger Delta region.

Women's protests are largely organized and driven by the struggle against the twin-layered level of domination that they suffer. This chapter draws a lot of its material from how grassroots women have formed their organizations and mobilized themselves 'from below' for protests, based on fieldwork in the oil-producing communities of Okerenkoko, Kokodiagbene, Ogboloma and Okoroba in Delta and Bayelsa states in the Niger Delta. It is also based on learning first hand from the women about their struggles against the state–oil partnership and male domination. Their responses show that, far from being undifferentiated, the struggle for resource control and self-determination by the ethnic minorities of the region is gendered. Apart from struggling against male and class domination, women play an important role in the Niger Delta resistance.

Okerenkoko and Kokodiagbene are both Ijaw communities within Gbaramatu Kingdom in South West Warri, Delta state. The kingdom is one of the richest in the country because of its huge deposits of crude oil, producing an estimated 400,000 barrels per day, and Kokodiagbene and Okerenkoko are major hosts to

Chevron-Texaco and the Shell Petroleum Development Company (SPDC). Gbara-matu has eight flow stations, operated by Chevron-Texaco and SPDC (Courson 2007). Some of these flow stations are situated within Kokodiagbene (operated by Chevron and SPDC) and Okerenkoko (operated by SPDC). Both communities are situated within the riverine areas and therefore their major economic livelihoods are fishing, subsistence farming and petty trade. In spite of both communities' contributions to Nigeria's wealth, the majority of the inhabitants are extremely impoverished, lacking the capability to fend for their families. Hence, both communities have been a site of land and environmental degradation, fuelling conflicts over 'scarce resources' between neighbours on the one hand, and between the communities and the state/oil companies on the other.

Okoroba, in the Nembe local government area, and Ogboloma, in Gbaraun Clan, are both Ijaw communities in Bayelsa state. While Okoroba is host to SPDC and the Nigerian Agip Oil Company (NAOC), Ogboloma also hosts SPDC. Okoroba is a riverine community, hence fishing is the main subsistence economic activity. Farming is also practised. Ogboloma is also a swampy area, but it has more land for farming. Both communities have suffered from oil spills and pollution recently.[1] There have been intra-community conflicts as well as conflicts between both communities and the oil companies, and women have not been left out of these conflicts in recent times. All the communities studied were ecologically balanced and self-sustaining before the emergence of the oil industry.

The root of women's violence in the case study areas of the Niger Delta region can be sought not only within the sphere of economic production but also in social and cultural structures. Women's experiences of oppression culminating in protests can be traced to the following: land ownership; household relations; socio-economic survival; and patriarchal relations between the state/oil industry and women.

As Ikelegbe and Ikelegbe (2006: 242) observed, 'women's groupings have not only become an active part of civil challenges and popular struggles, but have begun to appropriate traditional forms of resistance'. Examples of women resist-ance date back to the colonial era (van Allen 1972; Mba 1982), but more recently Urhobo women challenged oil companies in Ogharefe in 1984 and Ekpan in 1986. In the 1990s, the protests became better organized. Thus, the Federation of Ogoni Women Associations (FOWA) organized protests against Shell in Ogoniland between 1993 and 1995, while the Niger Delta Women for Justice (NDWJ) mobil-ized women to protest in 1999 in support of the Ijaw Youth Council's Kaiama Declaration, which sought among other things for control of oil by Ijaw people. Women from the Itsekiri and Ijaw ethnic groups also protested against the US oil MNC Chevron in Gbaramatu (Escravos) and Ugborodo, and Shell in Warri, between July and August 2002, blocking oil production until the company signed an agreement based on the women's demands (Ukeje 2004: 606–7).

Conflict: theorizing women's protests

Conflict is an inherent dimension of human and social relations. In the context of relations of production, it often involves struggles over power and resources/ rewards and can be expressed in the form of resistance to domination, dispossession and disempowerment. Wilson and Hannah (1990: 255) describe it as 'a struggle involving ideas, values and/or limited resources'. To Pruitt and Rubin (1986), conflict is a 'perceived divergence of interest or beliefs that the parties' current aspirations cannot be achieved simultaneously'. Conflict is made all the more pervasive in social relations by the problem of scarcity (in the midst of plenty) (CASS 2005). In most cases, states find it extremely difficult to mediate resource struggles and conflicts over 'who gets what, when and how'. In this case, struggles over scarce resources and the need to have access to them create horizontal inequalities and general inequities, which are usually expressed in conflictual terms.

Quite a number of theoretical studies have established the nexus between inequality, poverty and conflict. The frustration-aggression theory is one of the theories that can be used to explain women's protests in the Niger Delta in response to the exercise of power by oil capitalism against the interest of women who bear the exploitative burdens of the oil industry. The frustration-aggression theory suggests that individuals become aggressive when there are obstacles (perceived and real) to their success in life. Frustration in itself is the blocking of ongoing, goal-directed activity rather than an emotional reaction to the blocking (Berkowitz 1997: 182).

This theory is not without its own weakness, as perceived by Konrad Lorenz (1966) in his work *On Aggression*. Nevertheless, frustration-aggression theory has evolved sufficiently to explain protests, riots and, at worst, civil wars in countries, and is relevant in explaining the basis of women's protests in the context of dominant patriarchal relations in the Niger Delta region. Therefore to theorize women's war against big oil companies is, according to Turner and Brownhill (2003), to recognize the erasure of subsistence that corporate commodification entails, and both the imperative and the capacities of life-producers to stand against it.

Niger Delta women retain certain economic responsibilities as wives, mothers, fishers and farmers (even though they are not remunerated). In addition to being food producers, procurers and preparers, they are also expected to be major caregivers and, significantly, income-earners. However, the activities of oil multi-nationals, which have been operating in the region for over five decades, have been destroying the social and physical basis of subsistence and sources of income of rural women. Hitherto silenced, women in the oil-rich Delta have tapped into a history and narratives of women's resistance in their quest for justice and survival. This has also dovetailed with the contesting of their subordination to male power represented at the state, community and oil company levels.

Women's protests in the Niger Delta region

Traditionally in the Niger Delta region, women are faced with various forms of socio-economic oppression. These forms of oppression by the culturally dominant male population, which alienates women from the land that they live off, have been worsened by the depredations of the global oil industry operations in the region. It is within this context that this study examines the social 'patriarchal' relations between women and state–oil capitalism and how the former has been able to interpret the relations in the form of protests and conflicts against the latter. Since the discovery of oil in commercial quantities at Oloibiri in 1956, the Niger Delta region has increasingly been of immense economic importance to Nigeria. For instance, Nigeria's crude oil reserves as at 2007 were in the region of 36.2 billion barrels, while the natural gas reserves were estimated to be 182 trillion cubic feet (EIA 2007). Between 1970 and 2007, Nigeria's revenue from oil exports grew from US$300 million to a staggering US$55billion (Okonjo-Iweala et al. 2003: 1).

In spite of the huge returns on oil exports, the oil-producing Delta communities are experiencing a deepening crisis characterized by economic neglect, environmental insecurity and resource-control politics. Unfortunately, women are the most affected in this economy of oil because, in the cultural division of labour, Niger Delta women are mostly farmers and provide for family subsistence. Hence, they are always the first to recognize any threats to livelihoods, especially when affected by environmental degradation, and are quick to respond to those threats (Dankelman and Davidson 1988: 5–6; Peterson and Runyan 1999; Obi 2004b: 2). Ikelegbe (2005c: 254) describes the various ways in which the women of the Niger Delta region have suffered the consequences of oil exploration. They suffer immensely as a result of oil pollution of the creeks and rivers and the decline in fish stocks. Also, the canalization of the region to bring in heavy oil equipment destroys the fragile ecology, resulting either in the silting up of water bodies or the intrusion of salt water into freshwater bodies with disastrous consequences.

Beyond the economic impact, pollution adversely affects the social lives of women in the Delta. The effluents discharged into freshwater sources contain high amounts of toxic materials such as mercury, which are stored in fish, to be transferred into human beings who consume them. Studies in the Niger Delta have confirmed that its inhabitants who feed on aquatic animals take in a higher level of the cancerous chemicals and suffer the consequences (see Emeseh, this volume). When women's health is affected, invariably farming and fishing are also negatively affected. The problem is further compounded by the lack of early diagnoses and treatment as health facilities are not available in the rural areas.

Most times, oil MNCs deny any responsibility for this sad state of affairs. Owing to the Nigerian state's dependence on oil rents, it tends to overlook the negative practices of the oil industry in the region, and sends in security forces to crush any protests against, or popular demands on, oil MNCs. Although women are largely unwaged and their labour unremitted, oil capital exploits them as it commodifies and uses up 'free' nature, social service, built space and the production of paid and unpaid work (Turner and Brownhill 2003). In response, women express their anger at the perpetuation of the state–oil patriarchy that denies them access to economic and political opportunities, and violates them.

Organization of women's protests in the Niger Delta

Community women do not ordinarily organize themselves mainly for protests. They are generally very organized, and meet weekly, biweekly or monthly to discuss matters of common interest. In Ogboloma, community women hold meetings on a weekly basis; however, these are arranged without conflicting with their commitments to other existing welfare groups to which they belong, such as Ogboloma Ere Ogbo, Ama Miebi and Erewou Ogbo. Apart from the community women's group in Okerenkoko, there are groups such as the Trusted Ladies and Okerenkoko Yerinmene. In Kokodiagbene, groups such as Waritelemo Ogbo and Amatelemo Ogbo exist. In Okoroba community, there are similar community-based groups, but the chief among them is Okoroba Awar Ogbo, meaning 'Okoroba Women's Unity Club'; others include the First Ladies Club, and Ilaye Ila (meaning 'What concerns me concerns you').

These women's community associations serve as pressure groups and thrift societies (Osusu, Osisi), providing seedlings, farming and fishing implements, and regulating sales of agricultural produce by members. Sometimes, women take their marital and family problems to the groups for advice. Membership of these groups cuts across all sections of the community, irrespective of social status. As part of their membership commitment, community women pay a particular amount of money as dues every month and the funds are used for advancing women's interests. However, women collectively belong to the community women's associations such as the Ogboloma Community Women's Group and the Okerenkoko Women's Group, which constitute the major platform from which women mobilize themselves for protests and seek redress on issues affecting them in the communities.

Women leaders are highly respected and they can mobilize women within the community irrespective of the individual group they belong to. Thus, women are easily mobilized. Women leaders and members of the associations' executives need only to use the town crier to attract the attention of the women, go from house to house or use the market network, informing other women of whatever development or issue requires them to gather and take action.

While most men would not want their wives to be mobilized for protests and demonstrations for fear of being wounded or killed by the state security forces, women deliberately avoid involving men because of the probability of their seeking to take over their struggles, and possibly subvert the goals of the women's protests. Also, women are keen to avoid the likelihood that some men will hijack the protest and seek to influence or determine who shares in whatever benefits that may accrue from the protests. Fatima Wariyai, one of the women leaders in the 2002 Gbaramatu women's war, explained in an interview that, for fear of sabotage, men were kept out of the policy decisions that finally culminated in the protests.

The 2002 protest was mainly organized by the Gbaramatu women, including Kenyagbene women (International Crisis Group 2006a: 7). The protest was the result of the presence and activities of oil MNC operations, first in Okerenkoko (SPDC) and second in Kenyagbene (Chevron) for over thirty years, and the result-ant oil spills, gas flares and unfair treatment resulting from oil exploration and production activities. For example, owing to Chevron-Texaco's activities in the community, farms were being damaged, and rivers were covered with oil, therefore suffocating aquatic animals to death.[2] Moreover, there was no potable water in the host communities in Gbaramatu and people relied on the polluted streams and rivers for domestic use, exposing themselves to debilitating health infections and hazards. Rather than clean the oil spills, Chevron always complained of sabotage by indigenes, and generally intimidated them using police and military force. Women bore the brunt of sourcing alternatives to known means of livelihood for their families to survive. According to one of the women leaders in the crisis:[3]

> If you watch carefully, the problem of the Niger Delta is a different ball game altogether and that we the Ijaw women are the ones suffering the most is the most pathetic part in the whole story. If you move around our villages, you will shed tears for us. We live in thatched homes, our beds are terrible, our living conditions are poor. In short, most of us don't have what we could call a home of our own, yet we have all these oil companies on our land.

The immediate trigger of the conflict between the Ijaw Gbaramatu women (Kokodiagbene and Okerenkoko) and Chevron was when in May 2002 the oil company withdrew one of its boats, which used to ferry Kenyagbene women to Warri town on market days. Chevron's decision that women should proceed first to Escravos (a Portuguese word for slave port)[4] before boarding the boats was taken without consulting the Kenyagbene women who would be affected by the decision. Frustrated by this decision, an estimated six hundred women angrily mobilized and blocked the waterways, hindering Chevron-Texaco workers' passage to Escravos from the Abiteye flow station, as a way of showing their displeasure and bringing about a reversal of the decision.

However, Chevron reacted negatively by alerting the State Naval Patrol team, which came in gunboats and attacked and dispersed the unarmed women. The soldiers forcibly capsized the women's boats, throwing them into the river. In the process, a girl drowned and five boats were sunk. This single action by Chevron-Texaco, which had operated in Kenyagbene for over thirty years without putting anything back into the community, further intensified women's frustration, and the aggression that followed.[5] On 17 July 2002, Kenyagbene women, with support from other Gbaramatu women's leaders, who held emergency meetings in their various communities, including Kokodiagbene and Okerenkoko, took over as leaders of the collective, and marched down to the five Chevron flow stations located in the Niger Delta, including Kenyagbene-Abiteye, Makaraba-Otutuana, Dibi, Olero Creek and Opuekeba flow stations,[6] protesting over Chevron's action against Kenyagbene women, the dangers of oil exploitation in their communities, and the long-standing neglect of the area. The protest lasted for ten days.

At the beginning of the crisis, six women took over the security post while others went into the Chevron-Texaco offices and instructed the staff to vacate, except the security personnel and cooks who were cooking for the women. Chevron's planes and helicopters were barred from landing or taking off. The protesters worked on a shift basis, which provided the women with three hours per day in which they could go to their homes, freshen up, eat and resume the protest. Owing to the intensity of the protests, a total of 11,000 barrels per day of oil were shut in, resulting in a huge loss of income to Chevron and the Nigerian state. The women, particularly the elderly ones, also threatened to strip naked in protest, an act regarded locally as a curse. The prolonged protest and occupation of oil installations eventually forced Chevron-Texaco to the negotiating table, and culminated in the signing of a memorandum of understanding (MoU) between the oil company and the Gbaramatu women. However, the MoU was later overtaken by the Global Memorandum of Understanding (GMoU), which was signed in 2005 between Chevron-Texaco and the Gbaramatu leadership.[7]

Between August and October 2008, Okoroba women were locked in protest against Shell over an oil spillage that had occurred from Shell's pipeline. Okoroba has been a pathetic case of Shell's despoliation since 1991, when oil spills destroyed its freshwater swamp, including fish and periwinkles – the main sources of protein among local peoples, and a source of income for fishers. The recent spill originated from Okogbe community in Rivers state and made its way through the creeks to Okoroba community in the last quarter of 2008. The river was the only source of potable water, and its pollution by the oil spill had adverse consequences for the women, whose lives and health were seriously compromised.

As well as women bearing the burden of oil spillages, they are the ones responsible for fetching drinking water from brackish oil-polluted rivers and wells, and their families also suffer health problems after drinking toxic water.[8] In the words of a female interviewee: 'Shell don kill us finish, dem take our land, take our oil, take our health, take our food, take everything and dem no give us nothing, yet they expect us to keep quiet. Never again.'[9] A visit to the cottage

156

Blame on MNCs

hospital confirmed that, owing to the oil spillage, many people, particularly women and children, were hospitalized, and the death of a woman was recorded after she drank the polluted water from the river.[10] Sadly, no action was taken by Shell or the state to clean up the oil spill, whose toxic effects continue to pollute the community's main source of drinking water and destroy local livelihoods.

In a similar vein, Ogboloma community women protested against contractors handling the construction of the Gbarain Ubie Integrated Oil and Gas Project from 16 February to 21 March 2009. Although there had been deep-seated grievances caused by Shell's cavalier treatment of the community, especially women, the immediate cause can be located in the laying of a pipeline across the Taylor creek without due consultation with community women, who use the creek as an exit point to their farms and as a landing point any time their produce is transported from their farms to urban markets. According to the women's leader:[11]

> We cannot do without this river, even our going to the farm is by this river. We transport our food home through the river, and they want to block the creek, even our drinking water is from this creek [...] how are we to transport our fish home [...] that is why we are here, they should tell us how they want the women to cope when going to the bush and how we can transport our food home. They should come and tell us. If not, we shall fight with them.

Another factor that triggered the protest by the women was the incessant male deals with SPDC and SAIPEM (the contractor handling the Gbarain Ubie Gas Project). In response, Ogboloma women came together and appointed a female chief – something that was unprecedented in this male-dominated community – to mobilize the women. The protests resulted in the shutting down of the construction site, the demand for a separate community body for the women, to be headed by the women's leader (*Amananarau*), and the initiation of dethronement moves against Ogboloma's traditional ruler, suspected of having collaborated with other men in the community to collect compensation money from the company for the polluted land without consultation with the women. Under the leadership of the *Amananarau*, the women chased the contractor (SAIPEM) from the site and camped there for nine days, eating and sleeping in the open, vowing not to leave until their demands were met.

Factors engendering women's protests in the Niger Delta region

The problem of land: ownership and patriarchal relations In the Niger Delta region, land is an important asset, which is traditionally controlled by men. Culturally, in the four communities studied, men's dominance is perceived to be very strong both in the home and the community. The implication of the culturally constructed male dominance is that they dominate and exercise power in the decision-making process at the level of the community and their relationships with women. Findings show that women are not part of the traditional decision-making institutions in the area, but their opinions are sought and respected on some vital issues such as conflict mediation.[12] For example, in Gbaramatu Kingdom, women are not allowed to participate in most traditional affairs. Men constitute the membership of the Chiefs' Council and Community Development Committees, which are the decision-making organs. Though some communities have female chiefs who act as women leaders, tradition excludes them from the core decision-making organs. The structure of decision-making in these communities, and by extension the entire Niger Delta region, affects gender relations, property rights and land ownership. Land is culturally passed on from father to son (traditionally, women do not own land) or to a close male relative in the absence of a son to inherit the land.

Though there are portions of land that are communally owned, men own and control most of the land.[13] For example, in Okoroba the land is owned by families but essentially controlled by the men. In a polygamous household, the man shares his portion of land equally among his wives. A man can dispossess his wife of the land if a situation such as divorce arises. Unmarried women do not have the right to land in their parental homes, but as daughters they can assist mothers on their farms. As one female respondent explained, 'The men own the land but when it is time for farming the men will show the women where to farm and they will mark out the land for women to farm.'[14] In other words, men are the owners of the land and women are the owners of the food. It is important to note that whereas the woman is entitled to the proceeds of her farmland, the men share in it. But when an oil company takes over part of the land, the man's right to the land is automatically forfeited and made subject to the decision of the oil company, but the woman loses not only the land, but everything on the land without due compensation.

Compensation for loss of communally owned land paid by oil MNCs is mainly given to men, particularly elders and chiefs, who form alliances with the controllers of oil capital and state power, often getting rich while the women suffer impoverishment. Rather than sharing compensation payments equitably with their family members, they prefer to organize 'get together' (parties) for themselves, and/or they marry more wives, thus worsening women's already bad situation. As a member of this category of women put it, 'Sometimes their actions frustrate us, their wives [...]'[15]

In Ogboloma, women were denied the right to meet and negotiate with the SPDC for compensation alongside with the men. According to an Ogboloma man, 'Women are not allowed to negotiate with oil companies because as the heads of families, it is the sole right of men to protect and advance family's interests.'[16] While some wives could still benefit from compensatory 'ex gratia payments' made to their husbands, women who traditionally do not own land and are unmarried lose out completely on compensation payments, and this unfair segregation excludes women and adversely affects their economic sustenance.

It is against this background that Ogboloma women expressed their desire to put a stop to male domination as it had held the community back. In Kokodiagbene, prior to 2002, women were totally marginalized as men took all critical decisions without women's input, even though the women tilled the land. Since the 2002 'women's war', women have been involved in the making of some decisions affecting the community. However, to one Kokodiagbene's women's leader, women are still marginalized: 'But you know that men will be men, they want to take all the glory, hence when they have to make critical decisions, maybe on allocation of land or sharing of compensation, women are still sidelined and this means that women do not actually own anything. We are turned into their slaves.'[17]

Household relations Household relationships are at the heart of most societies, since families act as the primary cultural unit. The family is an important socio-economic unit, linked to the relations of production and culture. But in the Niger Delta region, while men are seen as pillars of households, women are always at the forefront of family and communal survival. In most cases, in a reversal of responsibility, women are the breadwinners in their families (Okon 2002). In spite of this all-important role, women tend to be marginalized from many issues and are prevented from gaining total authority over household matters.

In the four communities, evidence suggests that, compared to men, women contribute more economically to the family's upkeep by engaging in farming, fishing and petty trading. The only exception is in a case where a husband is a very successful businessman/oil contractor or is someone with a well-paid white-collar job.[18] In Okoroba, the women's leader noted, 'We train our children, pay their school fees, give them money for upkeep and our husbands give us just [a] little support.'[19] This tradition dovetails with the public space where women are not recognized in critical community decisions, especially those concerning land and relations with oil MNCs.

Socio-economic survival of women in the Niger Delta region The Niger Delta ecology largely influences the economic activities of rural women. Apart from farming, such women also engage in fishing for subsistence, collecting snails and periwinkles, weaving, fuelwood gathering, tapping of rubber trees and petty trading. For example, most women in Ogboloma engage in farming and petty trading as the oil-polluted river does not have enough fish to sustain the family, much less provide an occupation for an individual.[20] Owing to the closeness of Kokodiagbene and Okerenkoko to the sea, women engage in fishing and gathering of sea foods, which they combine with trading in fresh and smoked fish at the urban markets of Warri, Sapele and Koko. Some of them also engage in subsistence farming.

In all four communities, in addition to fishing, men engage in hunting, canoe carving, sculpture, brewing of local gin, trading and, in a few cases, menial labour in urban areas, whereas women's lives are tied to traditional farming and fishing. The expansion of oil capitalism in the region not only marginalizes women, but also disempowers them. In the four communities, women could not point to any female counterparts, young or old, who were employed in an oil MNC, whether Agip, Shell or Chevron-Texaco.

Women and state–oil industry domination Once the state government using the Land Use Act (LUA) legally acquires such land with or without paying compensation to its indigenous owners, the people are alienated from the land, and with it their livelihoods. The situation is more pathetic in the Niger Delta, where, owing to the strategic importance of the oil-rich lands, most of the oil-producing communities have lost their land rights to the state and oil companies. What they can lay claim to are just surface rights, but the granting of these is completely subject to the whims of officials in the oil companies and the Nigerian state.

Women also suffer from the pollution and gas flares attendant on oil production activities. In Okoroba community, the women's leader lamented the very frequent oil spills, which have destroyed the land and rivers, rendering the farms unproductive and the rivers devoid of living creatures for years.[21] In the same regard, an elderly woman noted angrily, 'Chevron is a curse and not a blessing to us at all [...] We used to get some food from our rivers before Chevron came but since it began oil exploitation, destroying our river, those species have also disappeared.' For example, an oil spill occurred in 2007, rendering most inhabitants of communities in Gbaramatu homeless and displaced for several days.[22] In response to the constant oil spills some women in Okerenkoko and Kokodiagbene have resorted to selling oil products in the local black market. Though this is risky, they claim it provides money for their daily household needs.[23]

In other cases, some young girls and even young married women engage in commercial sex work, mainly providing sexual services to oil company workers, in order to survive. This has been the case in Ogboloma, where many young girls prefer to go with rich(er) oil workers (mostly expatriates) to the chagrin of unemployed local men.[24] Oil workers and some local men use the wealth generated from oil to 'buy' women's bodies. There have also been instances of sexual violence against women. Although the prices of women's bodies are negotiated, the poor(er) women are often at a disadvantage and can hardly negotiate safe sex or reproductive health rights in the context of the multiple relations they maintain with rich(er) men. A consequence of the sex trade involving oil workers and some women in the region is the prevalence of sexually transmitted diseases (STDs), including HIV/AIDs.

Women's protests – successes or failures?

Though women's protests are not comparable with men's violent actions, such protests have paid off in some ways. In the cases of Okerenkoko and Kokodiagbene, the strategies employed achieved varying degrees of success. Though the protests occurred in 2002, it is only recently that some of the benefits have started trickling down to indigenes. Chevron-Texaco's GMoU outlines the stakeholders' commitment to participatory partnership, transparency and accountability (see Zalik, this volume). The company also invests in building community capacity for sustainable development and conflict resolution in the region (Adekoye 2006). Following Chevron-Texaco's example, Shell introduced the GMoU in all oil-operating communities. In Okoroba and Ogboloma, Bayelsa state, women were invited by Shell and Agip to negotiate with them, with promises that the GMoU would be implemented.

Women's groups now make their impact felt as Chevron now liaises with them on various issues in Gbaramatu. Though Chevron has not increased the scholarship for secondary school students, it increased tertiary institutions' scholarships to N60,000. An entrepreneurial development scheme was also launched by Shell in 2006 in Kokodiagbene, and buses were given to the community. A micro-credit scheme was introduced, which includes the granting of soft loans to women as a form of socio-economic empowerment. But as at the time of the study, women had not received them. According to one respondent, Faith Irite, 'We heard that the money has been released but we don't know to whom and where. Nevertheless, we are doing our own investigation to see whether it is true or not.'[25] But a Shell oil worker noted that 'Shell has worked out an empowerment scheme to give women a sense of belonging and partnership with the hope that the move will win peace.'[26] What should be noted is that, in all this, the power relations have remained skewed against the women, and remain in favour of the oil companies.

Beyond the aforementioned paltry outcomes, there are still running battles between the communities and oil MNCs over the non-fulfilment of the essential aspects of the GMoU. Both communities still lack good roads. Potable drinking water is non-existent and has to be brought in from Warri, which is about two hours' journey in a motorized speedboat. Those communities continue to suffer from oil spillages, which destroy their ecosystems and livelihoods, giving rise to new phases of protests, such as occurred in 2008 and were stopped by the brute force employed by the state's security forces.

Conclusion

Grassroots mobilization by women against the state–oil business partnership and dominant patriarchal relations in Niger Delta society has led to mixed results. The cases of Okerenkoko, Kokodiagbene, Ogboloma and Okoroba indicate that, beyond male domination, the domination by state–oil capitalism has triggered women's protests and resistance in rural communities of the Niger Delta. In spite of the peaceful nature of women's protests, the state, in support of oil MNCs, has deployed brutal force against women. In spite of some positive recorded outcomes, women in the oil-rich Niger Delta region are still marginalized and suffer brutalization in the course of the just struggles for gender rights in the context of the overall struggle for resource control and self-determination in the region.

This trend has become paramount even in the Nigerian state's bid to promote peace and development in the region. Women have been largely excluded from government's efforts to institutionalize peace and development in the Niger Delta. Out of the forty members of the Niger Delta Technical Committee appointed in 2009 to come up with a report and appropriate recommendations for peace and development in the region, only four are women.[27] The newly created Niger Delta Ministry has mainly men in positions of authority. To worsen the situation, the interests of women are not catered for in terms of the objectives of its establishment.[28] In the view of Chief Mamamu, 'as long as hardships continue, and as long as the economic livelihoods of the women [are] endlessly decimated by the oil companies without redress, the possibility of future conflicts by women should not be ruled out'.[29]

To address the challenges confronting women in the Niger Delta, the following recommendations are made to all stakeholders in the Niger Delta region, including men, traditional rulers, oil companies and the Nigerian state. Women's rights should be respected and women recognized as co-equals. Traditional structures and values that tend to marginalize women should be systematically dismantled through proactive social and civic policies. Women should be empowered to take part in decision-making at the family, community and public levels. This can be achieved through consistent advocacy of women's participation in decision-making pertaining to the oil industry, and through the education of traditional elite authorities, by human-rights-based civil society/community-based organizations on the need to open up the public space for women, and indeed to learn from them regarding the management of environmental/natural resources, conflict mediation and local development.

Another issue that needs to be addressed is land ownership by women, since it is now appreciated that land is extremely important to women's survival in the oil-rich communities. It is recommended that the state should embark on land reforms that would give women, married, single or divorced, rights to own land. This will give women, especially those who till the land, better opportunities to raise capital, earn better incomes, and have a stronger basis on which to demand compensation from oil MNCs when oil spills and related accidents occur. In addition, it will give them the autonomy to decide how to spend the compensation payments instead of being dominated by men, who appropriate such payments for personal use.

Oil multinationals should be sensitive to their corporate social responsibilities in the region, especially insofar as they affect the livelihoods and welfare of women. Responsible clean-ups of oil spills, provision of modern medical facilities and drugs associated with common and perceived potential diseases arising from oil activities must be provided. In the same regard, optimal conditions should be created for the employment and retention of qualified doctors and nurses in these communities. Second, education of girls and women should be very well taken care of by the state and the oil business. Special scholarships for girls and women's education and vocational training to the highest levels will resolve some problems, such as prostitution, and subsequently reduce the levels of sexually transmitted diseases in the region.

Finally, the state should negotiate and reach a social contract with Nigerian women. Gender should be mainstreamed in peacebuilding in the Niger Delta. The disarmament, demobilization and reintegration (DDR) aspect of the recently concluded amnesty programme glaringly shows the continued marginalization of women. Women should also be reintegrated, having suffered untold multiple physical, emotional, psychosocial and gendered violence from the state, oil multinationals and men in the oil-rich areas of the Niger Delta region. Without integrating women as a social category into the democracy and development projects, peace in the Niger Delta cannot be sustainable in the long run.

PART THREE

Oil MNCs' response(s)

12 | Corporate social responsibility and the Niger Delta conflict: issues and prospects

Uwafiokun Idemudia

Introduction

Corporate Social Responsibility (CSR) is a means by which businesses frame their attitudes, strategies and relationships with their stakeholders (Jenkins 2004). However, CSR remains an embryonic and contested concept (Windsor 2006). This is because critics and proponents hold different perceptions and understandings of the role and purpose of the corporation in society (Idemudia and Ite 2006a). Nonetheless, while there might be no consensual definition of CSR, the concept is often taken to mean that businesses have obligations to society that go beyond profit-making to include helping to solve societal and ecological problems (Idemudia 2008). Hence, it is no surprise that in the name of CSR, MNCs are at once being taken to task for exacerbating armed conflict and participating in its prevention and resolution (Berman 2000; Haufler 2004a). For example, Banfield et al. (2005) have noted that conflict-sensitive business and its promotion by public policy-making institutions represent an important part of a collective and multi-actor effort to create a more peaceful world.

The demand for active business involvement in issues of peace and conflict rests on the assumption that companies are inevitably a part of the local context as their activities impact on the environment and the lives of people in their areas of operation and they cannot separate themselves from the dynamics of local conflict. This is because corporate activities are bound to have either a positive or a negative impact on conflict dynamics but never a neutral one (Zandvliet 2005). Unfortunately, the interface between MNCs and conflict is yet to be fully understood (see Banfield et al. 2005; Zandvliet 2005). This is due to the fact that for most businesses conflict dynamics often enters into strategic business decisions largely in terms of 'political risk' and how it might affect business operations and profit.

In contrast, the reverse logic of how business decisions and operations impact on conflict dynamics is often neglected (Banfield et al. 2005; Zandvliet 2005). However, new insights have recently been generated with regard to the MNCs–conflict nexus. Banfield et al. (2005) have suggested that MNCs can have two kinds of impact on conflict: the impact of corporate operations on local relationships (micro-level impact) and the impact of foreign investment on the host country's political, economic and natural environment (macro-level impact), both of which are intertwined in ways that make them difficult to separate (see Haufler 2004a). Similarly, Nelson (2000) noted that MNCs can contribute to conflict prevention and management via core business operations, social investment programmes and engagement in policy dialogue and civic institutional building.

Business can play a role in conflict prevention and management by adopting CSR principles and practices (Bennett 2002). However, there has been limited explicit focus on the relationship between CSR initiatives and conflict. Haufler (2004b) noted that we still do not have sufficient empirical evidence to make any judgement on whether corporate conflict prevention initiatives do actually reduce conflict. Similarly, Ballentine and Nitzschke (2004) also noted that the CSR approach to managing conflict suffers from the absence of a sound analytical basis. Hence, there is an overarching need to further explore the extent to which CSR can serve as an effective vehicle for conflict prevention and management.

Conflict between local communities and oil MNCs in the Niger Delta provides a fertile ground for exploring these issues. The persistent incidences of oil workers being kidnapped, sabotage of oil facilities and human rights violations have had a negative impact on both government revenue and corporate profit (see Idemudia 2009a). As a result, after decades of initially rejecting CSR, oil MNCs have sought to secure their social licence to operate, legitimize their position, and respond to local and international criticisms by adopting CSR initiatives as a strategy for responding to and managing conflict in the region. However, despite the widespread adoption of CSR in the Nigerian oil industry, violence in the region has increased both in intensity and scale, and oil MNCs continue to be held responsible for a range of infractions by local communities (Idemudia and Ite 2006a). This situation suggests that there are gaps between the nature of and the quality of CSR initiatives aimed at changing the hostile attitude of local communities towards oil companies, and addressing the violent conflict in the Niger Delta. This chapter critically examines the CSR–conflict nexus in the Niger Delta and offers possible insights into ways of strengthening CSR as a strategy for managing corporate–community conflict.

Oil multinationals and the dynamics of CSR strategies in the Niger Delta: trends and issues

Nigeria's crude oil is extracted mainly from the Niger Delta (see Figure 12.1). The revenue derived from crude oil sales accounts for 40 per cent of Nigeria's GDP, 95 per cent of the country's total export revenue, and 80 per cent of government revenue. However, despite the region's immense contribution to national wealth, poverty and unemployment levels in the Niger Delta are higher than the national average. In addition, 70 per cent of the people live in rural communities with no access to basic social amenities like potable water, good roads, electricity supply and healthcare facilities (TCND 2008; Idemudia 2009b). It is against this background that corporate–community relations metamorphosed from being relatively peaceful in the 1960s to outright violence in the 1990s.

A defining moment in this transformation of community relations, due largely to oil MNCs' and governmental neglect, reflected in decades of oil-related environmental degradation in the region, was the 1990s grassroots-community peaceful protest led by the MOSOP. The fall-out from this protest and the subsequent negative international backlash for the reputation of oil MNCs pushed them to adopt CSR strategies as a method of managing corporate–community relations in the Niger Delta. The logic behind the adoption of CSR principles is that CSR initiatives that contribute to sustainable community development will address local grievances, and make peace more attractive than conflict. This is because local communities are unhappy with the deleterious impact of MNCs' operations in the region. CSR initiatives are therefore supposed to address local grievances, improve local livelihoods (that is, offer a peace dividend) and secure a social licence to operate (see Figure 12.1).

Oil MNC principles	Goal	Expected outcome
CSR initiatives	Community development	Conflict reduction and livelihood dividend

FIGURE 12.1 Conceptual linkage of CSR and conflict in the Niger Delta

The approach of most oil companies, like Shell, ExxonMobil, Total and Chevron-Texaco, to Corporate Social Responsibility in the Niger Delta has evolved over time through three main phases. The discovery of crude oil in commercial quantities in 1956 was followed by the first phase of the community relations strategy adopted by oil MNCs. This phase can be called the 'pay-as-you-go approach' to corporate–community relations. This is because in this first phase, the idea was to keep communities at arm's length as much as possible while securing local right-of-way (ROW). CSR was therefore largely an 'add-on' to MNCs' business strategy. Hence, oil companies gave local communities one-time gifts as they saw fit, and such gifts were often restricted to communities where either oil wells are located, or pipelines pass through (Idemudia 2009b).

Following a decade of the pay-as-you-go strategy, with no real substantive benefits accruing to local communities, and constant military repression of community protests, a volatile atmosphere characterized by a vicious cycle of protest, repression and conflict was created in the Niger Delta. Hence, by the 1990s, as a response to increased community protest (by MOSOP and other groups in the Niger Delta) over environmental degradation, limited employment, loss of livelihoods and widespread human rights violations, oil companies began to adopt the second generation of a corporate strategy on community relations.

This second phase was based on the acceptance of CSR as being critical to continued oil exploration. Consequently, most oil companies began to adopt a community assistance/community development model for engagement with host communities. However, problems associated with this model, such as poor community participation, lack of project sustainability and the tendency of community development projects to spur intra- and inter-community violence owing to competition for such projects, resulted in a shift towards the third phase of the corporate–community involvement strategy.

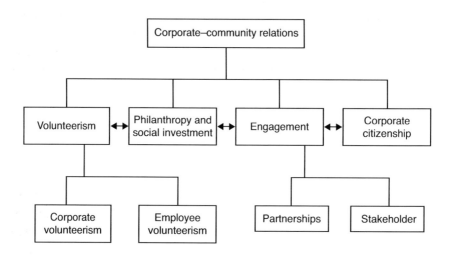

FIGURE 12.2 Corporate–community relations practices (*source*: author)

The third phase of community relations was based largely on the ideals of partnership. This is due to oil MNCs' need to reduce the skyrocketing cost of community relations[1] and to address the gaps associated with previous strategies. While some oil companies like Shell and Chevron have opted for an in-house-controlled corporate–community involvement model in partnership with local communities under the umbrella of a Global Memorandum of Understanding (GMoU), others, such as Total and Statoil, have adopted a corporate–community Foundation Model as the preferred strategy for corporate–community involvement (Idemudia 2009b). Nonetheless, the extent to which the present approaches to community relations have been able to address community grievances and developmental expectations remains questionable (Idemudia 2009a).

CSR practices in the oil industry often take one or more of several forms (see Figure 12.2). Figure 12.2 suggests that while businesses might opt to use only philanthropy and social investment as the avenues for addressing their CSR obligations, they can also simultaneously employ stakeholder engagement and volunteerism. These different CSR practices are not mutually exclusive and, in fact, most companies tend to engage with CSR through more than one form of CSR practice. For example, ExxonMobil employs philanthropy and employee volunteerism in implementing its CSR obligation in Akwa Ibom state. In addition, volunteerism can be either employee- or corporate-driven, and stakeholder engagement can be through partnership or stakeholder dialogue.

CSR–conflict nexus: conceptual framework

The understanding of CSR that informs much of the discussion here is that CSR entails the integration of social and environmental concerns into core business operations and in its interactions with stakeholders (van Marrewijk 2003). This definition of CSR goes beyond the limited conception of CSR as corporate philanthropy, which has been a subject of criticism. Similarly, the definition encompasses different ways through which business can contribute to conflict prevention and management as identified by Nelson (2000). It is therefore suitable for exploring the complex relationship between CSR and conflict. From a critical CSR perspective, the conflict around oil extraction in the Niger Delta is a function of the breakdown of stakeholder relationships (that is, government–local communities, corporate–community and business–government relationships).

This stakeholder perspective to the conflict in the Niger Delta has three principal ramifications for any critical discussions of the CSR–conflict nexus. First, it suggests that the analyst must accept that there are limits to what CSR can achieve with regard to conflict management. Second, oil MNCs affect conflict dynamics both directly via corporate–community relations and indirectly via the business–government relationship, given the nature of concessional agreements over oil extraction. Third, since CSR initiatives are not undertaken in a vacuum but within a specific context, the presence or absence of an enabling environment for CSR needs to be factored into any critical analysis (see also Banfield et al. 2005).

The analysis that follows proceeds from the assumption that oil MNCs can best contribute to conflict prevention and management through CSR initiatives that seek to maximize the potential positive social and economic impact of oil extraction while simultaneously actively seeking ways to minimize the negative impact of oil extraction on local communities. This proposition is consistent with the assertion of Ballentine and Nitzschke (2004) that in order to better understand the effectiveness of CSR in managing the impact of business in zones of conflict, we need to focus not only on the companies' 'capacity to promote peace' but also on the requirement that core business operations 'do no harm'.

Corporate Social Responsibility and conflict in the Niger Delta: opportunities and challenges

There are four dimensions to the Niger Delta conflict that define the 'conflict environment' in which oil MNCs operate. These are:

1 political/electoral conflict;
2 local community–government conflict, including attacks on oil MNCs, based on the perception that companies are proxies of government;
3 intra- and inter-community violence;
4 corporate–community conflict.

In practice, it is difficult to draw clear lines of distinction between these dimensions of the conflict because they are often intertwined owing to the centrality of oil to Nigeria's political economy. While the multidimensional nature of the Niger Delta conflict explains why there are limits to what CSR can achieve, the centrality of oil to conflict dynamics in the region highlights the significant latitude of opportunity for oil MNCs' leverage or buy-in to projects/ initiatives designed to prevent, manage and resolve conflict around their areas of operation. However, we argue that while CSR has the potential to contribute to conflict reduction in the region, a number of factors may constrain its effectiveness.

The CSR–conflict nexus: structural constraints

The structural factors that constrain CSR effectiveness are manifest in the capital-intensive nature of the oil industry, the logic of capitalist production and profitability, and a skewed CSR agenda. Employment opportunities in oil MNCs can contribute to conflict prevention and management through the improvement of socio-economic conditions in their host communities. Indeed, Haufler (2001) noted that the investments, economic activities and employment that oil MNCs bring can be an indirect means of promoting peace. Jobs in oil MNCs in Nigeria are among the highest paid in the country.

It is claimed by an oil MNC source that a single employee of an oil company takes care of between ten and fifteen members of his/her immediate and extended family (SPDC 2000). It is therefore common for local communities to demand and expect employment from oil MNCs operating within their communities. When such expectations are not met it is not unusual for conflict to ensue between youths and the oil companies (Idemudia 2007). Unfortunately, the potentially positive impact of employment opportunities in the oil industry on corporate–community tensions is often not realized, for reasons described later.

Drawing from personal experience, field study and direct observation,[2] only two core factors are highlighted here. First, the technical skills required for most jobs in the oil industry are often lacking in host communities owing to low levels of education and decades of political and economical marginalization of the Niger Delta region (see Ako, this volume). For example, only about 18.1 per cent of the respondents in the survey villages in Akwa Ibom state had tertiary education (see Table 12.1).

TABLE 12.1 Educational distribution of respondents by village (figures in brackets are percentages)

Education	Ikot Ebidang	Inua Eyet Ikot	Emereoke 1	Ikot Abasi Idem	Total
Secondary	9 (28)	37 (53)	15 (35)	3 (20)	64 (40)
Primary	14 (44)	7 (10)	13 (30)	1 (7)	35 (22)
Tertiary	2 (6)	21 (30)	6 (14)	0 (0)	29 (18)
No formal education	2 (6)	3 (4)	9 (21)	11 (73)	25 (16)
Others	5 (15.6)	2 (3)	0 (0)	0 (0)	7 (4)
Total	32 (100)	70 (100)	43 (100)	15 (100)	160 (100)

Source: Author's survey

A shortage of technical skills often means highly paid technical jobs that could have gone to members of host communities go either to people from other non-oil-producing communities or to expatriates. A male respondent in Iko village expatiated on the situation further, asserting that:

> You see, sometimes it is difficult to blame these oil companies. Our people are not educationally equipped for most jobs in the petroleum industry. It is therefore not possible for them to employ most of us, as we would like them to do. But most people don't know this as they just assume that once you go to university, a graduate is a graduate.

Second, oil MNCs have made some efforts to address the problem of lack of capacity in host communities by the establishment of training centres. An example is the Mobil training school in Eket, which aims to help build local capacity for low-skilled technical jobs in the oil industry. However, the impact of such initiatives is limited This is because of the capital-intensive – as opposed to labour-intensive – nature of the oil industry, as a result of which only a small number of jobs are created. For example, only about 9 per cent of the respondents in the survey villages have been employed by oil MNCs (see Table 12.2).

TABLE 12.2 Respondents' employment in oil MNCs by village (figures in brackets are percentages)

Employment in oil MNCs	Ikot Ebidang	Inua Eyet Ikot	Emereoke 1	Ikot Abasi Idem	Total
No	32 (100)	58 (83)	41 (95)	14 (93)	145 (91)
Yes	0 (0)	12 (17)	2 (5)	1 (7)	15 (9)
Total	32 (100)	70 100)	43 (100)	15 (100)	160 (100)

Source: Author's survey

Hence, the opportunity for conflict reduction via employment opportunities is severely limited. A chi-squared test of data in Table 12.2 yielded a significant result (chi-squared = 9.54; degree of freedom = 3; P = 0.23).

The result implied that there are differences in the number of people employed by oil MNCs across the survey villages. The relatively higher number of people hired in Inua Eyet Ikot is responsible for the deviation observed. This is because, unlike the other survey villages, Inua Eyet Ikot is the immediate host community of ExxonMobil, which can directly enforce the social licence to operate.

In addition, out of the fifteen people that oil MNCs employed, twelve had temporary employment and three had full-time employment (see Table 12.3). Generally, temporary employees or contract workers do not receive the same benefits as full-time employees. Consequently, the argument that a single employee of an oil MNC by virtue of his/her wages can take care of ten to fifteen people is not necessarily applicable to most host communities, since the argument fails to take into consideration that the bulk of the employment opportunities usually available to host communities are low-skilled temporary positions and do not pay as much as management positions.

TABLE 12.3 Nature of respondents' employment by village

Nature of employment	Ikot Ebidang	Inua Eyet Ikot	Emereoke 1	Ikot Abasi Idem	Total
Temporary	0	9	2	1	12
Full time	0	3	0	0	3
Total	0	12	2	1	15

Source: Author's survey

Furthermore, CSR in the Nigerian oil industry is structurally constrained by the logic of capitalist production and profitability. Given the cost that is often associated with CSR practices, oil MNCs continually choose profitability over making meaningful contributions to conflict prevention that might incur cost not compensated for in profit. This problem is particularly accentuated in the oil industry, where there are limited opportunities for competitive advantage and profitability often largely depends on the capacity to externalize the cost of production. For example, oil companies save significant amounts of money by using old oil pipelines and other installations instead of investing in new ones, which results in oil pollution and indirectly in corporate–community conflict (Frynas 1998).

In addition, CSR is a domain of political contestation as opposed to being an ideationally neutral terrain. For example, oil MNCs often seek to pass on as much as possible of the cost of CSR to government. They are able to do this by virtue of their control over operating costs in the joint venture contract (JVC). Similarly, instead of incurring the cost passed on by MNCs, the state is often willing to pass on such costs to local communities in the form of poor regulation of the oil industry. This is due to the fact that government would have to bear about 55 per cent of any additional cost of operation due to regulation. As such, environmental laws are framed in such a way that the oil industry could comply with them without taking on serious additional costly measures. For example, fines for violating the gas-flaring legislations were fixed at such insignificant rates that it made it more economically rational for MNCs to continue gas flaring and pay the fine rather than obey to the law (Frynas 2000).

Oil MNCs' efforts at conflict prevention and management are limited by virtue of the skewed nature of their CSR agenda. Oil MNCs can contribute to conflict reduction in the Niger Delta via active engagement with micro and macro CSR issues. Micro-CSR activities are typically directed at local communities directly affected by the companies' operations and by nature are 'benign' issues that benefit both the companies' reputation and community development. By contrast, macro-CSR issues are potentially 'malign' in the sense that oil companies run a potential risk of involvement in such issues (Gulbrandsen and Moe 2007).

Consequently, oil MNCs in the Niger Delta have largely pursued micro-level CSR activities, to the detriment of active engagement with macro-CSR issues. For example, while oil MNCs are known to build roads and schools in host communities, they generally tend to be less than active in the fight against corruption or the acknowledgement of the problem of 'resource curse'. Unfortunately, while attention to micro-CSR issues might address some aspects of local grievances that drive violence in the region, it is unable to deal with the root causes of grievances. This is because events at the micro level (that is, in the host communities) are often consequences of action or inaction at both state and national levels. Hence, conflicts in the region including the incidence of corporate–community violence are not simply a function of what oil MNCs have done or failed to do; rather, they are due to governance deficits that oil MNCs' actions or inactions have accentuated. Thus, addressing macro- and micro-CSR issues together is critical for the reduction of violence in the Niger Delta.

The tendency to pay less attention to macro-CSR issues in the Nigerian oil industry can be attributed to a number of reasons, but two are of particular relevance here. The first is the problem of collective action in the Nigerian oil industry. While oil MNCs' involvement in macro-CSR issues carries an enormous amount of risk for their bottom line, the benefits of such involvement are public goods (that is, there is real potential for free-riding). In an environment like the oil industry, where competition is fierce and corporate attitudes to CSR are diverse, rational utility-maximizing actors like oil MNCs are more likely to free-ride than to unilaterally incur costs associated with involvement in macro-CSR issues. This is especially the case given the voluntary nature of CSR. For example, ExxonMobil's tendency to oppose new standards of fiscal transparency, in contrast to BP's attitude, was reflected when ExxonMobil indirectly criticized BP for disclosing payments to the Angolan government (Skjearseth et al. 2004).[3]

Second, macro-CSR issues such as corruption, poverty and inequitable distribution of oil revenue, which Bennett (2002) sees as the three principal causes of conflict, also touch on issues of sovereignty and public authority, a traditional preserve of the nation-state. Consequently, oil MNCs often cite the lack of legitimacy and the associated problems of interfering in the domestic affairs of a sovereign state as reasons behind limited involvement with these issues in Nigeria. For example, Shell frequently turned to this argument to justify its failure to prevent massive human rights abuses by the Nigerian state during the Ogoni crisis and its principle of non-involvement in the flawed trial and the judicial killing of Ken Saro-Wiwa in 1995. However, while such concerns might be true, such assertions are often used to mask the strong element of self-interest that underpins oil MNCs' choice of inaction in these areas. This is because unilateral actions by oil MNCs on these issues mean they risk losing the goodwill of the Nigerian authorities, or even of falling out with them, with potentially severe business consequences. Hence, the neglect of macro-CSR issues is perhaps a deliberate effort by oil MNCs in the Niger Delta to avoid upsetting the Nigerian government and undermining their business interests.

The CSR–conflict nexus: CSR practices and systemic issues

Some host communities in the Niger Delta have benefited from oil MNCs' CSR initiatives. For example, ExxonMobil has provided roads, renovated schools, provided electricity and supported local clinics in Inua Eyet Ikot, its immediate host community. These amenities are often lacking in other neighbouring communities owing to governmental failure to provide them. However, corporate–community relations are often conflictual, even in the communities that have supposedly benefited from corporate social investment. Oil companies tend to attribute this situation to high community expectations, which might partly be the case.

But a careful analysis suggests that the real reason behind corporate–community conflict is the systemic deficiencies inherent in CSR initiatives at the levels of design and implementation. These deficiencies are both a cause and a consequence of violence in the region. For instance, in the rush to address violence in the region, some oil MNCs initiated CSR programmes which have also inadvertently fostered intra- and inter-community violence. Systemic deficiencies in CSR manifest themselves in the tendency to use CSR more as a business tool than a development tool, failure to integrate social and environmental concern into core business operations, and a disjuncture in corporate–community world views.

The overemphasis on the business-case logic in the design and implementation of CSR initiatives in the oil industry in the past decade has meant that core community needs like poverty reduction are often only partially targeted. Also, local knowledge is sidelined. Emphasis tends also to be laid on immediate host communities to the detriment of neighbouring host communities, which has often spurred inter- and intra-community violence.[4] Limited contextual analysis has meant that CSR initiatives have contributed to the breakdown of traditional institutions, and the proliferation of failed development projects in the Niger Delta.[5] In other instances, instead of constructive community engagement, which is cited as costly by oil MNCs, the monetization of community relations through cash payment to youths as 'sit-at-home allowance' under the 'pay-as-you-go' strategy has fuelled violence.[6] This is not only because such monies are used to purchase weapons for violent ends, but also because such a strategy implicitly rewards negative instead of positive behaviour (Idemudia and Ite 2006a; Zandvliet 2005).

It is important to acknowledge that the recent admission by Shell that it contributed to fuelling violence in the region has brought about a modest change in its corporate–community relations strategy in the form of a GMoU (see BBC News 2004; also Zalik, this volume). However, Idemudia (2009a) points out that while the GMoU strategy might offer an opportunity to mitigate the intra- and inter-community violence, its broader impact on poverty reduction, capacity-building and livelihood improvement remains debatable.

Furthermore, oil extraction in Nigeria is undertaken in a vulnerable ecology, where over 70 per cent of the population depends on fishing and farming (Figure 12.1). To complicate matters, the oil industry by nature is an enclave economy with limited forward and backward linkages to the broader economy. These conditions invariably make it paramount that integrating social and environmental concerns into core business operation is central to any CSR initiatives in the Niger Delta. Unfortunately, despite widespread claims by oil companies that they adhere to CSR principles, communities continue to bear the full brunt of the negative social and environmental externalities that arise from crude oil extraction. For example, between 2000 and 2004 roughly 5,400 incidences of oil spills were officially recorded (Onwuchekwa 2004). Recent empirical studies undertaken by Idemudia (2009a) and Olujide (2006) have shown that communities in the Niger Delta continue to identify inability to fish and farm, damage to house roofing, health problems and low crop yield as the most serious negative impacts of oil extraction in the region (see Emeseh, Oluwaniyi, this volume).

The failure of oil MNCs to adequately address the negative social and environmental impacts of their day-to-day operations on host communities means that community livelihoods are still in jeopardy, with no alternatives being created. Consequently, while oil MNCs engage in providing social infrastructure, the root causes of corporate–community conflicts are not being addressed. This explains why corporate–community relations continue to remain volatile in the region, despite widespread claims of CSR adoption by oil companies.

The categories used by community members in the Niger Delta to interpret and understand their relationship with oil MNCs are largely based on cultural values and traditional forms of relationships (Idemudia 2007). Hence, oil MNCs are seen as members of host communities that should, like every other member of the community, instinctively take into consideration community concerns in their decision-making process and treat community issues as priority issues without community pressure to do so.

In contrast, the worldview of oil MNCs is shaped by a pure market logic driven by profitability and the assumption that everyone will benefit from oil exploration activities (Jenkins 2004). They believe that as private enterprises, once they pay their taxes, government, and not they, should be largely responsible for community development and the redistribution of the wealth generated from oil exploration. This clash in worldviews and expectations between communities and oil MNCs invariably fosters the violation of the psychological contract[7] that exists between local communities and MNCs from the perspective of the communities (Idemudia 2007). This violation of the psychological contract provides fertile ground for the negative perceptions of oil MNCs, which feed into corporate–community violence. Wheeler et al. (2002) point out that while oil MNCs often focus on scientific evidence from scientific studies and other conventional environmental impact assessments (EIAs), which they consider useful, they ignore the issue of perception and constructed 'reality' from the perspective of the community. A case in point was when the host communities in eastern Obolo rejected the EIA carried out by Total (EPNL) for the Amenam/Kpono Oil and Gas Export Project (AKOGEP) because they strongly felt that the final report failed to address their environmental and economic concerns and that they stood to be most directly negatively affected by the project (Alexander's Gas and Oil Connections 2004). Indeed, a male resident of Iko village in eastern Obolo stated in an interview that:

> Most EIA reports not only fail to allow for sufficient community input but also they are in most cases biased in favour of the oil companies. Besides, corruption between oil MNCs and government officials often means EIA reports are not adequately verified by government officials before they are endorsed.

The failure to pay attention to the 'psychological contract' and to integrate community perceptions into the design and implementation of CSR initiatives has meant oil MNCs are often unable to secure community support. As such, they are not given the benefit of the doubt in the event of crisis or accidents, and violence is more likely to ensue in response to every corporate misdemeanour.

The CSR–conflict nexus: questions of an enabling environment

A critical perspective on the CSR–conflict nexus requires a focus on not just the actions and inaction of oil MNCs, but also on stakeholder reciprocal responsibility. Unfortunately, analysts often fail to realize that insisting on the social responsibilities of business in no way replaces or displaces the social responsibilities of other stakeholders (Idemudia 2008). Crucial to the effectiveness of CSR, therefore, is the presence or absence of an enabling environment and, by association, effective governance. According to Fox et al. (2002), an enabling environment implies a policy environment that encourages business activities that minimize environmental and social costs while at the same time maximizing economic gains. They point out that CSR is, at its core, a process of managing the cost and benefit of business activity to both internal and external stakeholders. Setting the boundaries for how these costs and benefits are managed is partly a question of business policy and strategy and partly a question of public governance.

Consequently, governments not only have an important role to play, but also how they play this role is critical to whether or not CSR will achieve the desired outcomes for stakeholders. Unfortunately, the rentier nature of the state, and the politics of anxiety that is informed by the complex nation-building project of the Nigerian state, have meant that the Nigerian government has been unable to adequately address its stakeholder responsibility and create an enabling environment for CSR.

TABLE 12.4 Public sector roles

Mandating	'Command and control' legislation	Regulators and inspectorates	Legal and fiscal penalties and rewards
Facilitating	'Enabling' legislation	Creating incentives	Capacity-building
	Funding support	Raising awareness	Stimulating markets
Partnering	Combining resources	Stakeholder engagement	Dialogue
Endorsing	Political support		Publicity and praise

Source: Fox et al. (2002)

Fox et al. (ibid.) identified mandating, facilitating, partnering and endorsing as the key public sector roles government can play in order to ensure an enabling environment for CSR (see Table 12.4). In Nigeria, a number of public sector institutions have been created by the state to engage with these different roles (see Table 12.5). However, the extent to which each of the state institutions has been able to deliver on its responsibility remains questionable, with ramifications for CSR capacity to reduce conflict in the Niger Delta. Available evidence suggests that in principle the Nigerian government might be taking its role in promoting CSR seriously. For example, to deal with the issue of corruption and lack of transparency in the oil industry, Nigeria was the first nation to sign up to the voluntary Extractive Industry Transparency Initiative (EITI) (see Table 12.5).

In addition, the Nigerian senate, with regard to its standard-setting obligations, unanimously passed the Oil and Gas Bill in 2004, which stipulates the social responsibility of oil MNCs operating in the country (Aziken 2004). However, in practice, governmental efforts to ensure an enabling environment for CSR have largely been inadequate. To take the example of mandating: while Nigerian environmental laws are said to be comparable to those of western Europe and North America (Hara 2001), a combination of limited technical and human capacity, corruption and institutional decay has largely meant poor enforcement of existing regulation.

Similarly, while the Nigeria Extractive Industry Transparency Initiative (NEITI) was set up to address issues of corruption and mismanagement, failure to extend this initiative to state and local government levels and the emphasis on governmental income over governmental spending have limited the positive impact of NEITI. For example, the former chairman of the Economic and Financial Crimes Commission (EFCC), Mallam Nuhu Ribadu, recently asserted that the Commission was about to commence the prosecution of thirty-one governors (out of a total of thirty-six) in the country for money laundering, the looting of state treasuries, diversion of funds and other corrupt practices (This Day News 2006; Ekpunobi 2006).

TABLE 12.5 CSR roles and government agencies

Public sector roles	Principal Nigerian government agencies
Mandating	Department of Petroleum Resources (DPR), and Federal Ministry of Environment
Facilitating	Nigeria Extractive Industry Transparency Initiatives (NEITI)
Partnering	Niger Delta Development Commission (NDDC), Ministry for Niger Delta
Endorsing	Federal, state and local government officers

In addition, despite a significant increase in the derivation principle monies allocated to the Niger Delta region, local communities have nothing to show for it (chapters by Ako, Ibaba, this volume). For example, despite an increase in oil revenue allocated to Rivers state (see Figure 12.4), local communities have no tangible benefits to show for such an increase in state government revenue.

Furthermore, the establishment of the Niger Delta Development Commission (NDDC) provided an important institutional mechanism to facilitate partnership between government and oil MNCs to promote development and therefore reduce conflict in the region. However, poor governmental funding has undermined the capacity of the agency. For example, although the federal government was required by law to make an allocation of N318 billion to the NDDC between 2001 and 2006, it provided only N93 billion (Guardian 2007).

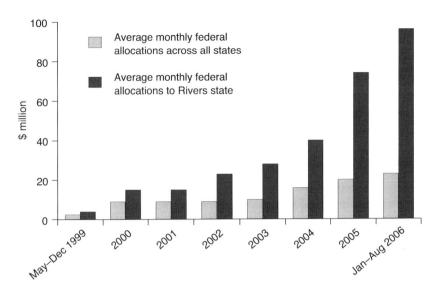

FIGURE 12.3 Comparison of monthly allocations to Rivers state and other Nigerian states (*source*: Human Rights Watch 2007d)

A critical examination of on-the-ground evidence thus suggests that an enabling environment for CSR practices in the Niger Delta is non-existent or at best ineffective (Ite 2004). The absence of an enabling environment for CSR in Nigeria due to government failures has three main consequences for CSR impacts on conflict reduction. The first is that it indirectly contributes to undermining CSR initiatives by reducing the positive impacts CSR can have on poverty alleviation and community grievance. The reality is that corporate efforts to meet community demands are negligible in the face of the huge scale of community needs that are not met owing partly to government failure to take on its fair share of responsibility. As a result, community grievance and a feeling of relative deprivation, which drives conflict in the region, persist despite oil MNCs' corporate social investments efforts.

The second consequence of the absence of an enabling environment relates to the inability of government to set minimum standards that oil companies are expected to conform to, and which would provide incentives for CSR practices. Poor regulation and a dearth of incentives for CSR initiatives within Nigeria suggest that oil companies are more or less left to their own devices regarding setting standards of operation. This absence of a minimum control mechanism has meant that oil companies are often tempted to break the law, at low cost and with little or no associated risk for doing so. This condition in turn makes it more economically rational for the oil companies operating in the region to break environmental and civil laws, which are deemed costly, as opposed to abiding by such regulations. Government failure therefore feeds into oil companies' reluctance to address the social and environmental externalities of oil extraction that often put them at loggerheads with host communities.

Emerging issues and conclusion

The foregoing analyses suggest that while structural factors constrain the effective engagement with CSR, systemic failures and the absence of an enabling environment limit the positive impacts of CSR on corporate–community conflicts. To strengthen existing CSR initiatives as a vehicle for conflict prevention and management, oil MNCs should seek to assess community perceptions through regular corporate–community workshops, research on community expectations and perceptions, and the extensive use of two-way communication channels. Assessing community perception allows oil MNCs to be responsive as opposed to being reactive. This is because, as community expectations and perceptions change, oil MNCs can also simultaneously adjust their CSR agendas and strategies accordingly so as therefore to be better able to pre-empt disjunctions in corporate–community expectations before they lead to a breakdown in relationships. However, assessing community perception is not straightforward as it can be subjected to elite or corporate capture and therefore efforts should be made to guard against this potential problem.

Second, oil MNCs must prioritize addressing the social and environmental cost of oil production by internalizing such costs through investment in environmental pollution reduction strategies and in alternative sources of livelihood in host communities. This would ensure that fewer people are displaced from their traditional sources of livelihood and that those displaced have alternative sources of livelihood. Addressing the social and environmental cost of oil extraction in an environment like the Niger Delta can be quite challenging given poor governmental regulation and the incidence of oil bunkering, which is common. However, more community involvement in the process of determining the cause of any incidence of oil spills would lead to more credibility in the process of determining the causes of oil spills and offer opportunities for dealing with the complex issue of compensation that is often a source of community grievance. In addition, development benefits should be increased in communities where oil pipeline sabotage has not occurred over a set period. Such an award scheme, directed not at individuals but at addressing common community needs, would serve as an incentive for communities to be more vigilant and discourage sabotage.

Third, oil MNCs need to actively engage in macro-CSR issues if they are to make a real contribution to conflict reduction. The present challenges can be partially managed through the adoption of a trisectoral partnership initiative as an avenue for addressing such issues. For example, active support for the Oil Producers Trade Section (OPTS) of the Lagos Chambers of Commerce working with civil society, and NEITI in dealing with the issues of transparency and accountability at federal, state, and local government levels, would go a long way in ensuring that transparency in the oil industry yielded some sustainable development benefits in host communities.

Finally, governments at various levels of Nigerian society must address the welfare and socio-economic priorities of its citizens. Issues of democratic governance, accountability and respect for the rights of the people must be integrated into a new culture of state-oil/company-oil community relations to create an enabling social environment for CSR to become an effective vehicle for conflict reduction. Local governments can actively pursue initiatives that facilitate CSR as well as work in conjunction with other tiers of government to endorse oil MNCs' CSR initiatives via award schemes for oil MNCs. Therefore, the institution of a coherent policy framework with the community as its main focus geared towards promoting and incentivizing CSR practices in Nigeria is crucial.

13 | Labelling oil, contesting governance: Legaloil.com, the GMoU and profiteering in the Niger Delta

Anna Zalik

In the first half of 2008, the attention of US and UK security institutions in the Gulf of Guinea[1] was further buttressed through the United Kingdom's promise of military aid to Nigeria. Directly acknowledged as a means of securing the Niger Delta region, the UK Foreign Office's announcement suggested how insurgent claims for a stake in extractive revenues have been effectively criminalized in global discourse (Barker 2008; Blitz 2008). In May 2009, the Nigerian military launched a full-scale attack on parts of the western Niger Delta, against fighters aligned to MEND. Some weeks later, in June, the Nigerian federal government offered amnesty to Niger Delta militants following weeks of this intensified offensive. The blurred distinction between the activities of resistance movements and gang violence were only deepened as a result – a range of armed groups could seek amnesty by turning in their guns, including those whose association with the Niger Deltan sovereignty movement was questionable.

The 2009 escalations in the 'oil war' only underlined the crucial role of the framing and definition of 'violence' and 'profiteering' in the Delta for the resolution of the region's ongoing crisis. Not only does the image of local 'profiteering' in the region, as presented to global audiences, influence the policy options advanced for *resolving* the so-called 'crisis', it has also influenced Deltan 'resistance' activities on the ground. As argued herein, social practices employed by Nigerian oil operators contribute to criminalizing non-violent protest. In the case of the emergent GMoU (Global Memorandum of Understanding) discussed further below, this is expressed in the banning of non-violent facility blockades; in the case of 'Legaloil.com', through the attempt to physically mark oil that has passed through contraband markets as distinct from its licit counterpart.

In contrast to the sympathetic portrayal of the Ogoni uprising in the 1990s or the 'Women's War' against Chevron in 2002, armed militia activity in the Delta has been depicted internationally as a kind of 'competitive thuggery'. To the extent that this was an accurate representation of post-electoral violence in 2003 and 2007, even Nigerian advocates of Deltan sovereignty and critics of global capital's role in the Niger Delta crisis are challenged in their portrayal of the region's armed movements. Indeed, the rise to prominence of major militant leaders often expresses the very political dynamics through which private capital and state agents have effectively criminalized community, and especially youth resistance in the Niger Delta.

The consent mechanisms employed by the transnational oil companies and their interlocutors have helped pathologize Deltan unarmed protest not only externally and internationally, but also in the minds of those most subject to the ravages of oil extraction. Indeed, in 2003, and even at present, many residents of the Delta's riverine region would refer to any facility takeover or shutdown as 'violence', a view promoted by industry in its emphasis on avoiding work stoppages and outlawing demonstrations.[2] Mainstream media and policy analyst representation play a role in this criminalization, through the use of terms like terrorism to describe the deepening ungovernability of the region. Ultimately, if a key tactic of unarmed resistance movements – such as blockades – becomes equated with 'violent' protest, few permitted options for demonstrating aggravation with industrial impacts remain: a result is the further radicalization of resistance movements.

This chapter examines two examples of industrial interventions that act as a discursive and practical criminalization of various forms of protest and popular claims in the Delta. In different forms, they aim to redefine the popular image of profiteering from the region's resources. Both seek to secure the extractive regime for industry: in one case through the actual policing of contraband activity and its physical marking as illicit, in the other through an institutional authority structure based on community–industry interaction that aims to guarantee the 'social licence to operate'. Accordingly, below I consider Legaloil.com and the Global Memorandum of Understanding (GMoU) as forms of industrial interventions which influence the terms of the debate on the Niger Delta's future and, specifically, the terms of industry's 'social licence'. I also consider how such interventions are challenged by the readings of contemporary resistance movements, and the implications of this contested process for the Niger Delta's current and future role in the global political economy of oil markets.

In the case of the GMoU, Chevron-Texaco and Shell, alongside other major transnational operators, have launched an initiative[3] to establish oilfield-wide corporate negotiation and governance structures. The initiative, the 'Global' MoU, seeks to displace previous 'host' community-by-community arrangements critiqued for fostering intra-communal resentment and violence. Concurrently, the commitments made by the community signatories circumvent the possibility of collective action among affected residents. Somewhat informed by the 'whole community'[4] concept, the GMoU process partially overlaps with and displaces local governance structures, whether chieftaincies or community development councils, with oil-industry-initiated and -sponsored administrative and decision-making mechanisms. In discussing the GMoU, this study locates its emergence in relation to (pilot) projects implemented in the areas of the Soku gas plant on the border of Rivers and Bayelsa states, as well as the Chevron-Texaco oilfields in the western Delta.

To begin, the chapter considers the implications of Legaloil.com. Legaloil.com's Internet presence aims to promote the discursive and material criminalization of the extra-institutional trade in crude oil, commonly refered to as 'oil bunkering' – equating it with the trade in conflict diamonds. The Legaloil.com website was established in the 2002/03 period, when control of this trade was said to have slipped increasingly out of the hands of the military and oil industry staff that previously directed it, into those of the armed youth that formerly served as their henchmen. Legaloil.com functions as a directly 'global' intervention that presents data concerning bunkered[5] shipments (the source of which is hard to verify or monitor, but becomes reified once presented as graphs and tables), tracks threats and attacks on installations, and endorses chemical fingerprinting as a means to distinguish between licit and 'illicit' oil. The site also seeks to present its data, and its proposals, as legitimized by Nigerian sources. Indeed, to be successful internationally, the 'legal oil' label requires reshaping to accord with the way exploitation in the Niger Delta is understood locally and globally, so that abusive relations of extraction come to be associated with bunkering activities, rather than the state-sanctioned operations of multinational oil companies that were much criticized in the 1990s.

Legaloil.com

The Legaloil.com website states that 'Tackling oil theft requires action on both the demand and supply side. It also requires attention to the root causes of the problem.' As it notes: 'Following the success of the "conflict diamonds" campaign and work on disarmament, there is a clear opportunity to address oil theft by including a focus on the market for the stolen oil in a comprehensive strategy that would include [measures of supply and demand].' On the 'supply' side, Legaloil.com calls for:

Law enforcement activities (e.g. monitoring 'oil theft hot-spots' and navy checks); Initiatives on corruption and transparency; Providing sustainable developmental alternatives to communities at the source of the theft (e.g. micro-credit schemes, community development projects); Tracking funds from oil theft and stopping associated revenue flows through banks.

On the demand side the website endorses:

'Fingerprinting' oil at source, during transport and at refineries; Auditing refineries for processing illegal oil; Establishing common industry-wide positions and action; Pressuring markets to only accept 'legal' oil.

Of course, the 'supply' and 'demand' sides of the oil bunkering equation require making links between production and consumption – that is, between Nigeria as the exporting source and various Northern/Western importers, including major strategic destinations such as the USA and the UK. In general, the promotion of 'relinking' between production and consumption in global commodity chains is a strategy endorsed by critics of economic globalization. From the perspective of these critics, local consumption may facilitate more just socio-economics, since consumers are less alienated from the source of these products and are able to more directly monitor the socio-environmental conditions surrounding these sources. To promote more equitable global trade relations, these advocates of 'local consumption' and fair trade often reveal the exploitative working and environmental conditions, deepened via neoliberal economic policies, that are common to many 'developing'-country industrial sites. It is these exploitative relations, following the now well-known theories of regional developmental gaps between global North and South, which allow for the accumulation of surplus capital in Northern, industrialized countries while surplus is extracted from the Southern former colonies.

This view has recently been reinvigorated among academics through critical geographer David Harvey's theorization of 'accumulation by dispossession', which he applied particularly to the USA's appropriation of strategic oil reserves in his 2004 book *The New Imperialism.* In the Deltan context, Harvey's view may be complemented by considering how the Nigerian state is consistently reconfigured as a 'joint venture' partner in the accumulation strategy common to transnational operators and some national oil companies. Here, Charles Tilly's insight on the historical sociology of the state and its security apparatus as the 'institutionalization of organized crime' bears repeating (see Tilly 1985); in the case of contemporary globalization the state serves as a facilitator of multinational corporate windfalls. Applying this perspective, what may be labelled 'legally regulated oil' arguably serves as a veneer for ongoing extractive relations.

Legaloil.com is, accordingly, an especially salient intervention in that it counters the view that recent capitalist expansion at the (so-called) global level amounts to ongoing 'accumulation by dispossession'. In the local Delta context, it also counters the insurgency's use of the language of 'resource control/ sovereignty' to frame bunkering as a rightful claim on locally extracted resources. Legaloil.com clearly asserts that the formal extraction of oil by the transnational industry is licit, thus underlining that 'resource control' via bunkering is illegal – and suggesting that its impacts are akin to popular notions of 'conflict diamonds' as the root of violence.[6]

A closer examination of oil bunkering beyond the scope of this chapter may suggest its role as a form of 'primitive accumulation' to which state and federal politicians may be closely linked.[7] As such, its link to more *oppositional* local struggles for resource control against the state may be attenuated, since individuals and sub-groups seek to profit from the bunkered resources, but these relations may indeed express cleavages between federal and state-level political office-holders. Indeed, a paper on the Legaloil.com website does allude to this, indicating that as a result of the disarming of militias following the 2003 elections, bunkerers turned to 'official means' of cargo theft via fraudulent bills of lading that would largely require involvement of those already operating in the 'licit' economy in order to be possible (Davis 2007). Uncited estimates in the paper put the amount stolen through these 'official' means as equivalent to that stolen via militias in the 2003/04 period, offering an approximate figure of 120,000 barrels per day (bpd) (ibid.: 13). The paper's author insightfully indicates that both the oil industry and the federal government would have to cooperate in order to shut down 'official' oil theft, an initiative which has not received sufficient international support to date.

Discursively, however, the main point of Legaloil.com is to focus attention on the militia activity/criminality surrounding the trade in bunkered oil as central to social violence and even ecological damage (due to sabotage), the latter particularly problematic given the huge amounts of gas flared by the multinationals in the Niger Delta. Here I understand bunkering not as the cause of socio-economic breakdown but as its consequence, revealing the problematic nature of the discursive reordering implied in the 'Legaloil' label. Legaloil.com's concept of oil certification suggests that bunkered oil is the culprit in socio-economic breakdown and 'aim[s] to hit the well-organised theft of oil by choking off the market for the stolen oil and interrupting the supply chain'. Instead of the 'Shell boycott' against the Ogoni killings,[8] then, the site encourages a bunkering boycott, using the conflict diamond campaign as a model. While the turf wars and proliferation of small arms around the oil bunkering industry may be compared to warlordism around conflict diamonds, oil and diamonds differ in a crucial respect from one another – one is a major source of energy required for contemporary global reproduction, the other is a trade based largely in a market of symbolic value and luxury goods. Arguably, the capital-intensive (i.e. fixed infrastructure and physical plant) nature of the oil industry shapes conditions of relative deprivation for local communities in a form far more pronounced than that of diamond mining.

In contrast to the 'predatory state' model with which conflict diamonds have been associated, the proliferation of arms in the Niger Delta has been partly linked for some years with the oil industry's security practices. Indeed, despite the *de jure* outlawing of 'stand-by payments' by oil companies to community youth, they remain commonplace, but with the added caveat that your firepower determines the payment's size. As one key informant put it in a 2006 interview in Port Harcourt: 'If you negotiate with an AK-47 they will pay you a price for that, with a pistol, a bazooka, a gunboat [...] they will pay you based on your coercive power.' Oil-bunkering-related proliferation has been closely tied to a protection racket fostered by industry, well documented in the late 1990s and early 2000s by groups like Human Rights Watch. This racket is in fact implicitly approved by foreign governments and industry in some clauses of the 'Voluntary Principles on Security and Human Rights', which sanctions the contracting of local residents as security providers (Zalik 2004).

Here it is also worth noting that President Yar'Adua's position concerning the Nigerian oil industry has recently been harnessed and 're-represented' by Legaloil.com. Yar'Adua also took various positions critical of oil MNCs. Indeed, he was identified in the *Financial Times* as having adopted a 'firm line' regarding the profits the multinationals have made from Nigerian production owing to high oil prices.[9] The mark of electoral 'illegitimacy' acted as a means to pressure him to adopt pro-market policies on oil rents and foreign investment. It is thus interesting that Legaloil.com cited the source ISN Security Watch as touting Yar'Adua as an originator of the proposal to fingerprint oil. A brief Internet search tied ISN Security Watch to the Hudson Institute, a conservative US security and economic policy think tank.

This subtle reframing of exploitation endorsed via Legaloil.com, I argue, is salient to current debates concerning the 'securing' of Nigerian oil and the Gulf of Guinea region more generally. In contrast, MEND and fellow travellers explicitly challenge the notion of 'legal' extraction and profiteering by government and multinationals. And the group(s) understand that questioning the Nigerian government's legitimacy is a tool not only for the Western powers that aim to secure the Delta, but for the insurgent groups said to subsist from bunkering. In response, corporate interests that lay claims to 'legitimacy' in oil extraction establish mechanisms which break social relations between insurgent groups and communities, creating shared identification – as stakeholders – between communities affected by extraction and the oil companies themselves. This is in part promoted through the terms of the evolving GMoU.

The GMoU

The emergence of the GMoU is embedded in successive paradigm shifts oil corporations employed in the wake of the Ogoni 'crisis'. It follows upon the various transitions from Community Assistance (CA) to Community Development (CD) to Sustainable Community Development (SCD) promoted by Shell Petroleum Development Company (SPDC) – now Shell Nigeria – and other transnational operators in the Delta since 2001 (Zalik 2004). As described by Lapin, the CD approach sought to mediate conflictual relations between communities and corporations by moving away from the explicit focus on 'giving things' under CA, which 'encouraged activism through its ad-hoc approach to community demands' towards a partnership approach that she describes as 'generally peaceful, leverag[ing] community and donor resources and build[ing] constructive ongoing relations with partners' (Lapin 2000). But the GMoU also reflects a deepening attention to the relationship between industrial 'security' and possible disputes over compensation payments. In the period when the

GMoU was under development, Shell began to implement a policy of non-compensation for spill damage, alleging sabotage.

This is problematic on a number of levels: not only because cases have been established where sabotage was in fact feigned by industry, but additionally because it acts as a form of collective punishment – basically promoting self-monitoring among community members. The GMoU in a sense takes this kind of collective/'global' treatment of stakeholders to the next level: that is, it creates legally binding requirements for community signatories to permit and facilitate ongoing operations (as such outlawing protest should local residents be dissatisfied). If one signatory from the 'recipient' side (affected communities) breaks the GMoU's terms requiring that a safe and unobstructed operating environment be provided to the industrial project, the corporation is not formally bound to *any* of the signatories.

In the case of the Chevron model in Delta state, a new set of community 'foundations'[10] are to be established through the GMoU, which are also to seek funds from non-governmental and multilateral sources, including the World Bank. This, explained a corporate representative, aims to address the fact that industry cannot pay for all the region's development needs. These new foundation-like bodies will operate alongside government-affiliated institutions, but in their initial establishment are *directly tied to* particular oilfield projects, with participant-representatives paid for their time via direct sitting allowances from the corporation.

The GMoU as implemented by a number of operators in 2006 consisted of a somewhat opaque set of committees, on which representatives of various levels of government and state bureaucrats sat alongside community representatives and oil industry operations and public affairs staff, and stages of implementation. The process is facilitated via mediating NGOs, but the corporation pre-determines the ordering of the process. In the case of both Chevron and SPDC the GMoU is (or was) intended to eventually encompass their entire areas of operation, replacing previous community-by-community agreements.[11]

The GMoU process employs an incentive structure similar to that used by Shell's previous Community Development and Sustainable Community Development models. Under this 'milestone' system, financing for future stages of implementation is not provided until 'community' representatives demonstrate that earlier stages have been completed. In the case of the GMoU, new oilfield-wide 'Project Advisory Committees' will eventually receive their own operating budget. But for this to occur, members must conclude an intra- and inter-community agreement concerning expected 'benefits' – infrastructure, jobs, etc. – associated with a given longer-term (oil development?) project. Based on this process, binding agreements (of approximately five years) are to be established with the company; these establish a set of promised developmental benefits to communities, the completion of which will rest upon these communities ensuring a 'non-conflictual' operating environment. In some cases, the GMoU contemplates the completion of so-called 'legacy' projects (otherwise known as abandoned projects, as one colleague put it), although certain informants indicated that responsibility for implementing these was to be assumed by state governments.

This chapter argues that the reshaping of industry–social relations through the whole community concept – and made legally binding via the GMoU – has (at least) two key thrusts, one that might be categorized as 'local', the other 'global'. The local involves shifting the conception of 'public–private' interests and territorial identification to reflect the actual delineation of a particular industrial oilfield or corporate project. Indeed, the 'clusters' and 'project advisory committees' created via the GMoU process change the way the population has laid claim to the natural resource base. Although in practice the general GMoU promotional materials claim that 'these communities are united either on historical (clan) or local government basis as approved by the relevant state government', key civil society informants indicated that in various cases only a handful of 'host communities' out of fifteen or more belonging to a particular clan were actually included in the committee structure for the GMoU. For instance, the 2006 draft GMoU for the Gbarain-Ekpetiama area (of Bayelsa state), extending over the local government area (LGA) of the same name as well as parts of Yenagoa LGA, states that it 'covers the range of SPDC's activities within Gbarain and Ekpetiama under the *area impacted by the Gbarain Integrated Oil and Gas Project*' (emphasis added).

The second policy thrust involves 'institutional' merging of public and private interests through the portrayal of the corporation as 'socially responsible' in global policy discourse. This is exemplified in the GMoU process through strategic partnership between industry, state institutions and non-governmental organizations, and SPDC indicates that the GMoU is part of the 'Sustainable Community Development' effort and not different from it. Emerging from the oil industry's globalized endorsement of corporate-driven sustainable development, the good corporation[12] is portrayed, in industrial public affairs pamphlets, as a central actor reshaping socio-environmental norms.[13] SPDC states, for instance, that the GMoU's key aspects include 'involvement of all production, assets and pipeline communities (Whole Community Concept); encouragement of people-based socio-economic development plans at communities and cluster levels; encouraged focus on Community Development Plan and Local Economic Empowerment and Development Strategy (LEEDS) as a basis for projects'. Through these practices, industry is discursively constructed as promoting 'sustainable development', but in a form that ties local economies to direct provision to oil industry contractors (a common example being micro-enterprise in the form of a woman or group of women selling bottled soft drinks at construction sites). In addition, problematic distributional questions are transferred to the 'cluster boards' for communities to dispute internally: 'The Cluster Development Board representing the communities will determine the sharing formulae based on the existing local understanding, with support from government and SPDC.'

Below, I consider an area where a precursor to the GMoU was piloted, in the Soku gas plant area, which eventually led to a pan-community mobilization of youth demanding that SPDC fulfil a series of developmental and employment requests; and then go on to provide some details of a GMoU agreement that exemplifies how pan-community mobilization is to be curtailed via legal obligation.

Soku: conflict transformation and territorial security

Privatized dispute settlement [...] infuses private activity with public purposes, eroding the foundations for accountability under the rule of law but, by virtue of self disciplining distinctions between public and private activities and politics and economics, is neutralized or sanitized of public content and function. (Cutler 2003: 239)

An examination of the Soku case, as an SDC precursor to the GMoU, suggests how earlier social divisions and territorial disputes were deepened through 'host community' policies. To remedy this, Shell's new approach proclaimed equal treatment of villages that had previously been managed via divisive 'host community' policies. Third-party mediation, through non-governmental organizations, sought to mediate conflict involving competing Kalabari and Nembe clans and sub-states (Rivers-Bayelsa). Concurrently, contracted NGOs, subsidized by global aid institutions, delivered welfare interventions that blurred compensation for historical environmental and social injustice with 'developmental projects'. As a precursor to the GMoU, this involved promoting shared identification with the Soku gas plant rather than with the states of Rivers and Bayelsa, or particular LGAs or communities; the privileging of new administrative and governance structures which managed oil industry payments independently of chiefs or community development councils (CDCs) (as exemplified in a particular Oil and Gas Committee in one of the three communities in the Soku cluster); and the oil industry's favouring of 'human development' (sometimes called 'economic empowerment') via income generation and micro-credit, which emphasized 'attitudinal change' alongside infrastructural development.

The gas supply plant at Soku provides the majority of SPDC's natural gas supply commitment to the Bonny liquefied natural gas plant, a $4 billion dollar joint venture between the NNPC and three other companies.[14] Its feed gas is provided by Shell, Elf and Agip at ratios of 53.3 per cent, 23.3 per cent and 23.3 per cent respectively. As is now widely known, in mid-June 2004 an internally commissioned report concerning Shell's role in Niger Deltan communal conflicts was leaked to the media. The leaked report provided cursory attention to *specific* cases of violence in the Delta, with the exception of conflict in the region adjacent to the Soku gas plant, involving the communities of Elem Sangama,

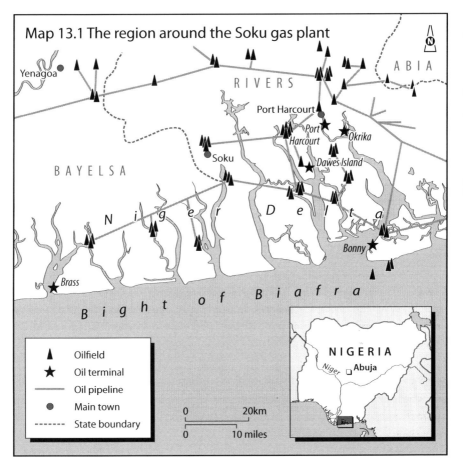

Map 13.1 The region around the Soku gas plant

Legend:
- ▲ Oilfield
- ★ Oil terminal
- Oil pipeline
- ● Main town
- ------ State boundary

0 20km
0 10 miles

NIGERIA
Niger □ Abuja

Oluasiri and Soku. According to the report, the region was selected as a case because it 'is the focus of the SCD [new Sustainable Community Development] pilot' which was to be driven by seven principles: 'the generation of robust profitability; the delivery of technical, economic, and commercial value to customers; protection of the environment; management of resources; the provision of respect and safeguards to people; working with stakeholders; and offering benefits to communities' (WAC Global Services 2003).[15] Thus the Soku pilot project aimed to (1) minimize any interruptions to extraction and (2) enhance the representational value of the company as a clean business, both of which serve to 'maximize shareholder value', or generate robust profitability. This is SCD's move to a 'whole new language' that focuses on 'processes rather than the blueprints understood by engineers'.

A few months after the report was leaked, in October 2004, the region surrounding the gas plant was evacuated as a result of a stand-off between rival armed militias led by Asari Dokubo and Ateke Tom, which raised tensions within the oil industry, also indicating the significance of the region to the broader regulatory context in the Niger Delta.

TABLE 13.1 State and clan affiliation of 'hosts' to the Soku gas plant

State	Clan	Community
Rivers	Kalabari	Soku – politically most powerful of the three communities
Rivers	Kalabari	Elem Sangama – smallest of three communities. Historical narratives connect them to Oluasiri by marriage. Destroyed in violence with Oluasiri in 1993 and rebuilt in 1996
Bayelsa	Nembe	Oluasiri – made up of fifty-two fishing settlements

The conflicts of the past decade between the Soku, Elem Sangama and Oluasiri communities mirror a longer disputed history for control over riverine trade routes between the Kalabari and the Nembe Ijaw.[16] While Soku and Elem Sangama belong to the Kalabari, Oluasiri is a Nembe community made up of fifty-two fishing settlements. Prior to 1996 the former two belonged to the same LGA and the latter to a different LGA in Rivers state. The creation of Bayelsa (out of Rivers) in 1996 established a political boundary between Nembe and Kalabari, but this did not remove the dispute over the gas plant region, now fuelled by competing claims of Rivers and Bayelsa state governments to oil revenues.

Soku is a relatively large Kalabari kingdom with which Shell negotiated from the 1960s, when the company began exploration in the area. Elem Sangama, a former fishing settlement, is not an offshoot of Soku per se, but does belong to the larger Kalabari clan, whose historical capital was at Abonnema. Although Soku and Elem Sangama lay competing claims to the gas plant they are in relative alliance as Kalabari communities. The Oluasiri communities, in contrast, historical outposts of Nembe, do not generally appear on maps of the region, have a less centralized authority structure, and generally practise 'traditional' or 'native' customs over Christianity.[17] Oluasiri's relationship with Shell is further complicated by the fact that Shell treats it as a single host community with regard to the Soku gas plant, despite its consisting of fifty-two fishing settlements.

Although it may not bear repeating, the delineation of oilfields by the oil MNCs through the act of naming and mapping has served to 'bound' communities in the area (for examples elsewhere, see Li 2001). Soku's claim to the gas plant, according to informants from outside the community, relates primarily to the fact that the plant was *named* for it, thus reflecting the oil industry's approach to demarcating installations territorially. One result is that in the NNPC-supported Environmental Impact Assessments for the gas plant carried out between 1997 and 2003, neither Oluasiri nor any of its major communities are referenced and Oluasiri continues to be absent from most accessible maps of the region (which are largely Shell products). In what might be referred to as a strategy of counter-mapping, legal advisers among Oluasiri community members and Bayelsa state sources refer to the site as the Oluasiri gas plant.[18] Elem Sangama, on the other hand, is careful not to place too much stress on laying claim to Soku, owing probably to its smaller size and because it is partially protected within Rivers state by its affiliation to the broader Kalabari kingdom.

Whole community mediation and its contradictions The new sustainable community development pilot project at Soku sought explicitly to displace the host community model. *Conflict Transformation* geared at 'attitudinal change' among communities and youth was pursued via NGO mediators. The transformatory process aimed to create a broad group of stakeholders through cross-community identification with *the company's* interests, rather than with particular communities or clans, while internalizing the conflict between the company in negotiations *among* host communities. Ideally, from the perspective of the company, the creation of the new 'whole community' would serve as a protective fence around the installation, excluding from claims-making those who do not share this stakeholder status.

Thus the notion that would become the 'global' in the GMoU was first shaped via affiliation with a particular industrial project/oilfield rather than with villages, clans or LGAs. In Soku this was to be achieved in part through the representational function of providing 'equivalent infrastructure' to each of the three communities. Externally the oil MNCs in the Delta have long argued that providing basic infrastructure to communities (i.e. connecting them to their own electricity grid or water source) creates unwieldy expectations; such services are the responsibility of the state agencies to whom they already pay corporate taxes. However, community residents observed the relative material opulence within the gas plant's residential area.[19] This shapes discontent in extractive sites, or 'relative deprivation', as sociologists at times describe it.

Despite the emphasis on 'whole community' mediation and equal treatment, one observes in the implementation of the community development projects a major contrast between Soku and Elem Sangama versus Oluasiri. A sort of equation of justice with equal treatment has not served to reconcile spatial and historical differences. Projects in Oluasiri, for instance, are complicated by conflicts between some of the fishing settlements, and also because the 'three' host communities are hardly equivalent in size or settlement structure. In Oluasiri there are fifty-two settlements to provide for, making the connection to the generator difficult. Electricity was at one point functional in some of the southernmost Oluasiri communities, but not during 2003. In Soku and Elem Sangama, on the other hand, the entire community was electrified through a generator.[20] The process of implementing the 'whole community' approach, then, has not led to the application of a comprehensive package of welfare benefits across all sites.

Both Elem Sangama and Soku have been altered significantly by sand-filling projects provided by SPDC. This relandscaping was essential to making Elem Sangama appear a sort of 'model' host community and thus a site for visitors on Shell tours. Relatively small in population size, and considered well organized and non-conflictual by Shell and the NGOs, it suggests to the visitor the sense of being taken to a 'plaster community' (one whose infrastructure is quickly constructed of plaster) in the middle of the Niger Delta. This was facilitated by the fact that Elem Sangama has been completely rebuilt since 1996, a project overseen by its specially constituted 'Oil and Gas Committee' – a sort of precursor to the community committees that participate in the GMoU clusters. The Elem Sangama Committee was favourably perceived by Shell, as it indicated the openness of the community to collaboration with the oil industry.

In Oluasiri a conflict between the southern and northern villages led to further displacement. Some community members indicated that up to 70 per cent of the population of the southernmost region was displaced during the inter-communal conflicts. The dispute also led to the temporary abandonment of the community by contractors charged with construction of the local cottage hospital, electricity and water projects. The leaked conflict report makes the following statement with respect to the contractors:

> On several occasions community representatives accused contractors of inciting violence in order to have their own project closed down. If work stoppage cannot be tracked to the contractor's behaviour, then contractors can claim compensation from SCIN [Shell Companies in Nigeria] to obtain: (a) contractual extensions; (b) exchange rate benefits on the Naira side of the contract for the duration of work stoppage; and (c) lost days due to 'force majeure'. For example, Saipam was awarded USD 20 million in claims due to community unrest at the Soku Gas Plant (by comparison, the CD budget was USD 2 million). (WAC Global Services 2003)

The promise of the whole community approach was thus stymied by the dominant characteristics of oil industry/social relations. Infrastructural projects are provided in response to grievances, yet these remain incomplete,[21] generating further discontent.

From the 'whole community' to the GMoU

Four years after the initial mediation among Soku, Elem Sangama and Oluasiri, the youth of the region found grounds for unity. In February 2005 youths from the Gas Plant Peace Committee, formed during the inter-community mediation, took collective action as 'landlords'. *This Day* reported on an ultimatum issued collectively by the youth associations of the three communities, related

to the fact that basic infrastructure – promised via the inter-community mediation – had yet to be completed.

> In the six-point petition, the groups stated that a lump sum of N15 million
> ($115,000 US) be paid to each of the three youth associations to prevent an
> impending feud between the oil company and the host communities due to the
> oil giant's insensitivity and neglect. (Mike Oduniyi, Lagos, 2005)[22]

It is the very possibility of such *collective action* which the new GMoU process
explicitly forbids. Here, citations from a 2006 GMoU demonstrate how this is
achieved. In particular, a review of these documents indicates that binding
terms are quite differently applied to the corporation and the communities.
For instance, while the company '*agrees to use its best endeavours to ensure* that
its Contractors award appropriate subcontracts to community contractors com-
mensurate with their capabilities and in line with (the Company's) contracting
procedures and Nigerian/Local Content Development goals',

> the Affected Communities/Clans and their representatives will ensure that the
> activities including those executed by [the company's] contractors are free from
> any form of harassment and disruptions by [the affected clans] throughout the
> duration of activities.
> The [affected clans] *agree to actively assist* the police and other law enforce-
> ment agencies in handling and prosecuting matters that may cause public
> disturbance or impede [the company's or the company's contractors'] ability to
> operate.
> No other benefits will be requested from the company or its contractors.

And a few other examples of the variant language employed, reflecting the
company's versus the affected communities' commitments:

> [The company] *shall put a process in place* to ensure compliance with en-
> vironmental standards in collaboration with the communities and regulatory
> agencies.
> The Affected regions: Provide [the company] and her contractors *at all times*
> with a conducive atmosphere for its operations and to take responsible steps to
> forestall and avoid disruptions to [the company's] activities.

The agreement indicates specific infrastructural commitments that would be
provided by the company, as well as a timeline of four annual payments to the
implementing body (or Project Advisory Committee, PAC) for the GMoU of the
region, and specific amounts to be offered in homage and courtesy payments,
at times of official visits. On this point, it should be noted that key respondents'
interviews in 2007 indicated that although the GMoU had been signed, funds had
yet to be disbursed by the corporation, suggesting a resurgence of the problems
that plagued earlier rounds of corporate–community negotiations.

Most significantly the final section on 'Penalty for Breach of GMoU' indicates that:

> All the benefits including SCD projects and programmes are conditioned to uninterrupted operations that may accrue to beneficiary communities and all parties agree that funding for these projects and programmes shall be suspended if there is *any disruption* to [the company's] and/or its contractors' operations during the period of the G-MOU [...]
>
> Any breach of this G-MOU on the part of [the company] especially from delay in disbursement of funds (taking into account Joint Venture Partner funding by more than 6 months), will attract a penalty, which is equivalent to an income generating project to the amount of N5. [Note: I can only assume that this is a typographical error and should read N5,000 or N50,000.]
>
> [The affected regions] expressly agree that breach or perceived breach of the G-MOU by [the company] or its Contractor shall not be a ground for disruption of [the company] or the Contractor operations but will use the grievance handling procedure to address their concern herein attached.

And so, to underscore the content of this final clause, 'non-violent' protest is made effectively illicit. Concurrently, the messy and highly charged business of distributing compensatory funds from industry to a range of stakeholders is offloaded on the affected residents themselves. In the process, community representatives to various implementing and advisory committees become accountable in the case of disputes.

Conclusion

Since the 1990s, the Niger Delta has operated in the global imagination as the site of oil-related contention par excellence. From the 'peaceful' protest of the Ogoni era and the pro-democracy movement that operated alongside it, the neoliberal democratization of the new millennium has been accompanied by a sort of 'democratization of violence' (Peterside and Zalik 2008), in which the weakening of state institutions of control is accompanied by a progressively more privatized market of industrial protection. As this protection market has increasingly constituted security *and* a threat to industry (by providing territorial 'security' alongside direct participation in the bunkering trade and commercial kidnappings – i.e. commodified *in*security), the USA and the UK have set up a military presence in West Africa in the form of US Africom, an extension of EUCOM (Lubeck et al. 2007; Keenan 2008b).

This chapter has examined how two industrial interventions respond to community and insurgents' 'resource control' claims and partially shape global understanding of profiteering and 'legality' in the Niger Delta crisis. While Legaloil.com is largely aimed at global traders and audiences in corporate bodies and security think tanks, the GMoU seeks to achieve the industrial 'social licence to operate' through oilfield-wide community development agreements within the Delta itself. Each of these corporate interventions is a discursive and practical project with real effects, reconstituting ideas of exploitation, greed and accumulation as applied to petroleum extraction from the Niger Delta region of Nigeria. Indeed, each defines a range of different claims against the transnational oil industry, in one case by connecting the contraband oil trade with armed violence, in the other by making non-violent protest effectively criminal.

As socio-industrial inputs into the Delta setting, the GMoU and Legaloil.com are today embedded in an ongoing exchange in the Delta. In this, multinational operators and the Nigerian government face off concerning state versus multinational responsibility for industry 'shortfalls' in a context of record oil profits. Concurrently, some state legislators and notably major transnational operators oppose the new National Petroleum Bill under debate in Nigeria. This reflects both the higher royalties and calls for transparency in reporting of extractive activity that such reforms demand from 'licit' operators.

14 | Conclusion: amnesty and post-amnesty peace, is the window of opportunity closing for the Niger Delta?

Cyril Obi and Siri Aas Rustad

Introduction

While the insurgency in the Niger Delta has been a source of instability, human suffering and threats to the interests of the petro-business alliance, it has dialectically opened up a new opportunity to address the problems of the region in a radical, holistic and sustainable manner. This knowledge is not lost on the Nigerian authorities. In his inauguration speech in May 2007, President Yar'Adua noted that: 'The crisis in the Niger Delta commands our urgent attention. Ending it is a matter of strategic importance to our country. I will use every resource available to me, with your help, to address this crisis in a spirit of fairness, justice, and cooperation.'

In 2008, concerned about the adverse domestic and international implications of the growing insurgency in the oil-rich region, the president launched several initiatives as part of a comprehensive plan to end the conflict, and promote peace, development and stability in the Niger Delta. Vice-President Goodluck Jonathan, an indigene of the Niger Delta, coordinated dialogue with various stakeholders in the region, and held consultations within and outside the country on how to bring lasting peace and development to the troubled region. However, by the end of 2008 it was evident that, although government had broadly accepted that the Niger Delta's problems required quick and urgent intervention, continued militia attacks and huge losses in oil production ensured that the 'military solution' was not about to be abandoned.

Peace initiatives under President Yar'Adua (2007–09)

Niger Delta peace summit In 2008 the federal government proposed hosting a peace summit that would include all stakeholders in the region – federal officials, ethnic minority leaders and oil companies. An experienced diplomat (Nigeria's former minister for foreign affairs in the 1990s) and UN Under-Secretary-General Ibrahim Gambari was nominated by government to mediate the summit. However, the Niger Delta groups rejected his candidacy because, as Nigeria's foreign minister during General Abacha's military regime, he had de-fended the execution of Ken Saro-Wiwa and eight Ogoni leaders, and had called

200

MOSOP a gang of common criminals.[1] The trial and execution of Ken Saro-Wiwa had been seen as another example of the federal government's insensitivity to the problems in the Niger Delta. After the execution of the 'Ogoni nine' the struggle in the Niger Delta became more violent.[2] Gambari, as a defender of a grievous assault on the region, was therefore seen as unacceptable, and subsequently withdrew from the role of mediator, leading to the cancellation of the summit. As the MOSOP president Ledum Mitee argued: 'If [...] the head of a process I am supposed to take part in [...] called me a common criminal, what am I supposed to think?'[3]

MEND rejected the idea of the summit, describing it as a 'jamboree' that was 'bound to fail'.[4] It also demanded that a MEND leader standing trial be released to take part in the Niger Delta peace process. In a meeting with Vice-President Goodluck Jonathan, the Niger Delta state governors and other prominent leaders from the region expressed the view that what the region needed was not another 'talk-shop', but recommendations that would lead to actions aimed at resolving the crisis. Thus, the exigent choice was to make a decision that would be based on consultations with, and acceptable to, both factions of the (Niger Delta and non-Niger Delta) elite. According to AllAfrica,[5] the Niger Delta leaders suggested to the vice-president that what the

> Federal Government should do is to set up a body to appraise the various reports that have been submitted on the way forward for the Niger Delta, from the Willink Commission of 1958 to 2007 and let the body come out with the things to be done or not done from the different reports, and then, the larger house like the stakeholders gathered, could be called to fine-tune and ratify the final report. (AllAfrica, 1 July 2009)

This set the stage for the establishment of the Niger Delta Technical Committee.

Niger Delta Technical Committee The Niger Delta Technical Committee was inaugurated on 8 September 2008. The committee was composed of forty-four members, mostly originating from the Niger Delta region (see Oluwaniyi, this volume). Ledum Mitee, the leader of MOSOP, was chosen to be the chairperson of the committee.[6] Their terms of reference were threefold: first 'to collate, review and distil various reports, suggestions and recommendations from the Willink Commission (1958) report to the present, and give a summary of the recommendations necessary for government action; second, to appraise the summary recommendations and present short-, medium- and long-term suggestions for dealing with the challenges in the Niger Delta; and third to make and present to government any other recommendations that would help the federal government achieve sustainable development, peace, human and environmental security in the Niger Delta region' (TCND 2008: vi).

After working for two months the committee visited the region, and reviewed over four hundred reports and documents from various sources and interests – local, national and global; and submitted its report to the president on 1 December 2008. At the core of the recommendations was the need for a (new) social compact with stakeholders in the Niger Delta as a strategy for building trust and confidence in the peace process. Others highlighted by the committee were:

- increased revenue allocation (derivation) to 25 per cent in the interim, with a gradual increase towards 50 per cent;
- establishment of a Disarmament, Decommission and Reintegration (DDR) Commission to address the Niger Delta militants;
- establishment of a Youth Employment Scheme by mid-2009;
- an open trial and unconditional bail for Henry Okah;[7]
- negotiation of an amnesty for those Niger Delta militants willing to participate in the DDR programme;
- strengthened independent regulation of oil pollution and an effective EIA process; ending of gas flares by December 2008;
- improved operational integrity of police and security forces;
- provision of 5000MW of power to the region by 2010;
- completion of the conversion to dual carriageway of the east–west road;
- rebuilding of health infrastructure;
- all outstanding funds to be paid out to the NDDC immediately. (Ibid.: 3, 73)

The Committee emphasized the need for quick, sincere and sustainable action to prevent the escalation of the conflict. It also commented on the lack of implementation of the recommendations of previous committees/reports. This was a strong indictment of previous governments, laying a large share of the responsibility for the escalating crisis in the Niger Delta on their doorsteps, and cautioning the Yar'Adua government not to repeat their mistakes. Although the report blamed the inability of previous administrations to act on recommendations on the 'lack of political will', it did not explain why such political will was lacking, but noted its impact – a breakdown of trust in the Niger Delta (ibid.: 59).

But, in spite of its warning, the federal government did not release a White Paper on the report of the Technical Committee of the Niger Delta. This inaction regarding the report cast some doubt on the sincerity of the federal government's efforts to solve the crisis in the region.[8] Although the ICG referred to the report as 'an opportunity to reduce the violent conflict significantly and begin long-term regional development in the oil-rich region' (International Crisis Group 2009: 1), it did not consider that the government would have other ideas. This was also complicated by the establishment of new institutions outside the terms of the report.

Niger Delta Ministry The last of the three major peace initiatives that the federal government initiated in 2008 was the establishment of a ministry for the Niger Delta on 10 September 2008. The timing of the creation of the ministry just after the creation of the Technical Committee, and before the Committee could make its recommendations, was a curious twist to the institutionalized response to the Niger Delta crisis, creating some confusion regarding the relationship between the ministry and the NDDC. According to Yar'Adua, 'The Niger Delta Ministry would co-ordinate our efforts to tackle the challenges of infrastructure development, environmental protection and youth empowerment in the region.'[9]

On 23 December 2008 the president appointed former Secretary to the Federal Government Chief Ufot Ekaette as the Minister of the Niger Delta, and Elder Godsay Orubebe as the minister of state in the ministry.[10] The scepticism about the ministry and appointments related to questions about the ability of the ministry to perform well given the fact that the 2009 federal budget had only allocated N50 billion (approximately US$340 million)[11] to it. Many argued that this budget would not allow the ministry to engage in any major development activities in 2009.[12]

Although both ministers originated from Niger Delta states (Chief Ufot Ekaette from Akwa Ibom and Elder Godsay Orubebe from Delta state), some Ijaw elites/elders were of the view that the minister should have been from one of the 'core' Niger Delta states and the Ijaw (the biggest ethnic group in the Niger Delta) community.[13] There was also controversy over the location of the ministry's headquarters in Abuja, and the decision to site liaison offices in the nine Niger Delta states.[14] Critics argued that placing the ministry's headquarters in Abuja would amount to locating it too far from the very region and people it was supposed to work with.[15]

It should be noted that while the government embarked on institutional reforms aimed at resolving the crisis in the Niger Delta, it continued to maintain and fund the Joint Task Force (JTF), which continued with a military campaign of crushing the militant insurgency in the region. In May 2009, a coordinated attack by the JTF on militant camps in Gbaramatu kingdom, and the bombardment of Okerenkoko, Oporoza, Kurutie, Kokodiagbene and Kunukuma communities, believed to provide shelter to militias in the western Delta, brought matters to a head. Although it successfully led to the destruction of several militia camps, none of the notable militia leaders was captured or killed. Also, the attacks led to a humanitarian emergency in the creeks, and created an internal displacement problem, with implications for security in neighbouring towns. Although movement in the region was restricted, reports of human rights violations during and after the attacks by government forces did not help matters for a government that was still contending with a credibility crisis following the flawed 2007 elections in the region and the country.

It was against this background that President Yar'Adua announced that a

Presidential Panel on Amnesty and Disarmament of Militants in the Niger Delta was being established to implement a presidential pardon. This proposal for the amnesty was presented to, and approved, by the federal executive council on 25 June, leading Yar'Adua to formally proclaim an amnesty, providing a sixty-day window (6 August to 4 October 2009) of 'unconditional pardon to all persons who have directly or indirectly participated in the commission of offences associated with militant activities in the Niger Delta',[16] in exchange for disarmament, rehabilitation and reintegration.

While a faction of MEND described the 2009 amnesty as unrealistic and insincere, others accepted it, and surrendered their weapons in well-publicized media events, often at the federal or state capital.[17] The faction against accepting the amnesty argued that the government should first release those militants who were being held captive. This was a clear reference to Henry Okah.[18]

The second objection to the amnesty was based on the continued presence of the JTF in the region and the view that the amnesty did not address the roots of the conflict. At the same time as President Yar'Adua presented the offer of amnesty, he also announced that the federal government had supplied the JTF with enough funds 'to acquire the proper capacity to be able to enforce law and order'.[19] Apart from indicating a level of ambivalence in the attitude of government towards the peace process, this created some difficulty in building trust and dialogue between the militants and the federal government.

Post-amnesty DDR: how wide a window?

By the end of the amnesty in October 2009, 15,000 ex-militants reportedly surrendered '2,700 sophisticated weapons and 287,445 ammunitions to the Presidential Amnesty Committee'[20] and moved into designated collection points and camps in six Niger Delta states.[21] Each ex-militant was promised a payment of N65,000 monthly, plus vocational training. The amnesty programme was not conceptualized along the lines recommended by the Niger Delta Technical Report. It was not the outcome of open negotiations or a formal peace agreement between the government and the militants. Rather, the consultations were at the highest levels of government, and involved members of the Niger Delta elite/elders and top government officials of Niger Delta origin negotiating with militia commanders.

Later, some such top commanders associated with a faction of MEND 'surrendered' at the presidential villa in Abuja. This public ceremony symbolized a 'public surrender' of 'repentant militants' to a 'benevolent' President Yar'Adua, who proceeded to 'forgive' them. He also instructed the chairman of the amnesty committee to open a dialogue and work with the ex-militants, whom he described as 'young, energetic and intelligent Nigerians'.[22] As Davidheiser and Nyiayaana (2010) have argued, the approach of the Nigerian state was to 'give' amnesty to militants 'who are perceived primarily as perpetrators of crimes against the state'. This underlined the superior authority and legitimacy of the state as a forgiving 'father-figure' ready to accept and reconcile with the 'prodigals', showing sympathy for the plight of the Niger Delta people.

The amnesty programme failed to address either the roots of the conflict or non-armed groups, who were victims of the violence in the region. Rather it moved hastily from conflict to a DDR process without a clear road map. This was perhaps based on the view that the greatest threats to petro-business were the armed militias and the proliferation of weapons in the region, and that once militias were taken out of the equation, stability would return. Thus, issues of transitional justice, abuses and acts of impunity committed by all sides to the violent conflict – government security forces and militias – were conveniently swept under the carpet, setting up a template for co-opting the most powerful militants and spoilers who could obstruct petro-business in the Niger Delta. It also sidetracked the issue of calling them and the military to account. The state-owned and -directed amnesty project was considered necessary to define/control the space of engagement, and reassert state power in the face of limited military victories, which had failed to stem the escalating insurgency threatening petro-business, the security of the country's maritime neighbours and international shipping.

While ex-militia 'commanders' enjoyed state patronage and largesse,[23] their erstwhile foot-soldiers in designated camps complained of the poor living conditions, lack of quality training facilities and programmes, and delayed payments of allowances (Davidheiser and Nyiayaana 2010). This led to their either abandoning the camps or resorting to violent riots in some instances, including in Benin, Yenagoa and Aluu, Port Harcourt, which resulted in many injuries and a few deaths.[24] There were also reports that apart from providing cover for the unemployed youth and miscreants 'to take advantage of the programme', some ex-militants were getting involved in violent crime.

The weaknesses of the DDR and the continued presence of the JTF in the region (after the 'disarmament' of local militias) raised concerns among local stakeholders. The Niger Delta Leaders, Elders and Stakeholders Forum, an elite group, openly called for the dissolution of the Presidential Amnesty Committee, and the removal of its chairman and minister for defence, retired general Godwin Abbe, from the implementation of the post-amnesty phase, since the disarmament process had been concluded. In his place, the group suggested that the ministers for the Niger Delta should lead the implementation of the development programme for the region.[25]

According to a panel set up in January 2010 to review the rehabilitation aspect of the DDR, about 80 per cent of the budget had gone on payments to consultants and contractors, leaving just 20 per cent for the rehabilitation of the ex-militants. The report also noted that 'the number of registered ex-militants had been "over bloated", many militants were still in detention, and criticized training programmes for falling short of acceptable standards and operating with inadequate facilities'.[26] This indictment of the disarmament and rehabilitation programmes also resonated with the views of other groups in the region and assumed greater urgency in the face of several developments. These included the continued absence of the president from the country owing to ill-health, growing pressures on the acting president (from 9 February 2010), Goodluck Jonathan, who was from the Niger Delta and a key architect of the post-2007 Niger Delta peace initiatives to rescue the post-amnesty programme.

On 2 December 2009, then Vice-President Jonathan dissolved the Presidential Committee on Amnesty and Disarmament and replaced it with five committees. These were: the Presidential Monitoring Committee on Amnesty, headed by a former managing director of the NDDC and the presidential adviser on the Niger Delta, Timi Alaibe; the Infrastructural Committee, chaired by the Minister of Niger Delta Affairs, Chief Ufot Ekaette; the Disarmament and Reintegration Committee, chaired by Minister of Defence retired general Godwin Abbe; the Oil and Gas Assets Protection Committee, chaired by the Minister for Petroleum Resources, Rilwanu Lukman; and the Environmental Remediation Committee, chaired by the Minister for Environment, John Odey.[27]

This act also indicated a shift in the centre of power in the post-amnesty project from the minister of defence to the emerging Jonathan presidency and the presidential adviser on the Niger Delta, Timi Alaibe – who was given the role of supervising the post-amnesty programmes. The decision was perhaps informed by Alaibe's closeness to the Jonathan presidency and the need to tap into his political networks, including his knowledge of local Niger Delta politics, and the militias in gaining traction for the rehabilitation and reintegration of ex-militants.

However, Jonathan's full assumption of the presidency, following the death of Yar'Adua on 5 May, led to further changes in the post-amnesty institutions. The appointment of a new set of ministers by President Jonathan created a vacuum as all but one of the leaders (Timi Alaibe) of the five committees were either dropped from the cabinet or reassigned, and reports claimed that the committees would be dissolved.[28] This left room for Alaibe and the Minister of Niger Delta Affairs, Godsay Orubebe (both Niger Delta indigenes), to take charge of post-amnesty rehabilitation, reintegration and development in the Niger Delta under the Jonathan presidency.

Alaibe announced a new phase in the post-amnesty DDR, based on 'transformative training for 20,192 militants', with the training of the first batch of 2,000 planned for June 2010. He reportedly explained that '300 experts' drawn from the United States, South Africa and Nigeria had been put in place for training ex-militants in non-violent conflict transformation.[29] Although the first batch of ex-militants graduated from the 'transformation' training camp coordinated by the Foundation for Ethnic Harmony of Nigeria (FEHN) in Obubra, Cross

River state, in July 2010, it was not to clear to them when the skills acquisition and resettlement component of the reintegration phase of the post-amnesty programme would commence.[30]

There is a school of thought that argues that the amnesty programme has become another arena for factional politics within the Niger Delta elite.[31] It is claimed, for example, that the political friction between the incumbent Bayelsa state governor, Timipre Sylva, and presidential adviser on the Niger Delta Timi Alaibe (allegedly believed to harbour gubernatorial ambitions) was reflected in the ways in which the two men competed in the bid to take sole credit for the surrender of militia leaders. Such views have persisted in the post-amnesty phase, with accusations having been made blaming certain political forces in the Niger Delta for sponsoring ex-militants who marched on Abuja on 7 July 2010 in protest against their exclusion from the training programme. This followed on the heels of a reported attack on Alaibe by some ex-militants during his visit to the Obubra training camp on 1 July.

Thus, the prospects for success for the post-amnesty programme under the new Jonathan presidency appear to be dogged by political wrangling within the Niger Delta elite, the politics within a Jonathan presidency poised to contest the 2011 elections, and the intermittent, piecemeal nature of the implementation of the post-amnesty DDR programme.

Conclusion: peering through a half-open, half-closed window

When President Yar'Adua was inaugurated in May 2007 he accorded the Niger Delta crisis top priority on his seven-point agenda. This culminated in the proclamation of the amnesty in May 2009, which led to a significant drop in violent militia activities in the region, and an increase in oil production figures (from less than 1 million to over 2 million barrels per day), but stopped short of being a comprehensive response to the deep-seated conflict in the region.

His successor, Goodluck Jonathan, has revived the post-amnesty process, promising to 'consolidate the gains of the amnesty program and do all that is humanely possible to prevent the Niger Delta from once again descending into a nightmare'.[32] Between the declarations of both presidents – one from outside, the other from the Niger Delta – lies a window of opportunity for a comprehensive resolution of the violent conflict that can either be opened further to advance justice, peace and development in the region, subverted, or left swinging between an uneasy state of no-war, no-peace.

The roots of the violent conflict While the current initiative focuses on the post-1999 aspect of the violence in the region, it neglects the underlying causes of the conflict which pre-date the discovery of oil in the region (see Ukiwo, Ukeje, Ako, Ahonsi, this volume). It is not clear that lessons learned from the failures of earlier institutional responses to the Niger Delta problem, which are well discussed in the report of the Technical Committee on the Niger Delta, have featured in the design of the amnesty and post-amnesty processes. Indeed, for reasons that remain unclear, the government has not responded to the recommendations of this committee. The response to the conflict has reflected more of a concern with the oil-related aspects of the violence, which, though significantly fuelling the conflict, are not its primary cause. Oil has deepened the volatile tensions and divisions within Delta society and increased the stakes in structural violence. However, such complex crises with connections to the oil economy require a much more engaged response embedded in social policies and democratic politics, not ad hoc programmes based on taking out, or co-opting, violent actors and colluding elites.

Peace: but at what price? The present approach, though reflective of some strategic thinking, does appear to be subordinated to an overall logic of 'buying peace'. Although figures are difficult to come by, nothing less than N400 billion has gone into the amnesty and post-amnesty programmes. A lot of this has been funnelled into contracts, fees, the co-optation of militia commanders, and the running of programmes, while the implementation of a comprehensive plan for the development of the region is yet to commence. Also, vast constituencies of people alienated by petro-business interests, but lacking the means of violence, have been invisible, and excluded from the post-amnesty deal. The question that remains largely unanswered relates to the extent of the sustainability of the current peace process.

It appears that those with the 'big guns' have gained the most from the deal – access to largesse from the government and oil companies, political relevance, and resources that can be deployed for future remobilization. The exclusion of grassroots organizations and the alienation of local knowledge and norms in the construction of peace-building mechanisms and processes raise some difficult questions about the sustainability of the internationally backed state-procured peace.

The international community also has a role to play in ensuring that peace is not at the cost of uninterrupted oil supplies. International support should be given to local groups monitoring the operators of the oil industry – and taking action on violations of rights, oil pollution and other acts that fuel local anger and protests against IOCs. Related to this is the role that international advocacy groups can play in building local capacities for negotiation, monitoring and advocacy. Support is also needed for strengthening local institutions in the areas of the regulation of the oil industry, governance, local entrepreneurial skills, job creation and development skills. The international community also stands to gain a lot from local knowledge about the Niger Delta environment and how its people have responded to ecological challenges over time. It is also important that this process should include mutual respect between global and local knowledge.

Accountability, democracy, justice and the politics of amnesty The amnesty and post-amnesty processes have so far largely remained top-down, elite-driven projects and have predominantly tilted in the direction of securitizing peace and development in the Niger Delta. Issues of popular participation, gender equity, democratic governance, dialogue and access to justice, so necessary for getting the people to ensure that their voices are heard and their interests represented and protected in the process – and legitimacy guaranteed – are played down in favour of those of the dominant elites and militia leaders. Thus, the amnesty and post-amnesty programmes have not been accountable to the people, but rather to the funders, who seem be driven primarily by an interest in stabilizing and securing the conditions for uninterrupted oil production in, and exports from, the region. Closely linked to this are the ways in which some politicians and elites from the Niger Delta have struggled over, or 'cornered', the post-amnesty project, in a context where capacities are weak, and factional politics undermine effective policy design and implementation (see Ahonsi and Ako, this volume).

As a civil society group observed, 'one critical problem that is often overlooked with regard to the Niger delta is that policy formulation is handed to political actors who have little or no experience with developing coherent and integrated plans. Their normal working environment – which consumes most available time – is focused on fire fighting political contests and dividing sources of patronage.'[33] What this view misses out is the issue of how (un)representative the political leadership of the Niger Delta region is, and the attendant high levels of corruption which are not even addressed by the post-amnesty programme. Post-amnesty may be seen more as an opportunity for patronage and positioning for future elections and political power. Under such conditions, issues of professionalism, competence and standards will likely be subordinated to serving the interests of a dominant few. Hence the lack of political will and weak capacity to transform the region will likely remain constraining challenges (Ako, Ahonsi, this volume).

In the final analysis, the way out of the complex violence in the Niger Delta lies in the inclusion of the social movements of the region that have emerged out of its history, and have consistently waged legitimate non-violent struggles for democratic and environmental rights, in the quest for sustainable peace. IOCs also need to transform company–community relations in equitable, participatory and developmental ways that respect and protect the people's rights and livelihoods. They should operate within transparent international environmental best practices and standards, and clean up the oil-polluted environment as part of a long-term strategy of promoting sustainable peace in the region.

Appeasing conflict entrepreneurs and implementing a post-amnesty DDR programme that fundamentally reinforces the dominant relations of power over oil extraction, backed by global oil power, without a corresponding comprehensive response to the critical issues relating to the roots of alienation, marginalization, exploitation, corruption, grievances, the youth and women's questions, and violence, portends ill for a half-open window for peace in the region. Also, the Niger Delta conflict cannot be resolved outside of the Nigeria citizenship question, but should be grounded in the age-old quest for democracy, social justice and equitable redistribution of resources, access to justice, redress and dignity for the majority of the people in the region (Obi 2010).[34]

From the foregoing, the resolution of the complex conflicts revolving around oil, and the inequities in the distributive politics of inclusion and exclusion, depend on the will and capacity of the Nigerian state, its institutions and political elite (of which the Niger Delta elite is a part) and oil MNCs to address the roots of the conflicts at several levels and sectors. A central part of this transformative social project must involve genuine local and national democratic participation, institutional and human capacity development, the empowerment of Niger Delta people, and the mainstreaming of gender relations in conflict transformation and development in the region. A more realistic solution to the conflict lies in a retreat from securitization into non-military engagement and dialogue with stakeholders as well as grassroots people in an open and participatory manner. Also important is reaching a comprehensive and consensus-based programme of Delta-wide socio-economic and infrastructural development.

Notes

Introduction

1 For example, the Associated Gas Reinjection Act of 1979 makes gas flaring in Nigeria illegal, but also gives the petroleum minister the power to grant exemptions to oil companies. Most oil companies prefer to apply for ministerial exemptions, or pay fines for gas flaring and continue breaking the law. The full implementation of the law has been repeatedly postponed by government, in 1984 and 2008, and has been put back to 2012.

2 By virtue of its location along the coast, the Niger Delta was integrated into transatlantic commerce from the fifteenth century onwards, when European merchants traded salt, spices, textiles and then slaves with local traders. In the nineteenth century, the trade in slaves was replaced by that in palm oil, giving way to the trade in petroleum in the second half of the twentieth century. This interaction had a far-reaching impact on the politics, cultures and socio-economic life of the people.

3 Shell D'Arcy commenced operations in 1938 after it was granted an oil concession over the Nigerian mainland by the British colonial government. This gave Shell a head start over other oil companies, which arrived on the scene over two decades later. It is an advantage that Shell has held on to ever since as the largest oil-producing company in Nigeria.

4 The principle of derivation provided that the revenue should be shared in proportion to the contribution by each state/region to the central/federal purse (the greater the amount contributed, the greater the amount received). Before the war, this principle had favoured the old regions based on their cash crop econo-

mies. But after the war (and the collapse of cash crop economies), the reversal of the principle implied that the same hegemonic ethnic groups retained control of the new source of national wealth, oil, even though their states no longer contributed the bulk of national wealth. Instead, the ethnic minorities whose states produced oil were alienated from the bulk of the oil wealth.

5 This is based on the observation that the increase in derivation from 3 to 13 per cent, resulting in a massive increase in federal revenue allocations to the Niger Delta states, has not had any visible developmental impact on the region; rather, several governors from these states and the political elite have amassed huge fortunes. Two such governors have been found guilty of corruption-related crimes, while another is wanted in the UK to answer to money-laundering charges.

6 Illegal oil bunkering refers to the theft of crude oil by tapping into oil pipelines, transporting the stolen oil in barges to oil tankers anchored offshore, for sale in neighbouring countries or farther afield. According to some estimates, Nigeria loses about a tenth of its annual oil production to oil bunkering.

1 The Nigerian state

1 Niger Delta leaders and activists rejected Professor Gambari's appointment because he had defended the hanging of Ken Saro-Wiwa and eight other Ogoni activists when he served as Nigeria's representative at the United Nations in 1995. See I. Chiedozie, 'Niger Delta summit: FG shops for Gambari's replacement', *Punch*, 7 July 2008.

2 This was in response to the position

of Niger Delta leaders and activists that what was needed was not another talking shop but implementation of recommendations of the reports of previous commissions and committees on the region.

3 The resolve of the committee to take independent and radical positions apparently influenced government's decision to ignore it. For instance, government pre-empted the report of the committee by establishing the Ministry of Niger Delta Affairs. See Ekekwe et al. (2010).

4 Formed towards the end of 2005, MEND is a loose coalition of militant groups that through systematic attacks on the oil industry seeks transfer of more resources to the oil-producing region. (See Ukiwo 2007; Watts 2008b; Asuni 2009.)

5 G. Oji and A. Ogbu, 'Ateke surrenders, pressure mounts on Tompolo', *This Day*, online version, 2 October 2009.

6 Transcript of presidential speech aired on *Weekend File*, NTA, 10 October 2009.

7 General Alex Ogomudia, chief of army staff, was chair of the Special Presidential Security Committee on the Niger Delta, empanelled by the Obasanjo administration. General Godwin Abbe was the chair of the Presidential Committee on the Amnesty, Demobilization and Rehabilitation established by President Yar'Adua. To emphasize the security perspective, Abbe was reassigned to serve as minister of defence shortly after his appointment. He was minister of the interior at the time of his appointment.

8 This is imperative as the protracted illness of President Yar'Adua raised concerns over the successful implementation of the post-amnesty programme. A bomb explosion linked to MEND, which disrupted a government forum on the Niger Delta in Warri in March 2010, is indicative of the fragility of the truce.

9 This chapter is primarily concerned with community, state and oil company conflicts. Other forms of violent conflicts in the region are intra- and inter-community conflicts (see Ojo 2002).

10 The first salvo was fired by the fiery Asari Dokubo shortly after being released from detention. The leader of the Niger Delta People's Volunteer Force (NDPVF) was peeved that during his detention a number of groups that had nothing to do with the struggles he was leading had emerged. He promised to ferret out this group. At the time of writing, neither Dokubo nor other militant leaders who made similar threats have arrested so-called criminals.

11 This refers to marshy or swampy land or to dirt generally. Chief Melford Okilo, the late veteran Niger Delta politician, used this term to refer to the Niger Delta peoples. The metaphor also captures the fact that they are poor and live in squalid conditions.

12 See G. Wahab, 'We want a share of our wealth', *Tell*, 25 January 1999, p. 36.

13 ERECTISM called for representation in Nigeria's federation on the basis of ethnicity and the right of people to control their resources and environment. (See Okonta 2008b.)

14 Among the major attacks orchestrated by MEND were the attacks on Bonga field, Nigeria's largest offshore oilfield, in June 2008, and Atlas Cove, Lagos, a major oil distribution artery, in July 2009.

15 See O. Ofiebor, 'Reign of violence', *The News*, 29 May 2006, p. 45.

16 For instance, most legislatures in the Delta are planning to pass executive-sponsored bills to make kidnapping and hostage-taking a criminal offence that will attract capital punishment.

17 This approach has been emphasized even when the armed forces increasingly recognize that security cannot address the issue in the absence of political decisions to address the fundamental grievance of people (see Federal Republic of Nigeria n.d.).

18 See A. Agbo, 'Voting against tokenism', *Tell*, 22 January 2007.

19 See *Newswatch*, 28 July 2008, pp. 58–60.

20 See 'Communiqué issued at the end of the special Ogoni National Congress held at Suanu Finimale Nwika

Conference Hall, Bori', *The Hard Truth*, 31 July–6 August 2008, p. 8.

3 The struggle for resource control

1 Part of the text of the communiqué issued at the end of the Third Summit of Southern States' Governors held in Benin City, Edo state, on 27 March 2001. See Senator David Dafinone, *Resource Control: The Economic & Political Dimensions*, on-line at the Urhobo Historical Society website, www.waado.org/nigerdelta/ essays/ resourcecontrol/Dafinone.html, accessed 22 April 2010.

2 The two reference cases, re Secession of Quebec [1998], 2 S.C.R. 217, and *Lalonde* v. *Ontario* (Commission de re-structuration des services de santé), 2001 CanLII 21164 (ON C.A.), defined federalism generally and specifically examined the Canadian conception.

3 *Attorney-General of the Federation* v. *Attorney-General of Abia State* (2001) 11 NWLR (pt. 725) 689.

4 According to the professor, agencies such as the Department of Petroleum Resources (DPR), which presently supervises the industry, and the Nigerian National Petroleum Corporation (NNPC), which partners the oil multinationals on behalf of the federal government, will be under the control of the body.

4 The question of access to justice

1 Such as the Universal Declaration of Human Rights 1948, the International Covenant on Civil and Political Rights 1966, the International Covenant on Economic, Social and Cultural Rights 1966, the International Convention on the Elimination of All Forms of Racial Discrimination 1965, the Convention on the Elimination of All Forms of Racial Discrimination against Women 1979, the Convention against Torture and Other Cruel, Inhuman or Degrading Treatment or Punishment 1984, the UN Convention on the Rights of the Child 1989, the International Convention on the Protection of the Rights of All

Migrant Workers and Members of their Families 1990, the Convention on Access to Information, Public Participation in Decision-Making and Access to Justice in Environmental Matters 1998.

2 See also see *Sarei* v. *Rio Tinto, PLC*, 456 F.3d 1069, 1073-74 (9th Cir. 2006).

3 *Beanal* v. *Freeport-McMoran* Inc. 969 F. Supp. 362 (E.D.La., 1997); Australian Council for Overseas Aid, *Eyewitness Accounts of West Papuan Resistance to the Freeport-McMoran mine in Irian Jaya, Indonesia and Indonesian Military Repression*, June 1994–February 1995, www. utwatch.org/corporations/freeportfiles/ acfoa.html, accessed 11 January 2009. While the veracity of these accounts is contested, they do provide some evidence of the existence of conflict in this resource-rich area and the issue of access to justice.

4 The recognition of collective rights is also a key feature of the African Charter on Human and Peoples' Rights, Banjul, Gambia, January 1981, OAU Doc. CAB/Leg/67/3/Rev 5 (1981); reprinted 21 ILM 59-68 (1982).

5 S.1 of the Land Use Act of 1979, now Cap 202, LFN, 1990.

6 S.29 (1) & (4) of Land Use Act.

7 Ss 2 & 3 of the Constitution of the Federal Republic of Nigeria, 1999.

8 S. 4 (2) (4), read together with Item 39 of Part 1 of the Second Schedule to the Constitution of the Federal Republic of Nigeria, 1999.

9 The Federal Environmental Protection Agency Act, 1988, Cap 131, LFN, 1990, as amended by Decree No. 59 of 1992 & Decree No. 14 of 1999. This law has now been repealed and replaced with the National Environmental Standards and Regulations Enforcement Agency (Establishment) Act 2007.

10 The Harmful Wastes (Special Criminal Provisions) Act, Cap 165, LFN, 1990.

11 Although recently the National Oil Spill Detection and Response Agency (Establishment) Act (NOSDRA) was enacted in December 2006, with the main objective of the agency being to detect

and respond to major oil pollution (see Section 5).

12 Section 3 of the Associated Gas Re-injection Act, Cap 26 LFN, 1990.

13 Federal High Court of Lagos Suit no. FHC/L/CS/573/96, which ruling was delivered on 17 February 1997.

14 See, for instance, *John Eboigbe and Others* v. *The Nigerian National Petroleum Corporation* (1994) 5 NWLR (pt.346) 649, where plaintiffs' ignorance of their legal rights prevented litigation until the action was statute-barred.

15 Although the Nigerian Legal Aid Scheme was introduced in 1976, it provided only for legal aid in respect of criminal cases. A further amendment in 1986 merely extended it to cover civil claims in respect of accidents. See Section 7 of the Legal Aid Act, Cap 205, LFN, 1990. See also A. Ibidapo-Obe, 'The jurisprudence of social justice in Nigeria', in W. Owaboye (ed.), *Fundamental Legal Issues in Nigeria: Essays in Honour of Justice Obaseki*, 1995, p. 188.

16 For instance, it took over fourteen years for the case of *Chief Joel Anare and Others* v. *Shell Petroleum Development Company Nigeria Ltd* Unreported Suit No. HCB/35/89, Delta State High Court, Ughelli Division, 27 June 1997, to be concluded in the trial court. The appeal process is set to take even longer!

17 *Owodunni* v. *Registered Trustees of Celestial Church & ors.* (2000) 10 NWLR (Pt.675) 315.

18 See, for instance, the case of *Amos and Anor* v. *Shell BP(Nig) Ltd* 4 ECSLR 486, where oil pollution of a waterway was held to be a public nuisance and therefore even a representative action was not sufficient.

19 See, for instance, *Allar Iron* v. *Shell-BP* Unreported Suit No. W/89/71, where a high court's reason for not granting an injunction was that nothing should be done to disturb the operations of the oil industry which 'is the main stay of this country's revenue'.

20 In *Onyoh* v. *Shell-BP* (1982) 12 CA 144, at 159-156, the court quite inexplicably decided not to grant the amount claimed even though it was fair so as not to 'sour the good relationship which exists between the parties in their positions of landlord and tenants'.

21 See *Social and Economic Rights Action Center and the Center for Economic and Social Rights* v. *Nigeria*, African Commission on Human and Peoples' Rights Comm. No. 155/96 (2001), available at www.serac.org/African percent 20Commn per cent20 Communication per cent20and per cent20Decision.doc; and *Jonah Gbemre* v. *Shell Petroleum Development Corporation of Nigeria Ltd and Ors* (suit no FHC/B/CS/53/05, Federal High Court, Benin Judicial Divison, 14 November 2005).

6 Changing the paradigm

1 An earlier version of this chapter was presented at the international workshop on Violent Conflict in the Niger Delta organized by the Nordic Africa Institute, Uppsala, Sweden, and the International Peace and Research Institute, Oslo, Norway, 18/19 August 2008.

2 Hard power refers to the deployment of large military forces, ruthless incarceration and suppression of dissent, brutal killings, etc., while soft power focuses on developmental interventions that meet the needs of the inhabitants of oil-producing areas in a sustained and sustainable manner.

3 Crude oil has consistently accounted for 65–95 per cent of Nigeria's foreign exchange earnings and about 40 per cent of the country's GDP. Under the subsisting revenue allocation formula, the three tiers of government share revenues from oil deposited in the Federation Account based on a formula that gives more than half to the federal rather than state and local governments.

4 Since crude oil displaced agriculture as the major component of gross domestic product in Nigeria in the late 1960s, successive governments have tinkered with the revenue allocation formula based on the principle of derivation, bringing it down from 100 per cent to 50 per cent and now 13 per cent.

5 It is important to note that matters relating to the Delta region featured on the agenda of the major European powers that attended the infamous Berlin Conference of 1884/85.

6 For a very interesting account of the exploits of the Royal West African Frontier Forces (RWAFF), see Asiegbu (1984: xxv–xxviii).

7 Two such ordinances were promulgated in 1912: the Collective Punishment Ordinance No. 67 and the Unsettled Districts Ordinance No. 15 (see C.O. 588/4 and C.O. 538/173/2).

8 C.O. 537/5783: Report of Police Adviser on his visit to Nigeria.

9 A similar fate befell the controversial multibillion Naira Police Equipment Fund, whose leadership, reportedly very close to the former president, Olusegun Obasanjo, is currently under investigation by the Economic and Financial Crimes Commission, the EFCC.

10 Perhaps the military authorities did not know that this was the same as the code name for the battered and badly bruised US military intervention in Mogadishu in 1993, which led to the death of eighteen American soldiers before the military was chased out by clan warriors.

11 'Navy reiterate readiness to ensure waterways safety', *The Tide Online*, 22 July 2007; 'RSG to assist navy fight criminality in N'Delta', *The Tide Online*, 22 July 2007.

12 'Sylva urges navy to increase presence in Bayelsa', *The Tide Online*, 27 August 2007.

13 'Navy holds sea exercise', *This Day Online*, 23 June 2008, available at www.thisdayonline.com.

14 It is estimated that between November 2005 and May 2007, 100 million barrels of oil were exported from Bonga, an oilfield of common interest to Britain/Shell (55 per cent), the United States/ExxonMobil (20 per cent), France/Elf (12.5 per cent) and Italy/Agip (12.5 per cent) respectively. In the aftermath of that attack, the price of crude oil went up by 91 cents (*Guardian*, 20 June 2008).

15 'Nigeria haemorrhages', *Guardian Online*, 20 June 2008.

16 'Revealed: why Bonga oil field was easy target', *This Day Online*, 24 June 2008, available at www.thisdayonline.com.

17 *Daily Trust*, 7 July 2008.

18 According to one estimate, there are at least 7,200 kilometres of pipelines, 159 oilfields and 275 flow stations (O'Neill 2006: 3).

19 According to Omeje (2006b: 488), Outsourcing Security Services Nigeria Ltd, a subsidiary of a major South African security corporation, presently supplies over three hundred unarmed security guards to Chevron.

20 There is still official denial of the existence of foreign private security outfits, or in plain terms mercenaries, in the Niger Delta. Some that have been mentioned in discussions include: Control Risk, Triple Canopy, Erinys, Armor Group, and ADS (interview, Port Harcourt, 2008).

21 Interview, Shell staff, Port Harcourt, 2007.

22 In a swift response, however, MEND argued that the actual amount paid to some fronts, operating as criminal gangs, was $25 million (shared by top commanders of the Joint Task Force, senior government officials in Delta state, the top management of the state-owned NNPC, etc. (See 'NNPC, MEND trade claims on pay to militants', *Guardian Online*, 24 July 2008.)

23 A very good example, but by no means the only one, is the location of Madagho military base just next to Chevron's Escravos plant, from where the American company mobilized troops to wreak havoc on recalcitrant communities – for instance, the Opia and Ikenya – in 1999. (See Human Rights Watch 1999b: 3–7.)

24 In early March 2009, the government of Equatorial Guinea accused the Nigerians, especially militants of the Niger Delta, of attacking the presidential palace in Malabo. See author's comments during a phone interview with Radio France International (RFI) on 23 March 2009. (See also Ukeje 2008.)

25 It is important to note that this is

a highly amorphous group, comprising indigenes and non-indigenes of the Niger Delta region. Given the spectre of violence and instability in the region, many Delta elites live in places like Abuja, the Federal Capital Territory and Lagos, but maintain regular contacts with their affiliates within the region.

26 A good example in this regard is the policy of the United States and Britain towards Nigeria and its troubled oil region. Rather than bring the enormous political and diplomatic leverage at their disposal to bear on the Nigerian leadership to embrace qualitative changes that bring relief to the people and promote genuine democratic consolidation, Washington and London have vacillated between indifference and preference for military rather than political solutions. See, for instance, 'Gulf of Guinea: Britain, Nigeria meet on security', *This Day Online*, 16 June 2008, available at www.thisdayonline.com; 'France to help tame Delta militants', *The Nation Online*, 28 June 2008; 'Niger Delta summit on agenda as Yar'Adua, Bush, Ban meet', *Guardian Online*, 5 July 2008.

27 It is estimated that this figure will rise to 25 per cent by 2015.

28 It has been estimated that the US Navy spent only ten ship days in the Gulf of Guinea in 2004, but by the end of 2007 the forces had been present all year round (Sorbara 2007: 56–8).

29 In 2003, the USA delivered two previously decommissioned Second World War ships to the NN.

30 See also 'Defence: Nigeria, UK sign MOU on capacity building', *This Day Online*, 13 June 2008, available at www.thisdayonline.com.

31 For a short discussion on the Britain-led Extractive Industry Transparency Initiative (EITI) launched in 2003, see Aaronson (2008).

8 'Mend Me'

1 Two exceptions are Clapham (1998) and Bøås and Dunn (2007).

2 See also 'Militants hit pipelines again', *This Day*, 22 April 2008.

3 Violence and conflict in key oil-producing countries facilitated a series of record prices from the beginning of 2008, as the market feared that supply would be insufficient to meet the demand from China and other growing economies in Asia. Investors moving into oil and other commodities as a hedge against the weakening dollar also caused part of the increase.

4 The 2007 Nigerian elections are generally seen as a violent farce and an orgy of corruption and electoral rigging. See European Union (2007) and Human Rights Watch (2007b).

5 After spending almost two years in prison awaiting the outcome of his trial, Okah was released in the spring of 2009 to boost the credibility of the government's amnesty offer. How much credibility this has added can, however, be questioned as there is every reason to believe that the part of MEND that most vocally has argued against accepting the amnesty offer is the faction that Okah belonged to.

6 See 'Militants hit pipelines again', *This Day*, 22 April 2008.

7 In 2007, the Rivers state government had a budget of US$1.4 billion. This was roughly five times the national average across all state governments. The tremendous wealth pouring into the coffers of the major oil-producing states such as Rivers has been mirrored by an equally large amount of waste and graft. In Rivers state, primary schools and basic health-care services have been left to crumble even as the state government budget has increased fourfold since 1999. Graft and patronage are the signatures of the government, not development and human security; see also Watts (2008a).

8 Sometimes also referred to as the 'Icelanders'.

9 This sections draws on Small Arms Survey (2007) and Human Rights Watch (2008).

10 For example, the 'Vikings' cult (aka Supreme Vikings Confraternity) was originally founded at the University of Port Harcourt in 1984. It has since expanded, and has members in universities all over

southern Nigeria. Its current and past members have been elected to high office, including in the Rivers state House of Assembly (according to rumours, in such high numbers that the Assembly should be renamed the 'Viking House'). Ateke Tom's NDV (Icelanders) were originally the 'street wing' of the 'Vikings'. Similarly, the campus-based cult the 'Klansmen' started the 'Deebam' as its 'street wing'.

11 Presumably to prevent them from 'bunkering'.

12 The Joint Task Force is made up of a combination of personnel from the police, military and the state security services, headquartered at Bori Camp (an army base in Port Harcourt). One can only speculate why it took so long before the Nigerian state intervened – one possible answer is that letting the armed groups 'kill' each other was seen as a cost-effective way of dealing with groups that had started to develop agendas and in-terests contrary to those of their 'masters'.

13 This is how it is argued in MEND parlance.

14 Two Norwegian and two Ukrainian employees of Trico Supply AS were kid-napped and taken from their ship. Trico Supply AS is a Norwegian affiliate of a US-based company, Trico Marine, which supplies marine support services to the oil and gas industry. The supply boat had been leased by Peak Petroleum. The men were later set free, unharmed. See Bøås (2006a, 2006b).

9 Popular and criminal violence

1 According to Davies (2009: 100–120), cults are violent urban/street gangs largely spun off from university fraternities that seek to define their authority over a given area. Examples include: Dee Well, Dee Gbam, Icelanders and Outlaws. Some of these cults later transformed either through mergers or by forceful integration or collapse into larger militias.

2 To many of the insurgents, oil bunkering is not a 'crime' as the oil they 'take' rightly belongs to them as indigenes of the Niger Delta. According to this logic,

the 'real thieves' are the outsiders: oil MNCs and the federal government, which take away the oil that does not belong to them.

10 Swamped with weapons

1 The common definition used for SALW was developed in 1997 by the UN Panel of Government Experts on Small Arms. They defined small arms as 'weapons designed for personal use' and light weapons as weapons 'designed for use by several persons serving as a crew'. More concretely this means that small arms include revolvers and self-loading pistols, rifles and carbines, sub-machine guns, assault rifles and light machine guns. Under light weapons we can find heavy machine guns, hand-held under-barrel and mounted grenade launchers, portable anti-aircraft and anti-tank guns, portable launchers of anti-aircraft and anti-tank missile systems and mortars of calibres up to 100mm (Bourne 2007).

2 These specific SALW are often referred to as the *weapons of choice* of non-state armed groups. Yet some analysts (e.g. Wezeman 2003) argue that SALW are primarily the *weapons of opportunity*, not of choice. Many insurgents would prefer more powerful – but also more expensive – weapons, but lack the necessary resources to obtain them.

3 Several analysts (e.g. Vines 2005) believe the real figure for illicit SALW circu-lating in the region is probably lower, but this does not reduce the problem, given the continuing trend of proliferation.

4 A survey in Bayelsa state in September 2005 confirms the wide range of weapons used by non-state actors in the Niger Delta (Isumonah et al. 2005).

5 Until 1999 violence between differ-ent armed groups was carried out with rudimentary weapons like machetes and bottles (Croft and Concannon 2006). A number of armed groups are still prim-arily armed with machetes, clubs, bows and arrows, although they also possess firearms. Increasingly, however, even the groups that have traditionally possessed

few guns are acquiring more of them (Florquin and Berman 2005). Besides SALW and more rudimentary weapons, armed groups in the Niger Delta also hold heavy weapons and explosives (WAC Global Services 2003) and probably possess remote-detonation, night-vision equipment and anti-aircraft missiles (Iannaccone 2007).

6 Most of the people living in the Niger Delta do not belong to the three major ethnic groups that dominate Nigeria (Yoruba, Igbo and Hausa-Fulani). The largest ethnic group in the Niger Delta is the Ijaw, collectively the fourth-largest group in Nigeria, but itself divided into different subgroups speaking their own dialect. Most of the 8 million people who consider themselves Ijaw live in riverine areas of Bayelsa, Delta and Rivers states, and in Port Harcourt, Warri and other towns on dry land. Other ethnic groups in the Niger Delta include the Ogoni, Itsekiri, Ikwerre, Urhobo, Edo and the Isoko (Human Rights Watch 1999b).

7 Examples of such communal strife are the violence between the Gberegolor community in the Ugheli South local government area and the Esama community in the Bomadi local government area (1996), between the Ogbe-Ijoh community and the Aladja (1996), between the Umasadge and Benekrukru communities in the Ndokwa East and West local government areas (1999), and between the Olomoro, Oleh and Emede communities in the Isoko South local government area (1998/99) (Abayomi et al. 2005).

8 A number of these youth groups were formed during the period of military rule and were initially supported by the military regime as sources of information and political influence over traditional community leaders who were not collaborating with the regime (WAC Global Services 2003).

9 Besides oil bunkering and arms trafficking, criminal armed groups are involved in money laundering, protection rackets, contract killings and a variety of other activities (Concannon and Croft 2006).

10 Although officially part of the police forces, SPY police officers de facto take their orders from the international oil companies, who also supervise and evaluate them. Their only association with the Nigerian police force is the limited training they receive shortly after being recruited.

11 The smuggling of weapons from peacekeeping missions to other conflict areas was confirmed by former ECOMOG commander, retired general Victor Malu (Bah 2004).

12 'Nigeria: army of illegal arm dealers', *This Day*, 8 December 2008.

13 Despite a rejection of this transfer by the Nigerian Senate, the territory was formally transferred to Cameroon in August 2008.

14 Guns 'made in Ghana' are known in West Africa for their reliability, accessibility and reasonable price. The Ghanaian gunsmiths do not produce their own ammunition, but design their firearms on the basis of the ammunition available on the open market (Aning 2005).

15 Some analysts (e.g. Vines 2005) argue that the illicit possession of and trade in SALW can be traced back to the failure to execute a comprehensive arms collection programme after the 'Biafran war', the civil war that raged through the south-eastern provinces of Nigeria between 1967 and 1970.

16 Although a very common practice in West Africa, there are no reports of arms transfers by foreign governments to armed groups in the Niger Delta (Florquin and Berman 2005).

17 Nigeria shares land borders with Niger, Benin and Cameroon. Besides these land borders, Nigeria also has 853 kilometres of coastline.

18 Several reports have appeared on the prices of SALW in the Niger Delta. Yet one needs to interpret these prudently since prices not only fluctuate greatly over time, but also vary considerably depending on the quality and age of the weapons, the location where they are sold and the interaction between local supply and local demand.

19 Between 1998 and 2004, arms collection initiatives collected more than 200,000 small arms in West Africa, of which at least 70,000 were subsequently destroyed. Such initiatives have also been undertaken in Nigeria. Over the years, the Nigerian government has collected tens of thousands of weapons and hundreds of thousands of bullets from armed political and criminal groups operating in the country. Yet the results of these disarmament processes are not always unambiguous. For more information on the problems that have arisen with the successive disarmament processes in Nigeria, see Florquin and Berman (2005).

11 Women's protests

1 They suffered environmental pollution on 29 November 2008, with an oil slick floating on the river and polluting the land.

2 Transport by boat from Warri to Gbaramatu cost N3,000 in August 2006.

3 Interview with Janet Ogoba, Warri, 28 August 2006.

4 The river was called Escravos because it served as the hub of the slave trade in Nigeria in the eighteenth century. Today, the Escravos is a tributary of the Niger river, ending at the Bight of Benin of the Gulf of Guinea, where it flows into the Atlantic Ocean, and Chevron's main production facility is located at the mouth of the Escravos river.

5 Interview with Chief Mrs Josephine Ogoba, Warri, 10 August 2006.

6 Information from focus group discussions held with women in Kenyagbene, 12 August 2006. The women include Sokari, Ebiere, Mrs Priye and Esther Igho.

7 The MoU is an agreement entered into with each community affected by oil corporations' activities. But the GMoU is a more comprehensive agreement, covering all oil communities or states at the same time, whether affected by oil spills or not. In this case, the state is divided into clusters of oil-rich communities and the clusters are governed by the same agreement based on the general needs of the people. The GMoU covers a period of five years, after which it can be evaluated and renegotiated.

8 Interview with Omiekuma Numo (the woman who first saw the spills and took the news to the Okoroba community), 26 February 2009.

9 Translated: 'Shell workers are wicked. They have taken our land, oil, health and food without compensation and they still expect us to keep quiet. Never again.'

10 The nurse on duty confirmed that patients suffered from dysentery after cooking in and drinking the water fetched from the river. One of the patients died owing to the failure of her family to rush her to the clinic before her case worsened.

11 Interview conducted with the Ogboloma women's leader Chief (Mrs) Pinaere Ayama, Ogboloma, 20 February 2009.

12 This fact was reiterated by Ogboloma women, including Ebiere Posa, Ruth Kemebidou, Ayaere Aladama, Friday Zidiba, Love Amaebi and Adi Kemepadei, in a focus group discussion on 20 February 2009.

13 An air of authority and power could be sensed in the discussions with men such as: Chief Opaminola Ezekiel, Okoroba compound chief; Chief Vincent Wobi, Ogboloma's landlord for Etelebou flow station; Chief Y. Z. Mamamu, Ogbeh Ijo community leader; and Mr Inimitie of Okerenkoko.

14 The statement was made by Mrs Obeite Ngolayefa in a group discussion with Okoroba women, 10 February 2009.

15 Focus group discussions with Kokodiagbene women such as Alaere Amaladei, Clarina Gbasa and Amaere Dorgu, in Kokodiagbene, 5 March 2009.

16 Interviews with Hezekiah Ibedangha, Ayakurai Freeman and Chief Vincent Wozi, Ogboloma, 10 and 11 March 2009.

17 Face-to-face interview with the Kokodiagbene's women leader Mrs Victoria Abadi, 5 March 2009.

18 Interviews with Karibo Olali (Okoroba), Ayakorai Freeman (Ogboloma),

Ezekiel Ibedangha (Ogboloma), 11 February 2009.

19 Interview with the Okoroba women's leader Mrs Selai S. Douglas, Okoroba, 16 February 2009.

20 Focus group discussions with women in Ogboloma, 9 February 2009.

21 In-depth interview with the Okoroba women's leader Mrs Selai S. Douglas, Okoroba, 11 February 2009.

22 E. Arubi, 'Nigeria: oil spill displaces 10 Ijaw communities', *Vanguard*, 13 February 2007.

23 Focus group discussions with women such as Ikiomoere Aladei, Janet Seiyefa, Beniere Sagbe and Warriere Nimitei, 10 March 2009.

24 Interviews with Chief Vincent Wozi, Ogboloma, 11 February 2009.

25 Interview with Faith Irite, secretary-general of Iyoroabu-Ebidou Ogbo, 10 August 2006.

26 Interview with the community development officer at the SPDC Unit, Yenagoa, Bayelsa state, 16 February 2009.

27 Interview with Deborah Laju Eda, founder and chairperson of the Coastal Women's Forum, Warri Delta state, 24 January 2009. The Technical Committee, which was inaugurated on 5 September 2009, comprised the following (F indicating female and M indicating male): Professor Ayebaemi (F); Atei Beredugo (M); Magnus Njei (M); Chibuzo Ugwoha (M); Ledum Mitee (M); Tony Uranta (M); Anyakwe Nsirimovu (M); Timi Alaibe (M); Prince Tony T. J. T. Princewill (M); Chief Olusola Oke (M); Col. Wole Ohunayo (M); Hon. D. L. Kekemeke (M); Barrister Cyril Anyanwu (M); Dr Sam Amadi (M); Dr Godswill Ihetu (M); Prof. G. M. Umezurike (M); Charles Edosomwan (M); Prof. Julius Ihonvbere (M); Admiral P. Ebhale (M); Ben Bouegbor (M); Senator Chief (Mrs) Stella Omu (F); Sam Amuka Pemu (M); Barrister Bernard Jamatiu (M); Dr Abel Dafighor (M); Nkoyo Toyo (F); Prof. Omafume Onoge (M); Prof. B. I. Ijomah(M); Chief I. Jemide (M); Lt Col. Paul E. Obi (M); Ukandi G. Ogar (M); Dr Youpele Banigo (M); Prof. Austin Ikein (M); Dr Lawrence Ekpebu (M); Chief John Anderson Eseimokumoh (M); Grace Ekong (F); Dr Kalu Idika Kalu (M); Chief E. C. Adiele (M); Chief Tony Esu (M); and Prof. Peter King (M).

28 Mr Ufot Ekaette is the Minister of Niger Delta Affairs and Elder Godsay Orubebe is the Minister of State for Niger Delta Affairs.

29 Interview with Chief Y. Z. Mamamu, community leader of Ogbeh Ijoh, 10 March 2009.

12 Corporate social responsibility

1 For example, in response to the increase in community violence Shell's community relations spending rose from $330,000 in 1989 to $43 million in 1998, to $67 million in 2002, and dropped back to $30.8 million in 2003 with the adoption of partnership.

2 Empirical data presented here are part of a broader study in which 160 households were surveyed and 130 interviews conducted in Akwa Ibom state. Field observation was also undertaken in Rivers, Bayelsa and Delta states between 2005 and 2008.

3 This was when Sonangol, the state-owned Angolan oil company, threatened to terminate BP's contract over BP's efforts to publish payments to government in 2002.

4 For example, the Nembe War in Bayelsa state and the Emouha versus Ogbakiri inter-community violence in Rivers state over development benefits from oil MNCs.

5 For example, Ukiwo (2008a) highlighted how youths in Evwreni in Delta state decapitated their traditional ruler over allegations of misappropriation of funds from oil MNCs.

6 For example, youths in Umuechem in Rivers state got a sit-at-home allowance under the guise of surveillance contracts from Shell.

7 The psychological contract is the implicit expectations that companies and communities have of each other; it typically remains beneath the surface of the relations and is dynamic, continually

changing and frequently unacknowledged (Burke 1999).

13 Labelling oil, contesting governance

1 As expressed since 2006 in the constitution of the US Africa Command.

2 At the 2003 SPDC Women's Peacebuilding Forum in Yenagoa this connection was made explicit, with women-as-mothers criticized for neglecting their 'duty' to foster good behaviour among their sons.

3 These had precursors in a number of areas near Soku and Cawthorne Channel in the immediately preceding years, discussed below.

4 Advanced by a key development NGO in the Niger Delta as substitute for problematic host community relations. I should note that a representative of the NGO that promoted the whole community model made clear to me by email that they in no way saw the GMoU as an accurate reflection of their idea – but rather as a negative manipulation of it.

5 As described in the October 2003 Legaloil.com Information Paper no. 1: 'Bunkering is a term used to describe the process of filling a ship with oil (or coal). "Illegal bunkering" as used in respect to oil is a euphemism for oil theft.'

6 In contrast to 2004, when Governor Alamieseigha asserted that 'no Ijaw man is lifting oil', today some of the region's militia leaders tend to equate bunkering with resource control. And despite the relatively unsympathetic global imagery provided of the Delta's 'insurgent' groups, their spokespeople nevertheless do manage to make their interpretation heard internationally.

7 Marx suggested primitive accumulation was a historically continuous process, a point taken up by Harvey through the notion of 'accumulation by dispossession'. In describing accumulation via state and private coffers at a recent conference at the University of Port Harcourt, Nigeria, Eskor Toyo distinguished between primitive accumulation and 'accumulation out

of the surplus generated by wage labour in an already formed capitalist enterprise'. Here we use this phrase to indicate that calls for local resource sovereignty may overlap with accumulation of capital in limited hands, or what Ekeh has called the 'primordial public' of the clan or family; these hands may have redistributive tendencies as per the 'first public' of the clan or family (Ekeh 1975).

8 In 1990 MOSOP, a representative organization of the Ogoni in the Niger Delta, presented the Ogoni Bill of Rights to the Nigerian government. The Bill protested about environmental degradation and livelihood destruction by Shell, and included a demand for political autonomy for the Ogoni. In response to mass community protests, the Nigerian military regimes of Generals Ibrahim Babangida and Sani Abacha, with the prompting of Shell, massacred hundreds of Ogoni and murdered the top leadership of their organization, including the charismatic president, Ken Saro-Wiwa, in 1995. In solidarity with the Ogoni and other Niger Delta communities, environmental justice organizations in Europe and North America initiated a boycott campaign against Shell's products.

9 In 2008 the now late President Yar'Adua made demands for increased royalties from oil majors. See, for instance, Green (2008a, 2008b).

10 Referred to, at times, by Chevron as a Community Trust and by Shell as a Regional Development Council. On this point, one informant noted that in some oilfields both of these bodies – one supported by Chevron and one by Shell – overlap with one another under each company's separate GMoU. In other places, a GMoU has been signed or established where another independent community development foundation along the lines of the 'Akassa Model' supported by the NGO Pro Natura International was already in existence.

11 This is not universally accepted. In Delta state in August 2006 various informants complained that to facilitate

the GMoU Chevron was requesting the cancellation of previous community-level memoranda of understanding which had not yet been fulfilled. Shell was addressing this problem through the designation of its 'legacy projects' team.

12 Or 'good corporate citizen' within the global polity.

13 As epitomized in Shell's pamphlet entitled 'There is no alternative' prepared for the 2002 Johannesburg World Summit on Sustainable Development.

14 NNPC – Nigerian National Petroleum Corporation. The recently released film *The Smartest Guys in the Room* reveals that Enron was involved in early financing for the LNG tanker project, which involved dubious deals with various banks to periodically assume ownership when in the red. Enron and Merril Lynch's involvement with a dubious scheme to provide energy to Lagos through offshore oil- and gas-burning projects was recently confirmed through the conviction of four Merrill Lynch and one Enron executive in a scheme that boosted their earnings and made the project appear profitable (Ackerman 2004).

15 I began fieldwork on this case during dissertation research in 2002/03; the coverage of it in the WAC report ultimately corroborated its acting as a 'model' for the new SCD approach.

16 E. J. Alagoa documents the colonial era war between the Kalabari and Nembe for control over riverine trade routes (Alagoa 1964: 88–90). What is referred to contemporarily as Nembe Town, made up of the neighbouring communities of Bassambiri and Ogbolomambiri, has received considerable attention owing to ongoing violence between groups of competing youth seeking security contracts for nearby flow stations (see Manby 1998; Kemedi 2003; Watts 2004).

17 SPDC staff tended to show greater sympathy and concern towards Elem Sangama, which they consider more organized and less confrontational.

18 See, for example, Bayelsa state sources at www.travelsyt.com/bayelsa1.htm.

19 The contrasting use of these arguments in academic discourse is seen in Okonta's (2008b) application of a rational-choice, limited-resource perspective to the struggle for Ogoni self-determination versus Peluso and Watts's (2001) critique of neo-Malthusian approaches to conflict by signalling that in fact it is surplus, not scarcity, which is conflict-inducing in oil-rich economies. It is the constructed scarcity which is key to fictitious market relations, following a Marxian approach. Nevertheless, the 'paradox of plenty' and construction of foreign goods as desirable are central to the production of 'oil subjects' and experienced scarcity is essential to this in the Nigerian context.

20 During interviews in 2003, Shell staff indicated that the company would not commit to broad-scale electrification projects owing to the tendency for such activity to create expectations in neighbouring communities. This policy appears to have changed owing to criticism from international NGOs, including Christian Aid and Catholic Relief Services, given that the 2003 SPDC People and Environment Report makes reference to planned electrification projects across the area surrounding the Soku gas plant. On a related note, Shell-financed water projects in each of the communities remained non-functional or incomplete, paralleling the state of affairs throughout the Delta. This general failure of water projects is documented in the 2002 External Stakeholders Review of SPDC projects, and by various observers.

21 Various major projects that I observed in 2003 remained incomplete in 2006 – including the hospital in Oluasiri.

22 Youth associations from the three host communities of Akuku-Toru Local Government of Rivers state and Nembe Local Government of Bayelsa state have jointly issued a fourteen-day ultimatum to SPDC demanding compensation for deprivation of work experience and empowerment opportunities due to them. The petition was signed by the presidents of the three youth federations: Mr Orusakwe

Aseimiegha, leader of the South-Youth Welfare Association T. O. F. Windah and president of the Eleme-Sangama Youth Movement, Comrade Soingo Benson Duke.

14 Amnesty and post-amnesty peace

1 Various newspapers and AllAfrica. com.

2 Interview with Ledum Mitee by Siri Rustad, December 2008.

3 BBC, 7 July 2008, news.bbc.co.uk/2/ hi/africa/7500472.stm, accessed 27 March 2009.

4 Nick Tattersall, 'Nigerian oil rebels reject Niger Delta Summit', Reuters, 17 June 2008, www.reuters.com/article/ idUSL17190258, accessed 17 May 2010.

5 AllAfrica, 1 July 2008, allafrica.com/ stories/200807010001.html, accessed 27 March 2009.

6 AllAfrica, 9 September 2008, allafrica.com/stories/200809090144. html, accessed 27 March 2009, and www. nigerdeltatechnicalcommittee.org.

7 Henry Okah is a leader of the Movement of the Emancipation of the Niger Delta. He was arrested and detained in Angola in February 2008, later deported to Nigeria and charged, among other crimes, with treason, terrorism, illegal possession of firearms and arms trafficking. Okah was later released under an amnesty package for Niger Delta militants.

8 www.vanguardngr.com/content/ view/33928/44, accessed 24 April 2008.

9 www.independentngonline.com/ news/tfpg/article01, accessed 12 September 2008.

10 allafrica.com/stories/200812260 150. html, accessed 27 March 2009.

11 Exchange rate as at 27 April 2009.

12 allafrica.com/stories/200901121 310.html, accessed 25 March 2009.

13 Ibid., accessed 25 March 2009.

14 www.vanguardngr.com/content/ view/27171/45/, accessed 29 April 2009.

15 allafrica.com/stories/200902120 104.html, accessed 29 April 2009.

16 Yar'Adua's Niger Delta Amnesty Proclamation, www.saharareporters.com/ index.php?option=com_content&view= article&id=3088:yaradua-qniger-deltaq-amnesty-proclamation&catid=42:exclusive &Itemid=160, accessed 17 May 2010.

17 Examples of militia leaders who handed in their weapons were: Government Ekpemupolo (Tompolo), Solomon Ndigbara (aka Osama Bin Laden), Ateke Tom, Ebikabowei Ben Victor (aka Boyloaf), John Togo, Africa Owei, 'Commander' Africa Ukparasia, 'Commander' Joshua McIver, Soboma Jackrich (aka Egberi Papa), Prince Amabiye (aka Busta Rhymes), Soboma George, Farah Dagogo, 'Commander' Ogunboss, Kile Selky Torughedi (aka Commander Young Shall Grow), 'Commander' Toruma Ngologo, and many others.

18 www.ngrguardiannews.com/ editorial_opinion/article01/indexn2_ html?pdate=190409&ptitle=The per cen-t20Amnesty per cent20Offer per cent20To per cent20Niger per cent20Delta per cent20Militants, accessed 20 April 2009.

19 www.thetimesofnigeria.com/Article. aspx?id=1620, accessed 16 April 2009.

20 Shehu Abubakar, 'Amnesty: 15,000 militants surrendered', *Daily Trust*, 9 October, www.news.dailytrust.com/ index.php?option=com_content&view =article&id=7554:amnesty-15000-militants-surrendered&catid=46:lead-stories&Itemid=140, accessed 18 May 2010.

21 The figures for surrendered weapons and ex-militants have not been independently verified and are believed to be overestimated.

22 Vincent Ikuomola, 'Yar'Adua receives Boyloaf, 31 other militia leaders', *The Nation*, 8 August 2009, thenationon lineng.net/web2/articles/13310/1/YarAdua-receives-Boyloaf-31-other-militant-leaders-/Page1.html, accessed 19 May 2010.

23 Daniel Alabrah, 'Amnesty Bazaar! Militants on spending spree', *Daily Sun*, 30 August 2009, odili.net/news/source/2009/ aug/30/503.html, accessed 11 April 2010.

24 Austyn Ogannah, 'Niger Delta

Amnesty riot: many, raped, two dead, UNI-PORT shut', *Punch*, 19 November 2009, thewillnigeria.com/mobile/general/3165-Niger-Delta-Amnesty-Riot-Many-Raped-Two-Dead-UNIPORT-Shut.html, accessed 18 May 2010.

25 Sola Adebayo, 'Dissolve amnesty committee, Niger Delta leaders tell FG', *Punch*, 9 November 2009, www.punchng.com/Articl.aspx?theartic=Art200911094234721, accessed 15 May 2010.

26 Akanimo Sampson, 'Niger Delta panel faults post-amnesty plan', *Next*, 22 January 2010, 234next.com/csp/cms/sites/Next/News/5515575-147/story.csp, accessed 19 May 2010.

27 Sola Adebayo, 'N'Delta: FG scraps amnesty committee, raises five new panels', *Punch*, 11 December 2009, www.punchontheweb.com/Articl.aspx?theartic=Art20091211285762, accessed 16 May 2010.

28 Sola Adebayo, 'N'Delta: FG bars ministers from supervising post-amnesty programme', *Punch*, 21 March 2010, www.punchng.com/Articl.aspx?theartic=Art2010032142213902010, accessed 23 March 2010.

29 Chiawo Nwankwo, 'Niger Delta: 2,000 ex-militants begin training in June – Alaibe', *Punch*, 13 May 2010, www.punchng.com/Articl.aspx?theartic=Art2010051330350, accessed 13 May 2010.

30 Sola Adebayo and Mike Odiegwu, 'Confusion as ex-militants depart rehab' camp', *Punch*, 11 July 2010, www.punchng.com/Articl.aspx?theartic=Art201007114142881, accessed 11 July 2010.

31 Chris Ajaero and Godfrey Azubike, 'The politics of the Niger Delta Amnesty deal', *Newswatch*, 17 August 2010.

32 Austin Ekeinde, 'Nigeria president pledges better security in delta', Reuters, 14 May 2010.

33 Akanimo Sampson, 'Group exposes conflict triggers in Niger Delta', ALLVOICES, 11 May 2010, www.allvoices.com/contributed-news/5799336-group-warns-about-niger-delta-exposes-conflict-triggers, accessed 18 May 2010.

34 Cyril Obi, 'Oil extraction, dispossession, resistance and conflict in Nigeria's oil-rich Niger delta', *Canadian Journal of Development Studies*, XXX(1/2), 2010.

Bibliography

Aaron, K. K. (2006) 'Human rights violation and environmental degradation in the Niger Delta region of Nigeria', in E. Porter and B. Offord (eds), *Activating Human Rights*, Oxford/New York: Peter Lang/Borne, pp. 193–215.

Aaronson, S. A. (2008) 'Natural resources, often a curse, can also serve the public', Yale Global Online, Yale Centre for the Study of Globalization, www.yaleglobal.yale.edu/article.print, accessed 19 June 2008.

Abati, R. (2009) 'Nigeria's future and the Niger Delta', *Guardian* (Lagos), 18 January, p. 70.

Abayomi, F., D. Atilade, M. Matswamgbe, U. Onwumah and O. Lawrence (2005) 'Report of a small arms and light weapons survey in Delta state', in O. Ibeanu and F. K. Mohammed (eds), *Oiling Violence: The Proliferation of Small Arms and Light Weapons in the Niger Delta*, Lagos: Frankad Publishers/Friedrich Ebert Stiftung, pp. 101–56.

Abbink, J. (2000) 'Preface: Violation and violence as cultural phenomenon', in G. Aijmer and J. Abbink (eds), *Meanings of Violence: A Cross Cultural Perspective*, Oxford: Berg.

Abdullah, I. and P. Muana (1998) 'The Revolutionary United Front of Sierra Leone: a revolt of the lumpen proletariat', in C. Clapham (ed.), *African Guerrillas*, Oxford: James Currey.

Abrahamsen, R. and M. C. Williams (2008) 'Selling security: assessing the impact of military privatisation', *ROAPE*, 15(1): 131–46.

Ackerman, D. (2004) 'Enron's Nigeria barge: the real deal', *Forbes*, 30 September.

Adejo, P. Y. (2005) 'Crime and the cross-border movement of weapons: the case of Nigeria', in A. Ayissi and I. Sall (eds), *Combating the Proliferation of Small Arms and Light Weapons in West Africa: Handbook for the Training of Armed and Security Forces*, Geneva: UNIDIR, pp. 93–9.

Adekoye, V. (2006) 'Distrust, root of the N/Delta crisis – Shell MD, Omiyi', *Daily Champion*, 25 July.

Ademoyega, A. (1981) *Why We Struck: The Story of the First Nigerian Coup*, Ibadan: Evans Brothers.

Adesopo, A. and A. Asaju (2004) 'Natural resource distribution, agitation for resource control right and the practice of federalism in Nigeria', *Journal of Human Ecology*, 4: 277–89.

Adewale, O. (1989) 'Oil spill compensation claims in Nigeria: principles, guidelines and criteria', *Journal of African Law*, 33: 91–104.

Afigbo, A. E. (2003) 'Britain and the Hydra in the Bight of Benin: towards a history of the abolition of the internal slave trade in the Oil Rivers and its hinterland, c. 1885–c. 1943', *African Economic History*, 31: 1–18.

Africa Action (1999) *Nigeria: Odi Massacre Statements*, www.africaaction.org/docs99/odi9912.htm, accessed 10 December 2008.

Agboton-Johnson, C., A. Ebo and L. Mazal (2004) *Small Arms Control in Ghana, Nigeria and Senegal*, International Action Network on Small Arms.

Agbu, O. (2004) *Ethnic Militias and the Threat to Democracy in Post-Transition Nigeria*, Research Report no. 127, Nordiska Afrikainstitutet.

Ake, C. (1996) *Capacity Building in Africa: Trends, Tasks and Challenges*, Paper prepared for the World Bank, Port Harcourt: CASS.

Ako, R. (2008) 'Resolving the conflicts in Nigeria's oil industry – a critical analysis of the role of public participation', PhD thesis submitted to the University of Kent at Canterbury.

— (2009) 'Nigeria's Land Use Act: an antithesis to environmental justice', *Journal of African Law*, 53(2): 289–304.

Akpan, E. R. (2003) 'Acidic precipitation and infrastructural deterioration in oil producing communities of Akwa Ibom state: a case study of Eket, south eastern Nigeria', *Global Journal of Environmental Sciences*, 2(1): 47–52.

Akpode, J. (2004) 'Niger Delta: the staying power of the militia', *This Day*, 12 October, p. 32, www.thisdayonline.com/archive/2004/10/12/20041012rep01.html, accessed 24 March 2009.

Akpuru-Aja, A. (2003) 'The state and the military: perspectives on Nigeria–USA military cooperation', *Strategic Analysis: A Monthly Journal of the IDSA*, XXVII(2), April–June.

Alagoa, E. J. (1964) *The Small Brave City-State: A History of the Nembe-Brass in the Niger Delta*, Madison: University of Wisconsin Press.

Albin-Lackey, C. (2007) *Chop Fine: The Human Rights Impact of Local Government Corruption and Mismanagement in Rivers State, Nigeria*, New York: Human Rights Watch.

Alemika, E. E. (1993) 'Colonialism, state and policing in Nigeria', *Crime, Law and Social Change*, 20(3): 187–219.

Alexander's Gas and Oil Connections (2004) *Nigerian Oil Producing Communities Cry Out over Environmental Neglect*, 14 October, www.gasandoil.com/goc/company/cna44113.htm, accessed 25 January 2006.

Allen, C. (1999) 'Warfare, endemic violence and state collapse in Africa', *Review of African Political Economy*, 81: 367–84.

Alper, B. S. and L. T. Nichols (1981) *Beyond the Courtroom: Programs in Community Justice and Conflict Resolution*, Lexington, MA: D. C. Heath and Co.

Alston, P. (2000) 'What is access to justice? Identifying the unmet legal needs of the poor?', *Fordham International Law Journal*, 24: 187–218.

Amakiri, S. F. (2003) *The Ijaws of the Niger Delta: Their Relevance in Nigeria Nation*, Paper presented at the First Pan Ijaw Conference, 28 February and 2 March, Port Harcourt.

Anaya, J. S. (2004) *Indigenous Peoples in International Law*, 2nd edn, Oxford: Oxford University Press.

ANEEJ (African Network for Environment and Economic Justice) (2004) *Oil of Poverty in Niger Delta*, Lagos.

Aning, E. K. (2005) 'The anatomy of Ghana's secret arms industry', in N. Florquin and E. G. Berman (eds), *Armed and Aimless: Armed Groups, Guns, and Human Security in the ECOWAS Region*, Geneva: Small Arms Survey, pp. 79–107.

Annan, K. (2001) 'Small arms, big problems', *International Herald Tribune*, 10 July.

— (2003) Secretary-General's Remarks to the Ministerial Meeting of the Security Council on Justice and the Rule of Law: The United Nations Role, 24 September, New York, www.un.org/apps/sg/sgstats.as p?nid=518, accessed 20 July 2006.

Anugwom, E. E. (2005) 'Oil minorities and the politics of resource control in Nigeria', *Africa Development*, XXX(4): 87–120.

Apter, A. (2005) *The Pan African Nation: Oil and the Spectacle of Culture in Nigeria*, Chicago, IL: University of Chicago Press.

ARD Inc. (2006) *Democracy and Governance Assessment of Nigeria*, Abuja: USAID-Nigeria.

Ashton-Jones, N. (1998) *The Human Ecosystems of the Niger Delta: An ERA Handbook*, Ibadan: Kraft Books.

Asiegbu, J. U. J. (1984) *Nigeria and Its British Invaders, 1851–1920: A Thematic Documentary History*, New York: NOK Publishers International.

Asuni, J. B. (2009) 'Blood oil in the Niger Delta', USIP Special Report, Washington, DC: United States Institute for Peace.

Asuno, B. A. (1982) 'Impact of oil industry on the environment', *Proceedings of Environmental Awareness Seminars for National Policy Makers*, 51, Lagos: Federal Ministry of Works and Housing/NNPC.

Ate, B. (1987) *Decolonization and Dependence: The development of Nigeria–US relations 1960–1984*, Boulder, CO: Westview Press.

Awobajo, S. A. (1981) 'An analysis of oil spill incidents in Nigeria: 1976–1980', in *The Petroleum Industry and the Nigerian Environment: Proceedings of an International Seminar Sponsored by the Nigerian National Petroleum Company*, Lagos: Federal Ministry of Works and Housing/Nigerian National Petroleum Company.

Aziken, E. (2004) 'Senate unanimously passes Oil and Gas Industry Bill', *Vanguard News*, 27 August, allafrica.com/stories/printable/200408270561.html, accessed 1 September 2004.

Bah, A. (2004) *Implementing the ECOWAS Small Arms Moratorium in Post-War Sierra Leone*, Ottawa: Canadian Peacebuilding Coordinating Committee.

Baldauf, S. (2009) 'Niger Delta militants vow more attacks', *Christian Science Monitor*, 21 June, www.csmonitor.com/World/Africa/2009/0621/p06s17-woaf.html, accessed 26 April 2010.

Ballentine, K. and H. Nitzschke (2004) 'Business and armed conflict: an assessment of issues and options', *Die Friedenswarte*, 75: 35–56.

Banfield, J., V. Haufler and D. Lilly (2005) 'Transnational corporations in conflict-prone zones: public policy response and framework for action', *Oxford Development Studies*, 33(1): 133–47.

Barker, A. (2008) 'UK offers Nigeria help to train security forces', *Financial Times*, 18 July.

Barret, L. (2008) 'Niger Delta: more security yes! Search and destroy no!', *This Day Online*, 26 June, pp. 1–2, www.thisdayonline.com.

Bayelsa State Government (2009) Press release, Office of the Chief Press Secretary, 3 August.

BBC (2006a) 'Nigerian troops burn Delta slums', London: BBC.

— (2006b) 'Tempting riches of Nigeria oil crime', London: BBC.

— (2009) 'Hopes and rusty guns in Niger Delta', London: BBC, 7 September.

BBC News (2004) 'Shell admit fuelling corruption', newsvote.bbc.co.uk/mpapps/pagetools/print/news.bbc.co.uk/2/hi/business/3796, accessed 25 September 2004.

— (2005) 'Oil giant admits Nigeria aid woes', 4 May, news.bbc.co.uk/2/hi/business/4512143.stm, accessed 9 May 2010.

Bennett, J. (2002) 'Multinational corporations, social responsibility and conflict', *Journal of International Affairs*, 55(2): 393–410.

Berkovitz, L (1997) 'Aggression, nature and nurture. The study of urban violence: some implications of laboratory studies of frustration and aggression', in J. C. Davies (ed.), *Why Men Revolt and Why*, New York: Free Press.

Berman, J. (2000) 'Boardrooms and bombs: strategies on multinational corporations in conflict areas', *Harvard International Review*, 22(3): 28–32.

Best, S. G. and D. von Kemedi (2005) 'Armed groups and conflict in Rivers and Plateau States, Nigeria', in N. Florquin and E. G. Berman (eds), *Armed and Aimless: Armed Groups, Guns, and Human Security in the ECOWAS Region*, Geneva: Small Arms Survey, pp. 13–45.

Billon, P. (2003) 'Buying peace or fuelling war: the role of corruption in armed conflicts', *Journal of International Development*, 15: 413–26.

Bisina, T. (2003) 'Legislator accuses Chevron of fuelling Warri crisis', *Daily Independent* (Lagos), 3 November, p. A6.

Blitz, J. (2008) 'Nigeria to tap UK security aid', *Financial Times*, 10 July.

BMCAA (Bayelsa State Micro-Credit Administration Agency) (2009) *Bayelsa*

State Poverty Baseline Survey: A Research Report.

Bøås, M. (2004) 'Rebels with a cause? Africa's young guerrillas', *Current History*, 103(673): 211–14.

— (2006a) 'Kampen om oljen i Nigeria', *Dagbladet*, 14 June, p. 56.

— (2006b) 'Oljebanditer?', *Dagbladet*, 20 August, p. 44.

— (2009) 'Terminology associated with political violence and asymmetric warfare', in W. Okumu and A. Botha (eds), *Domestic Terrorism in Africa: Defining, Addressing and Understanding Its Impact on Human Security*, Pretoria: ISS, pp. 7–13.

Bøås, M. and K. C. Dunn (2007) 'African guerrilla politics: raging against the machine?', in M. Bøås and K. C. Dunn (eds), *African Guerrillas: Raging against the Machine*, Boulder, CO: Lynne Rienner.

Bourne, M. (2007) *Arming Conflict: The Proliferation of Small Arms*, New York: Palgrave Macmillan.

Boutwell, J. and M. T. Klare (1999) *Light Weapons and Civil Conflict: Controlling the Tools of Violence*, Lanham, MD: Rowman and Littlefield.

Braathen, E., M. Bøås and G. Sæther (2000) 'Ethnicity kills? Social struggles for power, resources and identities in the neo-patrimonial state', in E. Braathen, M. Bøås and G. Sæther (eds), *Ethnicity Kills? The Politics of War, Peace and Ethnicity in Sub-Saharan Africa*, Basingstoke: Macmillan, pp. 3–22.

Braithwaite, J. (2002) 'Rewards and regulation', *Journal of Law and Society*, 29: 12–26.

Brehm, J. W. (1966) *A Theory of Psychological Reactance*, New York: Academic Press.

Burke, M. E. (1999) *Corporate Community Relations: The Principles of the Neighbour of Choice*, London: Quorum Books.

CASS (2005) *Enhancing the Capacity of Women Leaders of Community Organisations: Towards Peace Building in the Niger Delta Region*, Port Harcourt: CASS.

Cesarz, E., J. S. Morrison and J. Cooke (2003) 'Alienation and militancy in Nigeria's Niger Delta', *Africa Notes*, 16, CSIS, csis.org/files/media/csis/pubs/anotes_0305.pdf, accessed 9 May 2010.

Chankova, S., H. Nguyen, D. Chipanta, G. Kombe, A. Onoja and K. Ogungbemi (2007) *A Situation Assessment of Human Resources in the Public Health Sector in Nigeria*, Bethesda, MD: Abts Associates Inc.

Clapham, C. (1998) 'Introduction: analysing African insurgencies', in C. Clapham (ed.), *African Guerrillas*, Oxford: James Currey, pp. 1–18.

Cole, P. D. (2008) 'Why choke the goose?', *Financial Times Nigeria Survey*, July.

Coleman, J. S. (1986) *Nigeria: Background to Nationalism*, Benin City: Broburg and Wistrom.

Collier, P. and A. Hoeffler (2004) 'Greed and grievance in civil wars', *Oxford Economic Papers*, 56: 663–95.

Collier, P., A. Hoeffler and D. Rohner (2006) 'Beyond greed and grievance: feasibility and civil war', Working Paper no. 10, Centre for the Study of African Economies, Oxford.

Concannon, T. and J. H. Croft (2006) 'Growing violence in the Niger Delta poses risks to a broad range of stakeholders in the region', London: Stakeholder Democracy Network.

Cookey, S. (1974) *King Jaja of the Niger Delta*, New York: Nok Publishers Ltd.

Courson, E. E. (2007) 'The burden of oil: social deprivation and political militancy in Gbaramatu Clan, Warri South West Local Government Area, Delta State', Niger Delta Economies of Violence Working Paper no. 15.

Cramer, C. (2005) *Inequality and Conflict: A Review of an Age-Old Concern*, Identities, Conflict and Cohesion Programme Paper no. 1, United Nations Research Institute for Social Development.

Croft, J. H. and T. Concannon (2006) *Niger Delta Conflict: Basis Facts and Analysis*, London: Stakeholder Democracy Network.

Crummey, D. (1986) 'Introduction: the great beast', in D. Crummey (ed.),

Banditry, Rebellion and Social Protest in Africa, Oxford: James Currey, pp. 1–32.

CSN (Catholic Secretariat of Nigeria) (2006) *Nigeria: The Travesty of Oil and Gas Wealth*, Lagos: CSN.

Cutler, A. (2003) *Private Power and Global Authority: Transnational Merchant Law in the Global Political Economy*, Cambridge, Cambridge University Press.

Dankelman, I. and J. Davidson (1988) 'Land: women at the centre of the food crisis', in S. Sontheimer (ed.), *Women and the Environment: A Reader*, London: Earthscan, pp. 3–31.

Dappa-Biriye, H. J. R. (1995) *Minority Politics in Pre- and Post-Independence Nigeria*, Port Harcourt: University of Port Harcourt Press.

Davidheiser, M. and K. Nyiayaana (2010) *Demobilization or Remobilization? The Amnesty Programme and the Search for Peace in the Niger Delta*, Paper presented at the second International Conference on Natural Resource, Security and Development in the Niger Delta, held at the Niger Delta Wetlands Centre, Yenagoa, Bayelsa state, 8–11 March.

Davies, S. (2009) *The Potential for Peace and Reconciliation in the Niger Delta*, Coventry: Coventry Cathedral.

Davis, S. (2007) *Shifting Trends in Oil Theft in the Niger Delta*, Legaloil.com, 23 March.

Dike, K. O. (1956) *Hundred Years of British Rule in Nigeria, 1851–1951*, Lagos: Nigerian Broadcasting Corp.

Doom, R. and K. Vlassenroot (2001) 'Violent culture or culture of violence? Militia formation in eastern Congo', in F. Columbus (ed.), *Politics and Economics in Africa*, vol. 1, Huntington, NY: Nova Science Publishers Inc.

Douglas, O. (2001) 'A community guide to understanding resource control', www.waado.org/NigerDelta/Essays/Resource-Control/Guide_Douglas.html, accessed 14 December 2006.

— (2004) 'It is time to sit down for justice', Paper presented at the Niger Delta Youths Stakeholders Workshop organized by the Nigerian National Petroleum Corporation and Academic Associates and Peace Works, 16 April, Hotel Presidential, Port Harcourt, Nigeria, www.nigerdeltacongress.com/articles/it_is_time_to_sit_down_for_justi.htm, accessed 20 January 2009.

Douglas, O., V. Kemedi, I. Okonta and M. Watts (2004) 'Oil and militancy in the Niger Delta: terrorist threat or another Colombia?', Niger Delta Economies of Violence Working Papers Series 4.

Dunmoye, R. (2002) 'Resource control: which way forward?', *Nigerian Social Scientist*, 5(1): 49–53.

Dunning, T. and L. Wirpsa (2004) 'Oil and the political economy of conflict in Colombia and beyond: a linkage approach', *Geopolitics*, 9(1): 81–108.

Duodu, C. (1996) 'Shell admits importing guns for Nigerian police', *Observer*, 28 January.

Duquet, N. (2009) 'Arms acquisition patterns and the dynamics of armed conflict: lessons from the Niger Delta', *International Studies Perspectives*, 10(2): 169–85.

Eberlein, R. (2006) 'On the road to the state's perdition? Authority and sovereignty in the Niger Delta, Nigeria', *Journal of Modern African Studies*, 44(4): 573–96.

— (2009) 'Bomben und begnadigungen', *Konkret*, 9: 34–5.

Ebiri, K. (2008) 'Human capital development as growth option for Niger Delta: NDDC groaning under fund paucity?', *Guardian* (Lagos), 19 June, pp. 33–4.

Ebo, A. (2005) 'Small arms proliferation in Nigeria: a preliminary overview', in O. Ibeanu and F. K. Mohammed (eds), *Oiling Violence: The Proliferation of Small Arms and Light Weapons in the Niger Delta*, Lagos: Frankad Publishers/Friedrich Ebert Stiftung, pp. 1–35.

Edeogun, C. F. O. (2008) *Peace Building Strategies for Peace in the Niger Delta: A Comprehensive Four Phased Peace Model in the Nigerian State, Oil Industry and the Niger Delta*, Proceedings of international conference, Department of Political Science, Niger Delta University, Wilberforce Island, and Center for Applied Environmental Research, University of Missouri-Kansas City, at Yenagoa, Bayelsa state, 11–13 March.

Edwards, R. and I. White (1999) *The Sea Empress Oil Spill: Environmental Impact and Recovery*, Proceedings of the International Oil Spill Conference, Seattle, 7–12 March, American Petroleum Institute, Washington, DC, www.itopf.com/information-services/data-and-statistics/case-histories/documents/seaemp.pdf, accessed 4 August 2008.

EIA (2007) *Official Energy Statistics from the US Government*, US Department of Energy.

Ekeh, P. (1975) 'Colonialism and the two publics in Africa: a theoretical statement', *Comparative Studies in Society and History*, 17: 91–112.

— (1996) 'Political minorities and historically dominant minorities in Nigerian history and politics', in O. Oyediran (ed.), *Governance and Development in Nigeria: Essays in Honour of Billy Dudley*, Ibadan: Oyediran Consult.

Ekekwe, E., S. Okodudu and U. Ukiwo (2010) *Report on a Roundtable on the Technical Committee on the Niger Delta*, Port Harcourt: Institute for Petroleum Studies.

Ekpunobi, C. (2006) 'Corruption – EFCC names 31 governors – 15 in court next week', *Daily Champion*, 28 September, allafrica.com/stories/printable/200609280729.html, accessed 29 September 2006.

Elias, T. O. (1956) *Nature of African Customary Law*, Manchester: Manchester University Press.

Ellis, S. (2003) 'Violence and history: a response to Thandika Mkandawire', *Journal of Modern African Studies*, 43(3).

Emeseh, E. (2006) 'Limitations of law in promoting synergy between environment and development policies in developing countries: a case study of the petroleum industry in Nigeria', *Journal of Energy and Natural Resources Law*, 24(4): 574–606.

Emitimi, M. (2009) 'Massive fraud at Delta State Oil Producing Development Commission (DESOPADEC) by Chief Andy Osawota', Sahara News Reporters, 5 June, www.saharareporters.com/reports/petitions/2913–massive-fraud-at-delta-state-oil-producing-development-commission-desopadec-by-chief-andy-osawota.html.

Enweremadu, D. A. (2008) *The Vicious Circle: Oil, Corruption, and Armed Conflicts in the Niger Delta*, Conference proceedings, international conference on the Nigerian State, Oil Industry and the Niger Delta, organized by the Department of Political Science, Niger Delta University, Yenagoa, in collaboration with the Center for Applied Environmental Research, University of Missouri-Kansas City, 11–13 March, at Yenagoa, Bayelsa state, pp. 445–7.

Epstein, P. R. and J. Selber (2002) *Oil: A Life Cycle Analysis of Its Health and Environmental Impacts*, Cambridge, MA: Center for Health and the Global Environment, www.med.harvard.edu/chge/oil.html, accessed 2 April 2008.

ERA (Environmental Rights Action) (1999) *The Emperor Has No Clothes: The 1999 Constitution and the Niger Delta Peoples*, Benin City: ERA.

ERA/FoEN (2009) 'Visit to Gbaramatu displaced persons', Field Report no. 207, 19 June, www.eraction.org.

Eseduwo, F. S. (2008) 'Petroleum prospecting, state violence and hostage taking in Nigeria: a study of the Niger Delta region (1966–2007)', in *International Conference on the Nigerian State, Oil Industry and the Niger Delta*, Wilberforce Island: Department of Political Science, Niger Delta University.

Etekpe, A. (2005) *Minority Politics in Nigeria: The Case of the South-South and Middle Belt Regions*, Port Harcourt: Kemuela Publications.

— (2007a) *The Politics and Conflicts over Oil and Gas in the Niger Delta: The Bayelsa State Experience*, Port Harcourt: TowerGate Resources.

— (2007b) *Politics of Resource Allocation*

and Control in Nigeria, Port Harcourt: Harey Publications Co.

Etim, W. (2002) 'Activists warn Shell, AGIP against use of soldiers', *Post Express*, Lagos, 2 May, p. 6.

European Union (2007) *Declaration by the Presidency on Behalf of the EU on the Elections in Nigeria*, Brussels: European Union.

Fall, H. (2005) 'Border controls and cross-border crime in West-Africa', in A. Ayissi and I. Sall (eds), *Combating the Proliferation of Small Arms and Light Weapons in West Africa: Handbook for the Training of Armed and Security Forces*, Geneva: UNIDIR, pp. 85–91.

Federal Republic of Nigeria (n.d.) *Report of the Special Security Committee on Oil Producing Areas*, Unpublished.

Fekumo, J. F. (2001) *Oil Pollution and the Problems of Compensation in Nigeria*, Port Harcourt: F&F Publishers.

FGN (Federal Government of Nigeria) (2009) *Report of the Technical Committee of the Niger Delta November 2008*, Abuja: FGN.

Florquin, N. and E. G. Berman (eds) (2005) *Armed and Aimless: Armed Groups, Guns, and Human Security in the ECOWAS Region*, Geneva: Small Arms Survey.

FME (Federal Ministry of Education) (2006) *Education Sector Analysis*, Abuja: FME.

Fox, T., H. Ward and B. Howard (2002) *Public Sector Roles in Strengthening Corporate Social Responsibility: A Baseline Study*, Washington, DC: World Bank.

Frynas, J. G. (1998) 'Political instability and business: focus on Shell in Nigeria', *Third World Quarterly*, 19(3): 457–78.

— (2000) *Oil in Nigeria: Conflict and litigation between oil companies and village communities*, Hamburg: LIT.

Frynas, J. G. and G. Wood (2001) 'Oil and war in Angola', *Review of African Political Economy*, 28(90).

Fuller, L. (1980) 'Positivism and fidelity to law — a reply to Professor Hart', in J. Feinberg and H. Gross (eds), *Philosophy of Law*, Belmont, CA: Wadsworth Publishing Co.

Garuba, D. S. (2007) 'Contractual breakdown: small arms, intolerance and tragedy in Nigeria's Delta region', *AfricaFiles*, 5(4), www.africafiles.org/atissueezine.asp?issue=issue5.

Ghazvinian, J. (2007) *Untapped: The Scramble for Africa's Oil*, New York: Harcourt.

Global Policy Forum (2003) 'Navy, Shell, beef up security', 22 April, www.globalpolicy.org, accessed 19 June 2008.

Godnick, W., D. Klein, C. González-Posso, I. Mendoza and S. Meneses (2008) *Conflict, Economy, International Cooperation and Non-Renewable Natural Resources*, IfP/International Alert/INDEPAZ/PLASA/Socios Peru, www.initiativeforpeacebuilding.eu/pdf/Conflict_Economy_International_Cooperation_and_Non_Renewable_Natural_Resources.pdf, accessed 11 January 2009.

Green, M. (2008a) 'Nigeria demands $2bn taxes from oil majors', *Financial Times*, 22 May.

— (2008b) 'Nigeria warns on oil contracts', *Financial Times*, 22 January.

Green, P. and T. Ward (2004) *State Crime, Governments, Violence and Corruption*, London: Pluto Press.

Greenpeace (1994) *Shell-Shocked: The Environmental and Social Costs of Living with Shell in Nigeria*, Amsterdam: Greenpeace International.

Guardian (1999) 'Govt blames oil firms for Niger Delta crisis', *Guardian* (Lagos), 22 October.

— (2002) 'Government asks oil firms to clean up Niger Delta', *Guardian* (Lagos), 31 July.

— (2007) 'NDDC seeks National Assembly's intervention on N225b fund release', *Guardian* (Lagos), www.ngrguardiannewsngr.com/business/article03, accessed 13 October 2007.

Guhan, S. (2000) 'Thinking about governance', Working Paper Series 10(5), Harvard Center for Population and Development Studies.

Guichaoua, Y. (2006) 'The making of an ethnic militia: the O'odua Peoples

Congress in Nigeria', CRISE Working Paper no. 26.

Gulbrandsen, L. H. and A. Moe (2007) 'BP in Azerbaijian: a test case of the potential and limits of CSR agenda', *Third World Quarterly*, 28(4): 813–30.

Hara, O. K. (2001) 'Niger Delta: peace and co-operation through sustainable development', *Environmental Policy and Law*, 36(6): 302–8.

Haufler, V. (2001) 'Is there a role for business in conflict management?', in A. C. Crocker, O. F. Hampson and P. Aall (eds), *Turbulent Peace: The Challenges of Managing International Conflict*, Washington, DC: US Institute of Peace, pp. 659–76.

— (2004a) 'International diplomacy and the privatization of conflict prevention', *International Studies Perspectives*, 5: 158–63.

— (2004b) *The Politics of Conflict Prevention and Corporate Social Responsibility*, Annual Meeting of the International Studies Association, Le Centre Sheraton Montreal Hotel, Montreal, www.allacademic.com/meta/p73392_index.html, accessed 13 December 2008.

Hazen, J. M. and J. Horner (2007) *Small Arms, Armed Violence, and Insecurity in Nigeria: The Niger Delta in Perspective*, Occasional Paper, Geneva: Small Arms Survey.

Honwana, A. (2006) *Child Soldiers in Africa*, Philadelphia: University of Pennsylvania Press.

Horwood, J. (2008) 'Infectious disease surveillance update', *The Lancet*, 8: 669.

Houreld, K. (2009) 'Nigerian oil militants surrender rockets, guns', *Washington Times*, 23 August, www.washingtontimes.com/news/2009/aug/23/militants-surrender-weapons-in-amnesty-drive/.

Human Rights Watch (1995) *The Ogoni Crisis: A Case-Study of Military Repression in Southeastern Nigeria*, New York: HRW.

— (1999a) *Nigeria: Crackdown in the Niger Delta*, www.hrw.org/reports/1999/nigeria2/index.htm#TopOfPage, accessed 20 January 2009.

— (1999b) *The Price of Oil: Corporate Responsibility and Human Rights Violations in Nigeria's Oil Producing Communities*, New York/Washington/London/Brussels: HRW, www.hrw.org/legacy/reports/1999/nigeria/index.htm.

— (2002) *The Niger Delta: No Democratic Dividend*, New York: HRW.

— (2003) *The Warri Crisis: Fuelling the Violence*, New York: HRW.

— (2004) *Nigeria's 2003 Elections: The Unacknowledged Violence*, New York: HRW.

— (2005a) 'Violence in Nigeria's oil rich Rivers state in 2004', HRW Briefing Paper, February.

— (2005b) *Rivers and Blood: Guns, Oil and Power in Nigeria's Rivers State*, Washington, DC: HRW, www.hrw.org/legacy/backgrounder/africa/nigeria0205/.

— (2007a) 'The human rights impact of local government corruption and mismanagement in Rivers state, Nigeria', *HRW Reports*, 19(2A), January.

— (2007b) 'Criminal politics violence, "godfathers" and corruption in Nigeria', *HRW Reports*, 19(16A).

— (2007c) *Human Rights Watch, Nigeria*, 11 January, www.unhcr.org/refworld/docid/45aca2a316, accessed 19 January 2009.

— (2007d) 'Chop fine: the human rights impact of local government corruption and mismanagement in Rivers state, Nigeria', *HRW Reports*, 19(2A).

— (2008) 'Politics as war: the human rights impact and causes of post election violence in Rivers state, Nigeria', *HRW Reports*, 20(3A).

Iannaccone, A. (2007) *Toward a Reform Agenda for the Niger Delta*, Washington, DC: Center for Strategic and International Studies.

Ibaba, S. I. (2004) *The Environment and Sustainable Development in the Niger Delta: The Bayelsa State Experience*, PhD dissertation, University of Port Harcourt, Port Harcourt.

Ibeanu, O. (2000) 'Oiling the friction: environmental conflict management in the Niger Delta, Nigeria', Environmental Change and Security Project Report, 6.

— (2004) 'The rhetoric of rights: understanding the changing discourses of rights in the Niger Delta', *ACAS Bulletin*, 68(1): 16.

— (2005) 'The proliferation of small arms and light weapons in the Niger Delta: an introduction', in O. Ibeanu and F. K. Mohammed (eds), *Oiling Violence: The Proliferation of Small Arms and Light Weapons in the Niger Delta*, Lagos: Frankad Publishers/Friedrich Ebert Stiftung, pp. 36–56.

— (2006) *Civil Society and Conflict Management in the Niger Delta*, Monograph Series no. 2, Lagos: CLEEN Foundation.

— (2008) 'Affluence and affliction: the Niger Delta as a critique of political science in Nigeria', Inaugural lecture, University of Nigeria.

Ibeanu, O. and F. K. Mohammed (eds) (2001) *Oiling Violence: The Proliferation of Small Arms and Light Weapons in the Niger Delta*, Lagos: Frankad Publishers/ Friedrich Ebert Stiftung.

Idemudia, U. (2007) 'Community perceptions and expectations: reinventing the wheels of Corporate Social Responsibility practices in the Nigerian oil industry', *Business and Society Review*, 112(3): 369–405.

— (2008) 'Conceptualising the CSR and development debate: bridging existing analytical gaps', *Journal of Corporate Citizenship*, 29: 1–20.

— (2009a) 'Oil extraction and poverty reduction in the Niger Delta: a critical examination of partnership initiatives', *Journal of Business Ethics*, 90: 91–116.

— (2009b) 'Assessing corporate–community involvement strategies in the Nigerian oil industry: an empirical analysis', *Resource Policy*, 34(3): 133–41.

Idemudia, U. and U. E. Ite (2006a) 'Demystifying the Niger Delta conflict: towards an integrated explanation', *Review of African Political Economy*, 33(109): 391–406.

— (2006b) 'Corporate–community relations in Nigeria's oil industry: challenges and imperatives', *Corporate Social Responsibility and Environmental Management Journal*, 13: 194–206.

Idowu, A. A. (1999) 'Human rights, environmental degradation and oil multinational companies in Nigeria: the Ogoniland episode', *Netherlands Quarterly of Human Rights*, 17: 161–84.

Ifidon-Ekuerhare, E. (2009) 'Ibori – London court rejects suspects' plea', *Leadership* newspaper (Nigeria), 23 September, allafrica.com/stories/ 200909230707. html, accessed 25 April 2010.

Ikein, A. A. (1991) *The Impact of Oil on a Developing Country: The Case of Nigeria*, Ibadan: Evans Brothers.

Ikein, A. and C. Briggs-Anigboh (1988) *Oil and Fiscal Federalism in Nigeria: The Political Economy of Resource Allocation in a Developing Country*, Aldershot: Ashgate.

Ikelegbe, A. (2001) 'Civil society, oil and conflict in the Niger Delta region of Nigeria: ramifications of civil society for a regional resource struggle', *Journal of Modern African Studies*, 39(3): 437–69.

— (2005a) 'Encounters of insurgent youth associations with the state in the oil rich Niger Delta region of Nigeria', *Journal of Third World Studies*, 22(1): 151–81.

— (2005b) 'The economy of conflict in the oil rich Niger Delta region of Nigeria', *Nordic Journal of African Studies*, 14(2): 208–34.

— (2005c) 'Engendering civil society: oil, women's groups and resource conflicts in the Niger Delta region of Nigeria', *Journal of Modern African Studies*, 43(2): 24–70.

— (2006a) 'The economy of conflicts in the oil rich Niger Delta region of Nigeria', *African and Asian Studies*, 5(1).

— (2006b) 'Beyond the threshold of civil struggle: youth militancy and the militia-ization of the resource conflicts in the Niger Delta region of Nigeria', *African Study Monographs*, 27(3): 87–122.

Ikelegbe, A. and O. Ikelegbe (2006) 'Gender, resources and conflict:

233

the case of rural women and the oil economy in the Niger Delta region of Nigeria', *Nigerian Journal of Politics and Public Policy*, 4(1–6): 179–94.

Ikime, O. (1968) *Merchant Prince of the Niger Delta: The rise and fall of Nana Olomu, last governor of the Benin River*, Ibadan: Heinemann.

Ikporukpo, C. O. (1996) 'Federalism, political power, and the economic power game: conflict over access to petroleum resources in Nigeria', *Environment Planning C: Government and Policy*, 14: 159–77.

— (2003) *The Oil Industry and Communal Self-Destruction in the Niger Delta Region*, Paper presented at the First Pan Ijaw Conference, Port Harcourt.

— (2004) 'Petroleum, fiscal federalism and environmental justice in Nigeria', *Space and Polity*, 8(3): 321–54.

INC (Ijaw National Congress) (1996) *The Constitution of the Ijaw National Congress*, Port Harcourt.

— (1999) *The Ijaw Question*, Press release, 6 January.

— (2003) *First Pan Ijaw Conference Communiqué*, 2 March, Port Harcourt.

— (2008) *Briefs*, 25 November.

International Crisis Group (2006a) 'Fuelling the Niger Delta crisis', *Africa Report*, 118, 28 September.

— (2006b) 'Want in the midst of plenty', *Africa Report*, 113, 19 July.

— (2006c) 'The swamps of insurgency: Nigeria's Delta unrest', *Africa Report*, 115, 3 August, p. 36.

— (2007) 'Nigeria: ending unrest in the Niger Delta', *Africa Report*, 135, 5 December.

— (2009) 'Seizing the moment in the Niger Delta', *Africa Briefing*, 60, 30 April.

IRIN (2002) Nigeria: IRIN focus on the dangers of cross-border crime', New York: IRIN, www.irinnews.org/Report.aspx?ReportId=35434.

Isichei, E. (1973) *Ibo People and the Europeans*, London: Faber and Faber.

Islam, M. R. (1991) 'Secession crisis in Papua New Guinea: the proclaimed Republic of Bougainville in international law', *University of Hawaii Law Review*, 13: 453–75.

Isumonah, V. A., B. Tantua and J. Nengi (2005) 'The proliferation of small arms and light weapons in Bayelsa state', in O. Ibeanu and F. K. Mohammed (eds), *Oiling Violence: The Proliferation of Small Arms and Light Weapons in the Niger Delta*, Lagos: Frankad Publishers/ Friedrich Ebert Stiftung, pp. 57–100.

Ite, U. E. (2004) 'Multinationals and Corporate Social Responsibility in developing countries: a case study of Nigeria', *Corporate Social Responsibility and Environmental Management*, 11: 1–11.

Jackson, A. (2007) 'Nigeria: a security overview', *The Round Table*, 96(392): 587–603.

James, G. K., J. O. Adegoke, E. Saba, P. Nwilo and J. Akinyede (2007) 'Satellite-based assessment of the extent and changes in the mangrove ecosystem of the Niger Delta', *Marine Geodesy*, 30: 249–67.

Jenkins, H. (2004) 'Corporate Social Responsibility and the mining industry: conflicts and constructs', *Corporate Social Responsibility and Environmental Management*, 11: 23–34.

Jike, V. T. (2004) 'Environmental degradation, social disequilibrium, and the dilemma of sustainable development in the Niger-Delta of Nigeria', *Journal of Black Studies*, 34: 686–701.

Joab-Peterside, S. (2005) 'On the militarization of Nigeria's Niger Delta: the origins of ethnic militia in Rivers state', *Africa Conflict Profile*.

— (2007) *On the Militarization of Nigeria's Niger Delta: The Genesis of Ethnic Militia in Rivers State, Nigeria*, University of California Economies of Violence Working Paper no. 21, Berkeley.

Jones, G. I. (1963) *The Trading States of the Oil Rivers: A Study of Political Development in Eastern Nigeria*, London: James Currey.

Juma, C. (2006) *Redesigning African Economies: The Role of Engineering in International Development*, London: Royal Academy of Engineering.

Kabia, J. (2008) 'Greed or grievance?: Diamonds, rent-seeking and the civil wars in Sierra Leone (1991–2002)', in K. Omeje (ed.), *Extractive Economies and Conflicts in the Global South: Multiregional perspectives on rentier politics*, Aldershot: Ashgate, pp. 93–106.

Kaldor, M. and Y. Said (eds) (2007) *Oil Wars. How Wars over Oil Further Destabilise Faltering Regimes*, London: Pluto Press.

Kalu, U. E. (1980) *The Rise of British Colonialism in Southern Nigeria, 1700–1900*, New York: Exposition Press.

Karl, T. L. (1997) *The Paradox of Plenty: Oil Booms and Petro-States*, Los Angeles: University of California Press.

Keen, D. (2000) 'Incentives and disincentives for violence', in M. Berdal and D. M. Malone (eds), *Greed and Grievance: Economic Agendas in Civil Wars*, Boulder, CO: Lynne Rienner, pp. 19–42.

— (2007) *Complex Emergencies*, London: Polity Press.

Keenan, J. (2008a) 'US militarization in Africa', *Anthropology Today*, 24(5).

— (2008b) 'Demystifying Africa's security', *Review of African Political Economy*, 35(118): 634–44.

— (2009) *The Dark Sahara: America's War on Terror in Africa*, London and New York: Pluto Press.

Keili, F. L. (2008) 'Small arms and light weapons in West Africa: a stock-taking', *Disarmament Forum*, 4: 5–11.

Kemedi, D. V. (2003) 'Community conflicts in the Niger Delta: petro-weapon or policy failure?', Berkeley Environmental Politics Working Paper, 12.

Kew, D. and D. L. Phillips (2007) 'Seeking peace in the Niger Delta: oil, natural gas and other vital resources', *New England Journal of Public Policy*, 21(2): 154–70.

Khakee, A., N. Florquin, S. Torjesen, S. Cattaneo, P. Dreyfus, R. Stohl and R. Stoicescu (2005) 'Sourcing the tools of war: small arms supplies to conflict zones', in Small Arms Survey (ed.), *Small Arms Survey 2005: Weapons at War*, Oxford: Oxford University Press, pp. 159–77.

Khan, S. A. (1994) *Nigeria: The Political Economy of Oil*, Oxford: Oxford University Press.

Kingsbury, B. (1998) 'Indigenous peoples in international law: a constructivist approach to the Asian controversy', *American Journal of International Law*, 92: 414–57.

Kiwanuka, R. N. (1988) 'The meaning of "people" in the African Charter on Human and Peoples' Rights', *American Journal of International Law*, 82: 80–101.

Klare, M. (2004) *Blood and Oil*, London: Penguin.

Klare, M. and D. Volman (2006) 'America, China and the scramble for Africa's oil', *Review of African Political Economy*, 33(108).

Lapin, D. (2000) *The Leveraged Buy-in: Creating an Enabling Environment for Business through Strategic Social Investments*, Richardson, TX: Society for Petroleum Engineers.

Lash, K. A., P. Gee and L. Zelon (1998) 'Equal access to civil justice: pursuing solutions beyond the legal profession', *Yale Law and Policy Review*, 17(1): 489–501.

Latour, B. (1986) 'The powers of association', in J. Law (ed.), *Power, Action and Belief: A Sociology of Knowledge?*, London: Routledge.

Le Billon, P. and F. El Khatib (2004) 'From free oil to "freedom oil": terrorism, war and US geopolitics in the Persian Gulf', *Geopolitics*, 9(1): 109–37.

Le Sueur, A. (2000) 'Access to justice rights in the United Kingdom', *European Human Rights Law Review*, 5: 457–75.

Leton, M. (2008) 'Oil and the urban question: fuelling politics and violence in Warri', Niger Delta Economies of Violence Working Paper, Series 8.

Lezhnev, S. (2005) *Crafting Peace: Strategies to Deal with Warlords in Collapsing States*, Lanham, MD: Lexington Books.

Li, T. M. (2001) 'Boundary work: community, market and state reconsidered', in A. Agarwal and C. Gibson (eds), *Communities and the Environment: Ethnicity, Gender, and the State in*

Community Based Conservation, New Brunswick, NJ: Rutgers University Press, pp. 157–79.

Lindsay, H. B. (2006) 'Shell shocked', *The Dominion*, dominionpaper.ca/environment/2006/03/20/shell_shoc.html.

Lindsay, M. (2005) 'The security threat to oil companies in and out of conflict zones', *Oil and Gas Review*, 2: 1–4.

Llewellyn, K. (1940) 'The normative, the legal, and the Law-Jobs Theory: the problem of juristic method', *Yale Law Journal*, 49: 1355–400.

Lohor, J. (2003) 'Warri crisis: FG considers full-scale military action: House requests judicial commission as violence worsens', *This Day* (Lagos), 20 August, www.thisdayonline.com/news/20030820news01.html, accessed 20 August 2003.

Lombard, L. N., E. G. Berman, N. Florquin and G. McDonald (2006) 'A constant threat: armed groups in West Africa', in Small Arms Survey (ed.), *Small Arms Survey 2006: Unfinished Business*, Oxford: Oxford University Press, pp. 247–93.

Lorenz, K. (1966) *On Aggression*, New York: Taylor and Francis.

Lubeck, P., M. Watts and R. Lipschutz (2007) 'Convergent interests: US energy security and the "securing" of Nigerian democracy', *International Policy Report*, Washington, DC: Center for International Policy, February.

Lyons, M. (2004) 'A case study in multinational corporate accountability: Ecuador's indigenous peoples struggle for redress', *Denver Journal of International Law and Policy*, 32: 701–32.

Mackinlay, J. (2002) *Globalisation and Insurgency*, Adelphi Papers no. 352, London: International Institute for Strategic Studies.

Mamdani, M. (1996) *Citizen and Subject: Contemporary Africa and the Legacy of Late Colonialism*, Princeton, NJ: Princeton University Press.

Manby, B. (1998) *The Price of Oil: Corporate Responsibility and Human Rights Violations in Nigeria's Oil Producing Communities*, New York: Human Rights Watch.

Mangete, E. D. O., U. E. Dambo and M. E. Amaegbe (1999) 'Health', in J. E. Alagoa (ed.), *The Land and People of Bayelsa State: Central Niger Delta*, Port Harcourt: Onyoma Research Publications, pp. 321–32.

Manifesto of the Niger Delta (2006) *Justice or Charity? Manifesto of the Niger Delta*, Port Harcourt.

Mba, N. E. (1982) *Nigerian Women Mobilized: Women's Political Activity in Southern Nigeria, 1900–1965*, Berkeley: Institute of International Studies, University of California.

Mbanefoh, G. F. and F. O. Egwaikhide (1998) 'Revenue allocation in Nigeria: derivation principles revisited', in K. Amuwo, R. Suberu, A. Agbaje and G. Herault (eds), *Federalism and Political Restructuring in Nigeria*, Ibadan: Spectrum Books, pp. 213–31.

McIntyre, A., E. K. Aning and P. N. N. Addo (2002) 'Politics, war and youth culture in Sierra Leone', *African Security Review*, 11: 3.

McKenzie, K. (2006) 'Fiscal federalism and taxation of nonrenewable resources', in R. Bird and F. Vaillancourt (eds), *Perspectives on Fiscal Federalism*, Washington, DC: World Bank, pp. 247–65.

McLean, I. and A. McMillan (2003) *Oxford Concise Dictionary of Politics*, Oxford: Oxford University Press.

Médard, J.-F. (ed.) (1991) *Etats d'Afrique Noire*, Paris: Karthala.

— (1996) 'Patrimonialism, neopatrimonialism and the study of the post-colonial state in sub-Saharan Africa', in H. S. Marcussen (ed.), *Improved Natural Resources Management – the Role of Formal and Informal Networks and Institutions*, Roskilde: Roskilde University Press, pp. 76–97.

Mehlum, H., K. Moene and R. Torvik (2006) 'Institutions and the resource curse', *Economic Journal*, 116: 1–20.

Mertz, E. (1994) 'A new social constructionism for socio-legal studies', *Law and Society Review*, 28: 1243–65.

Michalski, J. (2006) 'The careless gate-keeper: Sarei v. Rio Tinto, plc, and the expanding role of US courts in enforcing international norms', *Tulane Journal of International and Comparative Law*, 15: 731.

Mkandawire, T. (2002) 'The terrible toll of post colonial rebel movements in Africa: towards an explanation of the violence against the peasantry', *Journal of Modern African Studies*, 40(2).

Mustapha, A. R. (2008) 'Challenges for Nigeria's foreign policy in the post-Cold War era', in A. Adekeye and A. R. Mustapha (eds), *Gulliver's Troubles: Nigeria's Foreign Policy after the Cold War*, Scottsville: University of KwaZulu-Natal Press.

Naagbanton, P. B. (2008) *The Proliferation of Small Arms, Armed Groups and Violent Conflicts in the Niger Delta Region of Nigeria*, Paper presented at the 'International Workshop on the Niger Delta', Nordiska Afrika Institutet/ International Peace Research Institute Oslo, Oslo, 18/19 August.

Naanen, B. (1995) 'Oil producing minorities and the restructuring of Nigerian federalism: the case of the Ogoni people', *Journal of Commonwealth and Comparative Politics*, 33(1): 46–78.

Nafziger, E. W. (2006) 'Development, inequality and war in Africa', *Economics of Peace and Security Journal*, 1(1): 14–19.

NDDC (Niger Delta Development Commission) (2006) *Niger Delta Regional Development Master Plan*, Port Harcourt: NDDC.

Nelson, J. (2000) *The Business of Peace*, London: Prince of Wales Business Forum, International Alert Council on Economic Priorities.

Next (2009) 'Representatives want Niger Delta ministers sacked', *Next*, 20 November, 234next.com/csp/cms/ sites/Next/News/National/5483865-146/ Representatives_want_Niger_Delta_ ministers_sacked.csp.

— (2010) 'Ending gas flaring may ruin economy, says agency', *Next*, 16 April, 234next.com/csp/cms/sites/Next/ Home/5555542-146/story.csp.

Niger Delta Natural Damage Assessment and Restoration Project (2006) *Report*, Abuja: Ministry of Environment, Nigerian Conversation Foundation, WWF UK, CEESP-IUCN Commission on Environmental, Economic and Social Policy, www.ncfnigeria.org/ inthenews/news_feeds.php?article=21, accessed 9 May 2010.

Niger Delta Standard (2009), 19 May.

Nnoli, O. (1978) *Ethnic Politics in Nigeria*, Enugu: Fourth Dimension Publishers.

Nodland, A. and O. Hjellestad (2007) *Security in the Niger Delta: Background, Incidents, Forecast*, Bergen: Bergen Risk Solutions AS.

Nonet, P. and P. Selznick (1978) *Law and Society in Transition: Toward Responsive Law*, New York: Harper and Row.

Nsirimovu, A. (2005) 'Report of a study on Small Arms and Light Weapons (SALW) proliferation in Rivers state', in O. Ibeanu and F. K. Mohammed (eds), *Oiling Violence: The Proliferation of Small Arms and Light Weapons in the Niger Delta*, Lagos: Frankad Publishers/ Friedrich Ebert Stiftung, pp. 157–95.

Nwajiaku, K. (2005) 'Between discourse and reality: the politics of oil and Ijaw ethnic nationalism in the Niger Delta', *Cashiers d'Etudes Africaines*, 178(2): 457–96.

Nwideeduh, S. B. (1999) 'Education', in J. E. Alagoa (ed.), *The Land and People of Bayelsa State: Central Niger Delta*, Port Harcourt: Onyoma Research Publications, pp. 321–32.

Nzongola-Ntalaja, G. (1999) 'Ethnicity and state politics in Africa', *African Journal of International Affairs*, 2(1).

Oates, W. (1999) 'An essay on fiscal federalism', *Journal of Economic Literature*, 37(3): 1120–49.

Obi, C. (1997a) *Oil, Environmental Conflict and National Security in Nigeria: Ramifications of the Ecology–Security Nexus for Sub-Regional Security*, ACDIS Occasional Paper.

— (1997b) 'Globalization and local

resistance: the case of the Ogoni versus Shell', *New Political Economy*, 2(1).

— (2004a) *The Oil Paradox: Reflections on the Violent Dynamics of Petro-Politics and (Mis) Governance in Nigeria's Niger Delta*, University of Leipzig Papers on Africa – Politics and Economics Paper no. 73, Leipzig.

— (2004b) 'Global, state and local intersections: power, authority and conflict in the Niger Delta oil communities', in T. M. Callaghy, R. Kassmor and R. Latham (eds), *Intervention and Transformation in Africa: Global–Local Networks of Power*, Cambridge: Cambridge University Press.

— (2006) *Youth and Generational Dimensions to the Struggle for Resource Control in the Niger Delta: Prospects for the Nation-State Project in Nigeria*, CODESRIA Monograph Series, Dakar: CODESRIA.

— (2007) 'The struggle for resource control in a petro-state', in P. Bowles et al. (eds), *National Perspectives on Globalisation*, Hampshire and New York: Palgrave Macmillan.

— (2008a), 'Enter the dragon? Chinese oil companies and resistance in the Niger Delta', *Review of African Political Economy*, 35(117).

— (2008b), 'Reflections on West Africa's security in the context of the global war on terror', *Legon Journal of International Affairs*, 5(1).

— (2009a) 'Nigeria's Niger Delta: understanding the complex drivers of violent oil-related conflict', *Africa Development*, XXXIV.

— (2009b) 'Scrambling for oil in West Africa?', in R. Southall and H. Melber (eds), *A New Scramble for Africa?*, Scottsville: University of KwaZulu-Natal Press.

— (2009c) 'Structuring transnational spaces of identity, rights and power in the Niger Delta of Nigeria', *Globalizations*, 6(4).

— (2010) 'Oil extraction, dispossession, resistance and conflict in Nigeria's oil-rich Niger Delta', *Canadian Journal of Development Studies*, 30(1/2).

Obilade, A. O. (1979) *The Nigerian Legal System*, London: Sweet and Maxwell.

Ogbodo, A. (2009) 'Militants' disarmament: rough road to armistice', *Guardian* (Lagos), 16 August, p. 71.

Ogbu, A. (2008) 'Naval chief: warships not for N'Delta', *This Day Online*, 8 April, www.thisdayonline.com, accessed 6 August 2008.

Ojakorotu, V. (2008) 'The internationalization of oil violence in the Niger Delta region of Nigeria', *Alternatives: Turkish Journal of International Affairs*, 7(1): 92–113.

Ojeifo, S. (2008) 'Senate considers increased funding for navy in 2009', *This Day Online*, 8 June, www.thisdayonline.com, accessed 6 August 2008.

Oji, G. (2007) 'Dicon's unique parting gift for Obasanjo', *This Day*, 24 May.

Ojo, O. J. B. (2002) 'The Niger Delta: managing resources and conflicts', Research Report No. 46, Ibadan: Development Policy Centre.

Ojudu, B. (2004) 'Gun smuggling in the Niger Delta', *World Press Review*, 16 November.

Okoh, R. N. (2001) 'Cost–benefit analysis of gas production in Nigeria', in *Natural Resource Use, the Environment and Sustainable Development*, Proceedings of the NES 2nd Annual Conference, Port Harcourt, 29/30 August, Port Harcourt: NES.

Okoko, K. (2003) 'Our common future', Address presented at the First Pan Ijaw Conference, Port Harcourt, 28 February and 2 March.

Okoko, K. and S. I. Ibaba (1997) 'Oil spillages and community disturbances: the SPDC and the Niger Delta experience', *Nigerian Journal of Oil and Politics*, 1: 56–69.

Okon, E. J. (2002) *A Report of the Niger Delta Women for Justice (NDWJ) on the Delta Women's Siege of the American Oil Company, Chevron-Texaco, in the Delta State of Nigeria*.

Okonjo-Iweala, N., C. Soludo and M. Muhktar (2003) 'Introduction', in *The Debt Trap in Nigeria: Towards a*

Sustainable Debt Strategy, Trenton, NJ: Africa World.

Okonta, I. (2005) 'Nigeria: chronicle of a dying state', *Current History*, May.

— (2006) *Behind the Mask*, Niger Delta Economies of Violence Working Paper no. 11, St Peter's College, Oxford University.

— (2008a) 'The disease of elephants: oil rich "minority" areas, Shell and international NGOs', in A. Adekeye and A. R. Mustapha (eds), *Gulliver's Troubles: Nigeria's foreign policy after the cold war*, Scotsville: University of KwaZulu-Natal Press, pp. 116–39.

— (2008b) *When Citizens Revolt: Nigerian elites, Big Oil and the Ogoni struggle for self-determination*, Lagos: Ofrima Publishing.

Okonta, I. and O. Douglas (2001) *Where Vultures Feast: 40 years of Shell in the Niger Delta*, Benin City: ERA/FoEN.

Oliveira, R. (2007) *Oil and Politics in the Gulf of Guinea*, New York: Columbia University Press.

Ololajulo, B. O. (2006) *Rural Change and the Impact of Development Intervention on Ilaje people in Ondo State, Nigeria*, Unpublished PhD thesis submitted to the Institute of African Studies, University of Ibadan.

Olori, T. (2004) 'Porous border fuelling gunrunning', Inter Press Service News Agency, 22 April.

Olujide, M. G. (2006) 'Perceived effects of oil spillage on the livelihood activities of women in Eastern Obolo Local Government Area of Akwa Ibom state', *Journal of Human Ecology*, 19(4): 259–66.

Omeje, K. (2004) 'The state, conflict and evolving politics in the Niger Delta, Nigeria', *Review of African Political Economy*, 31(101): 425–40.

— (2006a) *High Stakes and Stakeholders: Oil Conflict and Security in Nigeria*, Aldershot: Ashgate.

— (2006b) 'Petrobusiness and security threats in the Niger Delta, Nigeria', *Current Sociology*, 54(3): 447–99.

Omonobi, K. and O. Okhomina (2003)

'Ijaw leaders named as sponsors of kidnappers', *Vanguard*, Lagos, 4 December, p. 7.

Omotola, J. A. (1990) 'The quantum of compensation for oil pollution: an overview', in J. A. Omotola (ed.), *Environmental Laws in Nigeria Including Compensation*, Lagos: Faculty of Law, University of Lagos.

OMPADEC (Oil Minerals Producing Areas Development Commission) (1993) *Quarterly Report*, 1(1), October.

O'Neill, T. (2006) 'The curse of black gold: hope and betrayal in the Niger Delta', *National Geographic*, February.

Onwuchekwa, O. (2004) '5,400 spills threaten Niger Delta – Ugochukwu', *Daily Champion*, 24 November, allafrica.com/stories/printable/200411240494.html, accessed 25 November 2004.

Onyige, P. U. (1979) *The Impact of Mineral Oil Exploitation on Rural Communities in Nigeria: The Case of Ogba/Egbema District*, PhD thesis, Centre of West African Studies, University of Birmingham.

Orere, O., J. Adiorho, K. Ebiri, R. Chikereuba, E. Willie, A. Akpan, I. Akpan-Nsoh, H. Oliomogbe and A. Aliu (2009) 'Mended and with faith, the amnesty can still be steered to safe anchor', *Guardian* (Lagos), 14 August, pp. 21–3.

Orobator, E., F. Ifowodo and E. Edosa (2005) *Federal State and Resource Control in Nigeria*, Benin City: F. Parker Publishing Co.

Osaghae, E. E. (1995) 'The Ogoni uprising: oil politics, minority agitation and the future of the Nigerian state', *African Affairs*, 94: 325–44.

Osaghae, E., A. Ikelegbe, O. Olarinmoye and S. Okhonmina (2007) *Youth Militias, Self Determination and Resource Control Struggles in the Niger-Delta Region of Nigeria*, www.ascleiden.nl/Pdf/cdpnigeriaRevisedOsaghae[1]2.pdf, accessed 1 May 2010.

Østby, G., R. Nordås and J. K. Rød (2009) 'Regional inequalities and civil conflict in 21 sub-Saharan countries, 1986–

2004', *International Studies Quarterly*, 53(2): 301–24.

OVPN (Office of the Vice-President of Nigeria) (2007) *Leadership, Good Governance and the Resolution of the Niger Delta Crisis*, Abuja: The Presidency.

Oyebode, A. (2004) *Law and the Management of a Petroleum Economy: Revisiting the Nigerian Crisis*, Ikeja: Setop Arts Productions.

Oyefusi, A. (2007) *Oil and the Propensity to Armed Struggle in the Niger Delta Region of Nigeria*, Post-Conflict Transitions Working Paper no. 8, Washington, DC: World Bank.

Peel, M. (2005) *Crisis in the Niger Delta: How Failures of Transparency and Accountability are Destroying the Region*, Briefing Paper, Chatham House African Programme, July.

PEFS (Programme on Ethnic and Federal Studies) (2004) *The Niger Delta Question: Background to Constitutional Reform*, PEFS Monograph New Series no. 8, Ibadan: PEFS.

Peluso, N. and M. Watts (2001) *Violent Environments*, London: Cornell University Press.

Penal Reform International and Bluhm Legal Clinic of the Northwestern University School of Law (2007) *Access to Justice in Africa and Beyond: Making the Rule of Law a Reality*, Louisville, KY: National Institute for Trial Advocacy.

Pepper, S. L. (1999) 'Legal ethics: access to what?', *Journal of the Institute for the Study of Legal Ethics*, 2: 269–88.

Peterside, S. and A. Zalik (2008) 'The commodification of violence in the Niger Delta', in L. Panitch and C. Leys (eds), *Violence Today: Actual and Existing Barbarism – Socialist Register 2009*, London: Merlin Press.

Peterson, V. S. and A. S. Runyan (1999) *Global Gender Issues*, Boulder, CO: Westview Press.

Pham, P. (2007) 'Next front? Evolving United States–African relations in the "war on terror" and beyond', *Comparative Strategy*, 26(1).

Powell, C. B., S. A. White, B. Baranowska-

Dutkiewicz, D. D. Ibiebele, M. Isoun and F. U. Ofoegbu (1985) 'Oshika oil spill environmental impact: effect on aquatic biology', in *The Petroleum Industry and the Nigerian Environment: Proceedings of an International Seminar*, Lagos: Federal Ministry of Works and Housing/Nigerian National Petroleum Company.

Preboye, P. I. C. (2005) *The Core Niger Delta: Iduwini Clan*, Ibadan: Rural Development Nigeria Ltd.

Pruitt, D. and J. Rubin (1986) *Social Conflict: Escalation, Stalemate and Settlement*, New York: Random House.

Raji, W. et al. (eds) (2000) *Boiling Point: The Crisis in the Oil Producing Communities in Nigeria*, Lagos: CDHR.

Rashid, A. (2001) *Taliban: the Story of the Afghan Warlords*, London: Pan Books.

Reno, W. (1998) *Warlord Politics and African States*, Boulder, CO: Lynne Rienner.

— (2000) 'Shadow states and the political economy of civil wars', in M. Berdal and D. Malone (eds), *Greed and Grievance: Economic Agendas in Civil Wars*, Boulder, CO: Lynne Rienner.

Reuters (2008) 'Nigeria rebels attack Shell oil pipelines', 21 April, www.alertnet. org/thenews/newsdesk/L21129451. htm.

Rice, S. and S. Patrick (2008) *Index of State Weakness in the Developing World*, Washington, DC: Brookings Institution.

Rich, P. (ed.) (1999) *Warlords in International Relations*, Basingstoke: Macmillan.

Richards, P. (2005) 'New war: an ethnographic approach', in P. Richards (ed.), *No Peace, No War: An Anthropology of Contemporary Armed Conflicts*, Oxford: James Currey, pp. 1–21.

Ross, M. (1999) 'The political economy of the resource curse', *World Politics*, 51.

— (2004) 'How do natural resources influence civil war? Evidence from thirteen cases', *International Organizations*, 58.

Sagay, I. (2001) 'Federalism, the Constitution and resource control: my response', *Guardian* (Lagos), 13 August.

Saro-Wiwa, K. (1995) *A Month and a Day: A Detention Diary*, New York: Penguin.

Schärf, W. and D. Nina (2001) *The Other Law – Non-State Ordering in South Africa*, Lansdowne: Juta Law.

Scheinin, M. (2005) 'What are Indigenous Peoples?', in N. Ghanea and A. Xanthaki (eds), *Minorities, Peoples and Self-Determination: Essays in Honour of Patrick Thornberry*, Leiden: Martinus Nijhoff Publishers/Brill Academic.

Shawcross, W. (2000) *Deliver Us from Evil: Peacekeepers, Warlords and a World of Endless Conflict*, New York: Simon & Schuster.

Shaxson, N. (2007) *Poisoned Wells: The Dirty Politics of African Oil*, London: Palgrave Macmillan.

Skjearseth, J. B., T. Kristian, P. Swanson, A. C. Christiansen, M. Arild and L. Lunde (2004) *Limits to Corporate Social Responsibility: A Comparative Study of Four Major Oil Companies*, Lysaker: Fridtjof Nansen Institute.

Small Arms Survey (2005) *Small Arms Survey 2005: Weapons at War*, Oxford: Oxford University Press.

— (2007) *Small Arms, Armed Violence and Insecurity in Nigeria: The Niger Delta in Perspective*, Geneva: Small Arms Survey.

— (2009) *Frequently Asked Questions*, www.smallarmssurvey.org/files/sas/home/FAQ.html#FAQ6, accessed 24 March 2009.

Sorbara, M. J. (2007) 'The United States and maritime security in the Gulf of Guinea', *Petroleum Africa*, July, pp. 56–8.

Soremekun, K. (1984) *Nigerian Petroleum Policy*, PhD thesis submitted to the Department of International Relations, Obafemi Awolowo University.

— (1995) 'Oil and the democratic imperative in Nigeria', in D. Olowu, K. Soremekun and A. Williams (eds), *Governance and Democratization in Nigeria*, Ibadan: Spectrum Books, pp. 97–109.

Soremekun, K. and C. Obi (1993) 'The changing pattern of foreign investments in the Nigerian oil industry', *Africa Development*, XVIII(3).

SPDC (Shell Petroleum Development Company of Nigeria Limited) (2000) *Creating an Enabling Environment for Sustainable Development in the Niger Delta*, www-static.shell.com/static/nigeria/downloads/pdfs/enabling_env_delta.pdf, accessed 1 September 2004.

— (2003) 'Unwarranted threat on EA Field', *Daily Independent*, Lagos, 1 December, p. A7.

— (2008) *Overview of SPDC Operations*, SPDC Oil Seminar for Academics, Port Harcourt, 5/6 November.

Survival (1999) Publication of the Chicoco Movement, 1, August.

Tamuno, T. (1978) *The Evolution of the Nigerian State: The Southern Phase, 1898–1914*, London: Longman.

— (1998) 'Nigerian federalism in historical perspective', in K. Amuwo, R. Suberu, A. Agbaje and G. Herault (eds), *Federalism and Political Restructuring in Nigeria*, Ibadan: Spectrum Books Ltd, pp.13–33.

— (2000) *The Niger Delta Question*, Port Harcourt: Riverside Communications.

— (2005) *The Ijaw Ethnic Nationality and the Nigerian State*, Paper presented at Ijaw World Summit, 23–25 February, Yenagoa, Bayelsa state.

— (2008) *The Geographic Niger Delta*, Conference proceedings, International Conference on the Nigerian State, Oil Industry and the Niger Delta, organized by the Department of Political Science, Niger Delta University, in collaboration with the Center for Applied Environmental Research, University of Missouri-Kansas City, 11–13 March, at Yenagoa, Bayelsa state, pp. 916–30.

TCND (2008) *Report of the Technical Committee on the Niger Delta*, www.stakeholderdemocracy.org/uploads/Other%20publications/Nigeriareport.pdf, accessed 15 October 2009.

Tell (2008a) 'Hostage economy: oil firms flee Niger Delta', *Tell* (Lagos), 9 June.

— (2008b) *Tell* (Lagos), 18 August.

The News (1999) 'Obasanjo condemned for the situation in Nigeria', *The News* (Lagos), 6 December.

This Day News (2006) 'Ribadu in Senate – 31 governors under investigation', 28 September, allafrica.com/stories/printable/2000609280012.html, accessed 29 September 2006.

This Day Online (2008) 'Soldiers raze Agge, Bayelsa Town', 8 May, www.thisdayonline.com/nview.php?id=118828, accessed 8 May 2008.

— (2009) 'Oil spill: FG to sanction 66 firms', 5 March, www.thisdayonline.com/nview.php?id=137273, accessed 5 March 2009.

Thomas, T. S., S. Kiser and W. D. Casebeer (2005) *Warlords Rising: Confronting Violent Non-State Actors*, Lanham, MD: Lexington Books.

Tilly, C. (1985) 'War making and state making as organized crime', in P. B. Evans, D. Reuschemeyer and T. Skocpol (eds), *Bringing the State Back In*, Cambridge: Cambridge University Press, pp. 167–91.

Transnational Crisis Project (2010) 'Antidote to violence: lessons for the Nigerian federal government's ten per cent community royalty from the oil company experience', *Niger Delta Report*, 1, Washington, DC: TCP.

Turner, E. T. and S. L. Brownhill (2003) 'Why women are at war with Chevron: Nigerian subsistence struggles against the international oil industry', *Journal of Asian and African Studies*, 39(1/2): 63–9.

Turner, L. (1978), *Oil Companies in the International System*, London: Longman.

Tyler, T. R. (2006) *Why People Obey the Law*, 2nd edn, Princeton, NJ: Princeton University Press.

Uche, C. U. and O. U. Uche (2004) 'Oil and the politics of revenue allocation in Nigeria', Working Paper no. 54, Leiden: African Studies Centre.

Udonwa, N. E., M. Ekpo, I. A. Ekanem, A. V. Inem and A. Etokidem (2004) 'Oil doom and AIDS boom in the Niger Region of Nigeria', *International Electronic Journal of Rural and Remote Health Research, Education, Practice and Policy*, rrh.deakin.edu.au/published articles/article_print_273.pdf, accessed 22 November 2008.

Ukeje, C. (2001a) 'Youth, violence and collapse of public order', *Africa Development*, XXVII(1/2): 337–66.

— (2001b) 'Oil communities and political violence: the case of Ijaws in Nigeria's Delta region', *Journal of Terrorism and Political Violence*, 13(4): 15–36.

— (2004) 'From Aba to Ugborodo: gender identity and alternative discourse of social protests among women in the Oil Delta of Nigeria', *Oxford Development Studies*, 32(4): 605–17.

— (2008) *Oiling Regional Insecurity? The Implications of the Niger Delta Crisis for Security and Stability in the Gulf of Guinea and West Africa*, Paper read at the Third Annual Conference of the European Network of Excellence GARNET, Sciences Po, Bordeaux, 16–20 September.

— (2009), *From Oil Rivers to the Niger Delta: The Paradoxes of Domination and Resistance in Colonial Nigeria*, Paper read at the Africa Conference, University of Texas at Austin, April.

Ukeje, C. and W. Adebanwi (2008) 'Ethnonationalist claims in southern Nigeria: insights from Yoruba and Ijaw nationalisms since the 1990's', *Ethnic and Racial Studies*, 31(3): 563–91.

Ukiwo, U. (2007) 'From "pirates" to "militants": a historical perspective on anti-state and anti-oil company protests in the western Niger Delta: the case of the Ijaw of Warri', *African Affairs*, 106(425): 587–610.

— (2008a) 'Nationalization versus indigenization of the rentier space: oil and conflict in Nigeria', in K. Omeje (ed.), *Extractive Economies and Conflicts in the Global South: Multiregional Perspectives on Rentier Politics*, Aldershot: Ashgate.

— (2008b) 'Horizontal inequalities and insurgency in the Niger Delta', in *The Nigerian State, Oil Industry and the Niger Delta*, Proceedings of international conference, Department of Political Science, Niger Delta University, Wilberforce Island, and Center for Applied

Environmental Research, University of Missouri-Kansas City, at Yenagoa, 11–13 March.

UNDP (United Nations Development Programme) (2005) *Nigeria Human Development Report 2005*, Abuja/New York: UNDP.

— (2006) *Niger Delta Human Development Report*, Abuja: UNDP.

United Ijaw States (2010) *Kaiama Declaration*, Communiqué of the All Ijaw Youth Conference, 11 December 1998, www.unitedijawstates.com/kaiama. html, accessed 25 August 2010.

van Allen, J. (1972) 'Sitting on a man. Colonialism and the lost political institutions of Igbo women', *Canadian Journal of African Studies*, 6(2): 165–81.

van Marrewijk, M. (2003) 'Concepts and definitions of CSR and corporate sustainability: between agency and the communion', *Journal of Business Ethics*, 44(2/3): 95–105.

Veitch, S. (2007) *Law and Irresponsibility: On legitimation of human suffering*, Abingdon: Routledge-Cavendish.

Versi, A. (2007) 'The Ibrahim Index on African governance', *African Business*, 336: 13–24.

Vickers, M. (2000) *Ethnicity and Sub-Nationalism in Nigeria: Movement for a Mid-West State*, Oxford: Worldview Publishing.

Vines, A. (2005) 'Combating light weapons proliferation in West Africa', *International Affairs*, 81(2): 341–60.

Volman, D. (2003) 'The Bush administration and African oil: the security implication of US energy policy', *Review of African Political Economy*, 30(98): 573–84.

von Kemedi, D. (2003) *Community Conflicts in the Niger Delta: Petro-Weapon or Policy Failure? Economies of Violence and Governable Spaces in the Niger Delta, Nigeria*, Working Paper 03-12.

WAC Global Services (2003) *Peace and Security in the Niger Delta: Conflict expert group baseline report*, www.shell2004.com/2007/shell_wac_report_2004.pdf.

Watts, M. (1999) *Petro-Violence: Some Thoughts on Community, Extraction, and Political Ecology*, UC Berkeley Workshop on Environmental Politics Berkeley Workshop on Environmental Politics Working Papers WP 03–WP 12, Berkeley: Institute of International Studies, University of California.

— (2004) 'Resource curse? Governmentality, oil and power in the Niger Delta, Nigeria', *Geopolitics*, 9(1): 50–80.

— (2007) 'Petro-insurgency or criminal syndicate? Conflict and violence in the Niger Delta', *Review of African Political Economy*, 34(114).

— (ed.) (2008a) *Curse of the Black Gold: 50 Years of Oil in the Niger Delta*, New York: Powerhouse Books.

— (2008b) 'Anatomy of an oil insurgency: violence and militants in the Niger Delta, Nigeria', in K. Omeje (ed.), *Extractive Economies and Conflict in the Global South: Multiregional perspectives on rentier politics*, Aldershot: Ashgate, pp. 51–74.

Watts, M., I. Okonta and V. Kemedi (2004) *Economies of Violence: Petroleum, Politics and Community Conflict in the Niger Delta, Nigeria*, Niger Delta Economies of Violence Working Paper Series 1.

Weber, M. (1947) *The Theory of Social and Economic Organization*, London: William Hodge and Co.

— (1954) *Weber on Law in Economy and Society*, Cambridge, MA: Harvard University Press.

Wezeman, P. (2003) *Conflicts and Transfers of Small Arms*, Solna: Stockholm International Peace Research Institute.

Wheeler, D., H. Fabig and R. Boele (2002) 'Paradoxes and dilemmas for stakeholder responsive firms in extractive sector: lessons from the case of Shell and the Ogoni', *Journal of Business Ethics*, 39(3): 297–318.

Williams, F. J. (2005) *Kaiama Declaration, Seven Years Later: An Assessment*, Paper presented at the Ijaw World Summit, 23–25 February, Yenagoa, Bayelsa state.

Willink Commission (1958) *Report of the*

Commission Appointed to Enquire into the Fears of Minorities and the Means of Allaying Them, London: HMSO.

Wilson, G. L. and M. S. Hannah (1990) *Group in Context*, New York: McGraw-Hill.

Windsor, D. (2006) 'Corporate Social Responsibility: three key approaches', *Journal of Management Studies*, 43(1): 93–114.

Worika, I. L. (2001) 'Deprivation, despoliation and destitution: whiter environmental and human rights in Nigeria's Niger Delta', *ILSA Journal of International Comparative Law*, 8(1): 1–30.

World Bank (1995) *Defining an Environmental Development Strategy for the Niger Delta*, vol. 1, Washington, DC: World Bank.

— (2008) *Niger Delta Social and Conflict Analysis*, Washington, DC: World Bank.

Yates, D. A. (2006) *The Scramble for African Oil*, Paper presented to the tri-annual International Political Science Association's World Congress, Fukuoka, 9–13 July.

Yuille, L. K. (2004) 'No one's perfect (not even close): reevaluating access to justice in the United States and western Europe', *Columbia Journal of Transnational Law*, 42: 863–924.

Zalik, A. (2004) 'The Niger Delta: petro-violence and partnership development', *Review of African Political Economy*, 31(101): 401–24.

Zandvliet, L. (2005) 'Assessing company behaviour in conflict environments: a field perspective', in K. Ballentine and H. Nitzschke (eds), *Profiting from Peace: Managing the Resources Dimensions of Civil War*, Boulder, CO: Lynne Rienner, pp. 185–206.

Contributors

Babatunde A. Ahonsi, an applied social scientist, is presently Country Director for the Population Council in Nigeria.

Rhuks Ako is a lecturer at the University of Hull Law School, UK. His research interests include public participation, minority and environmental rights, and justice issues in Nigeria's oil industry.

Morten Bøås is Research Director at Fafo's Institute for Applied International Studies. He has published extensively on different aspects of African politics and conflict. Bøås's work has been published in journals such as *Modern African Studies*, *Third World Quarterly*, *Africa Spectrum*, *Politique Africaine* and *Journal of Intervention and Statebuilding*. His latest published books in English include, *African Guerrillas: Rage Against the Machine* (2007), with Kevin Dunn, and *International Development*, vols I–IV (2010), with Benedicte Bull.

Nils Duquet is a senior researcher at the Flemish Peace Institute (Belgium), where he conducts academic and policy-oriented research and prepares policy advice. His research focus is on the legal and illegal arms trade, the dynamics of armed conflict, and the importance of oil for the arms acquisition of insurgent groups in sub-Saharan Africa.

Engobo Emeseh, is currently a lecturer in the Department of Law and Criminology, Aberystwyth University, Wales, UK. A former British Council Chevening Scholar, and a Ford Foundation (IFP) doctoral fellow, her broad area of research is environmental law and policy.

Ibaba Samuel Ibaba is a senior lecturer with the Department of Political Science, Niger Delta University, Wilberforce Island, Bayelsa State, Nigeria. He engages in research focused on conflict analysis, peace building and development. His professional memberships include the International Political Science Association (IPSA) and International Studies Association (ISA).

Uwafiokun Idemudia is an assistant professor of international development and African studies at York University in Toronto. His work focuses on the links between natural resources, business and development in Africa.

Augustine Ikelegbe teaches comparative politics and public policy at the Department of Political Science, University of Benin, Benin City, Nigeria. He has

245

researched and published extensively on identity and resource conflicts and the roles of youth, gender and civil society in conflicts.

Oluwatoyin Oluwaniyi is a lecturer in the History/International Relations Department at Redeemer's University, Ogun State, Nigeria. Her current areas of research are in conflict and conflict resolution, post-conflict reconstruction, and gender and youth issues.

Kayode Soremekun is a professor of international relations at Covenant University Ota, Nigeria, where he doubles as Dean of the College of Development Studies and Head of the Department of Political Science and International Relations.

Charles Ukeje earned a doctorate in international relations at the Obafemi Awolowo University, Ile-Ife, Nigeria, where he is also currently based. He previously taught African Politics and Development at the Department of International Development, Queen Elizabeth House, University of Oxford, UK.

Ukoha Ukiwo is a lecturer at the Department of Political and Administrative Studies, University of Port Harcourt, Nigeria. He was CRISE scholar at St Cross College, University of Oxford, and has held research positions at the Centre for Advanced Social Science (CASS), Port Harcourt and the Institute of International Studies, University of California, Berkeley. He has published widely on democratization, identity politics, conflicts and the Niger Delta region of Nigeria.

Anna Zalik is a faculty member in environmental studies at York University in Toronto, Canada. Her ongoing research examines the global political economy of oil and the merging of aid and security policy in strategic extractive sites, with fieldwork concerning state and subject formation and corporate regulation in southern Nigeria, Mexico's Gulf region and the Canadian northwest. From 2005–07 she was a Ciriacy Wantrup postdoctoral fellow in natural resource studies and political economy at the University of California at Berkeley. She holds a PhD in development sociology from Cornell University.

Index